Look for the Dog

An Illustrated Guide to
Victor
Talking Machines

by:
Robert W. Baumbach

"His Master's Voice" trademark
used with permission of RCA Corporation

Stationery X-Press · Post Office Box 207 · Woodland Hills · CA · 91364

ISBN 0-9606466-0-4

Library of Congress Cataloging in Publication Data

Baumbach, Robert W., 1945-
   Look for the Dog.

    Bibliography: p.
    Includes index.
    1. Victor Talking Machine Company - Catalogs
    2. Victor Talking Machine Company - History. I. Title
TS2301.P3B35   621.389'33   81-18461
ISBN 0-9606466-0-4   AACR2

© 1981, 1984, 1989, 1990 by Robert W. Baumbach

All rights reserved. Except for the purposes of a review written for inclusion in a magazine, newspaper, or broadcast, no part of this publication may be reproduced, stored in a retrieval system, or transmitted in any form or by any means, electronic, mechanical, photocopying or otherwise without the express permission of the copyright owner.

TABLE OF CONTENTS

USER'S GUIDE vii

INTRODUCTION ix

VICTOR IDENTIFICATION 1

    Model Summary 4

    Sales Summary 8

CHAPTER I

    The Early Years 9

    The Victor 17

CHAPTER II

    The Development of the Victrola 45

    How Victrolas Were Made 59

    The Victrola 69

    Period Victrolas 121

CHAPTER III

    The Orthophonic Era 149

    The Orthophonic Victrola, Electrola
      and Radiola 161

CHAPTER IV

Victor Accessories..............................227

CHAPTER V

Victor Patents..................................237

BIBLIOGRAPHY....................................254

APPENDIX

Service Information............................257

INDEX..324

User's Guide

This book is a compilation of the pertinent data on each of the "Talking Machines" manufactured by the Victor Talking Machine Company during its 29-year existence and is intended to be used just as one might use a collection of original catalogs. Each Victor model is described with particular attention paid to relating it to other models in the Victor line-up, indicating how the company's products molded, and were in turn molded by, the public's developing tastes and interests. Whether the reader is a dedicated collector or an arm-chair enthusiast, it is anticipated that this book will be a valuable aid in placing any model into perspective with each of the others manufactured by Victor, as well as offering some interesting insight into the times and conditions which created it.

When reviewing the individual instrument specifications given in this book, it must be remembered that variations from the published specifications were not uncommon. Victor was always willing to honor special requests from customers. Sound boxes and horns were easily interchanged between many different models. These and other parts were also sold separately for the purpose of updating older machines. Cases of woods other than those listed as available are sometimes discovered today, and other examples of special order customizing are known. Slight changes in trim, cabinet dimensions, mechanical features, etc., were being made continuously throughout the life of any model. Some Victrolas may have been made in more than a dozen variations, all of which appear identical on casual inspection. It is not the author's purpose, therefore, to document every variation in each model, but rather to present in a logical manner the development of the Victor Talking Machine through the use of the company's own published data.

This format was chosen because it could best convey the spirit of that period in American life - almost creating the impression that the reader were shopping for a new phonograph in those pre-Depression days.

The purist may object to the use of the word "phonograph" in describing products of the Victor Talking Machine Company, as this word was the trademark of Thomas Edison and originally described only those machines using vertically cut records. However, as the word has fallen into common usage as a generic term describing all forms of audio record players, its use can be justified.

The author has supplemented the normal "catalog" information contained within these pages with production quantities (from formerly private company files), introduction and discontinuation dates (from publications which were intended strictly for the trade), and service information (originally provided for the exclusive benefit of the dealers). This last section is of particular value to collectors today, as it describes the techniques recommended by the manufacturer in order to obtain peak performance from these instruments. By following the advice given in these service notes, it is possible for the collector to enjoy a musical performance in the manner in which Victor intended many decades ago.

Introduction to the Third Edition

In the period of time since the first edition of this book was printed, additional information regarding the Victor Talking Machine Company has been located by the author. Notebooks which are believed to be the work of B. L. Aldridge, a former Victor and RCA employee, who was also a company historian, were discovered. These notebooks contain a record of Victor and RCA products, and are noteworthy in that production figures for most instruments are recorded within them. These production figures, previously published by the author as a supplement to earlier editions of this book, are now included in the summary information charts which can be found on pages 4 through 7. The chart on page 8, which was included in the previous editions of this book, is also the work of B. L. Aldridge, and was originally published by him in his book *The Victor Talking Machine Company*.

Within the notebooks attributed to Mr. Aldridge are also contained wisps of information on Victor products which were never listed in the traditional sources which supplied the bulk of the information for this book (company sales brochures, parts lists, repair manuals or trade journals).

As an example, a production of 662 is listed for a **Victrola XIII**. Such an instrument is listed nowhere else in the company literature, but with such a small production, it was apparently quickly pulled from production for some reason or another - possibly for no reason other than it's "unlucky" nomenclature. Its price of $250 would make it actually more expensive than a **Victrola XIV**, and the same price as the **Victrola XVI**, which would seem to violate Victor's own hierarchical numbering system. As 1920, the year of reported introduction of the mysterious **Victrola XIII**, was near the time when the company was both experimenting with console style cabinets and changing their nomenclature for roman numerals to Arabic numerals, it is possible that this instrument was the same as one of the more familiar instruments of a different name, although none of the later instruments is an obvious candidate for a re-named Victrola XIII.

Small mysteries such as this remain even a decade after the original research into this book. In larger terms, however, Look for the Dog remains an invaluable source of information an insight into the products of the Victor Talking Machine Company, and the men and times which created it.

While this book was originally conceived as a collector's guide for a relatively obscure but growing hobby, time has modified its roll. *Look for the Dog* has given a certain organization and sense of history to a hobby which has grown in significant ways since this book was published. As the premier manufacturer of talking machines in this country, and the major force in the growth of the industry throughout the world, Victor was the leader. The story of Victor, as told through its products, is then, in a great way, the story of the industry.

Victor's story is also the story of America, and the great opportunities which it provided. For those who think that it is a story unique to the early part of this century; that people can no longer start from a garage and create great trend setting, lifestyle changing industries within a few short years, need to look no further than Silicon Valley. It is no coincidence that this update is being written and typeset on a Macintosh - a product which was virtually inconceivable when the first edition of this book was being penned a decade ago.

The parallels between Apple Computer and the Victor Talking Machine Company are remarkable. Both were begun by ambitious young men with a dream of a product and an industry which were not shared by many of their piers. These men did not invent their industry, but were indisputably responsible for shaping its growth. Victor's and Apple's influence on American, and the world, is difficult to overstate.

Both companies had the distinction of being in the right place at the right time. Their growth was a result of providing a product which was right for the times. Software played a critical roll in both companies. For Victor, this meant quality recordings by the top stars of the day, and creating a catalog of selections unmatched by others. Apple found an initial gold mine in a single piece of software (VisiCalc), which in itself was reason enough to buy an Apple. This first great piece of business software was soon joined by many others, and soon Apple had the largest catalog in the business.

Intentionally or not, Apple followed Victor into the schools. Both companies knew that by shaping young minds in these formative years, the future business of the company would receive a great boost.

The author is willing to bet that we will not have to wait sixty years to read a collector's guide to Apple Computers.

VICTOR IDENTIFICATION

Victor nomenclature followed several patterns throughout the years, and an understanding of them makes the task of identifying any Victor easier. The very earliest Victor talking machines were given alphabetic designations beginning with A. Thus there were Victor types A, B, C, D, and E (plus a toy hand powered machine that apparently did not warrant inclusion in this series). These designations must have seemed too pedestrian, for Eldridge Johnson soon concentrated on nomenclature which conveyed the regal status he felt the instruments deserved. The earliest instrument of this type was the Monarch. Variations on this theme were the De Luxe, the Special, and the Junior Monarchs, followed by the Royal (which may have been a tribute to his good friend and business associate Belford Royal). With the introduction of the rear-mounted tone arm, the phonographs were crowned by kingly titles such as Victor III (pronounced "Victor the Third"). This was carried over into the Victrola identification and Roman numerals served to identify all Victors until 1921, when they were slowly replaced with Arabic numbers. In nearly all cases, however, a higher number within any series identified the more expensive and deluxe instrument.

With the advent of the Orthophonic Victrolas in 1925, Victor introduced a short-lived series of romantic names (such as Granada). These soon gave way to a two-part numeric designation, where the first number indicated the approximate style of the instrument (4's were Victrolas with small horns, 8's had larger horns, 9's had radios, 10's had record changers, etc.) and the second number indicated an approximate position (either chronologically or by cost) within the series. Victor was thoughtful in assigning instrument identifications, and, as will be seen, generally left room within each series for future models. A problem was encountered, however, when they wanted to introduce a rear-mount phonograph which was smaller and cheaper than the Victor the First. They called it, out of neccessity, the Victor 0 (Victor the Zip?).

Attached to nearly every machine as it left the factory was a small ID plate which listed the model designation and serial number. These plates were usually located adjacent to, or under, the turntable, and provide the easiest means of establishing the history of any given Victor product today. Generally, the model designation is the first character, or set of characters, stamped into the ID plate. It is interesting to note that the famous Victor trade mark did not appear on the earliest plates, in spite of the fact that it had been used in advertising prior to the incorporation of the Victor Talking Machine Company.

Early Victors with names, such as Monarch, had the first letter of the name stamped into the plate for identification. The Monarch Special, as an example, carried the designation "MS", while the Royal was known as the type "R", and so forth. The later Orthophonic Victrolas with names had the entire name stamped into the ID plate. The charts on the following pages provide a speedy reference for the correlation of ID plates to model names or numbers. The charts also note the few machines which did not have ID plates, and indicate how these instruments may be identified.

Shortly after the first Victrola models were introduced, Victor recognized that a quick way to differentiate between inside and outside horn instruments was needed. This differentiation came in the form of a "VV" prefix, for Victor Victrola, on the ID plates of all of the spring-driven concealed-horn talking machines (a "VE" -for Victrola Electric - was used on Victrolas with electrically powered motors). At the same time, outside horn machines, which were referred to by the company as "Victors", gained the notation "Vic" (or alternately just "V") preceding the model number.

When the Orthophonic Victrola was introduced in 1925, a new and less expensive electric motor, for use with alternating current only, was made available as an option on several Orthophonic Victrola models. In order to differentiate between Victrolas with either of the two electric motors (so the dealer could easily tell from reading his invoices if he had the desired instrument in stock), an "x" appeared after the model number of instruments with the new motor. Victrolas with the older universal style motor continued to use only the "VE" prefix. When the new Victor Electrolas (with electrical amplification) were introduced in 1926, an "E" suffix was added to the ID plate.

The number following the model designation on the ID plate is the serial number. As a general rule, these serial numbers indicate the number of instruments of the same model designation made prior to the one under examination. A Victrola the Sixteenth, as an example, with an electric motor was considered a different model than the same machine with the standard spring motor, so that it is quite possible to find a "VE-XVI" with a low serial number of one or two hundred in spite of the fact that the "VV-XVI" had been in production nine years by the time that the electric motor option was introduced. A spring motor powered "Sixteenth" made on the same day would have had a serial number of several thousand.

A second source of information was applied to all but the very earliest Victor machines in the form of a printed patent information sticker. It was usually located on the bottom of the case on both floor and table models, but could also frequently be found on the back or inside the record storage compartment of Victrolas. These sheets are useful in pinpointing the date of manufacture of the machine to which they are attached, as they contain a printing date in the bottom corner. Since the sheets were updated on a regular basis to include all the latest patents, the date of manufacture of the phonograph was seldom more than a year or two later than the date appearing on the sheet. An exception to this statement might apply to machines with sheets dated in mid-1917, since Victor revised its licensing notice at this time and supplied new notices for the dealers to paste on all machines in their stock.

Victor (Outside Horn) Summary

ID Tag	First Year	Production	Comments	Page Number
$3.00	1901		Hand powered	19
A	1901		Type A - Continuation of Berliner design	20
B	1901		Type B - Similar to Trademark Gramophone	21
C	1901		Type C - Front-mount Victor	22
D	1903		Type D - The first Victor with a twelve-inch turntable	23
E	1902	60,000	Production estimated based on 30% of total 1901-05	24
M	1901	50,000	Production estimated based on 25% of total 1901-05	25
MD	1901	500	Monarch DeLuxe production estimated by author	27
MS	1902	11,000	Production estimated at 8% of total 1901-04	26
P	1902		Type P - Given as Premium	28
R	1902	19,000	Production estimated based on 23% of total 1902-03	29
Z	1903		Type Z	30
Jr.	1909	15,884	Victor Junior (ID Decal on case)	31
0	1908	50,640	Victor 0	32
I*	1903	94,135	"Victor the First"	33
II*	1902	125,249	"Victor the Second"	35
III*	1902	103,702	"Victor the Third"	36
IV*	1902	33,056	"Victor the Forth"	37
V*	1903	50,840	"Victor the Fifth"	38
VI*	1904	16,000	Production estimated from parts lists	39
XXV**	1913	19,000	Production estimated from parts lists	40
-	1906	500	**Auxetophone** - Pneumatically amplified Victor	42

All "Victors" contained spring motors. Where no production is shown, it indicates that the production is presently unknown.

* May be preceded with "V" or "Vic"
** Roman Numeral may be preceded with "V" or "Vic" or "VV"

Victrola (Inside Horn) Summary

Model	First Year	Production	Comments	Page Number
V-IV	1911	609,000	"Victrola the Forth" - Table model	70
V-VI	1911	693,417	"Victrola the Sixth" - Table model	71
V-VIII	1911	185,542	"Victrola the Eighth" -Table model	72
V-IX	1911	569,394	"Victrola the Ninth" - Table model	73
V-X	1910	506,000	"Victrola the Tenth" - Upright or table model	74
V-XI	1910	853,918	"Victrola the Eleventh" - Upright or table model	76
V-XII	1909	4,913	"Victrola the Twelfth" - Table model	78
V-XIII	1920	662	There are no known illustrations of this instrument	
V-XIV	1910	264,604	"Victrola the Fourteenth" - Upright	80
TLA	1906	2,500	Production estimate based on page 8	82
V-XVI	1907	196,000 *11,954*	"Victrola the Sixteenth" - Upright	85
V-XVII	1916	18,698 *2,524*	"Victrola the Seventeenth" - Upright	88
V-XVIII	1915	3,407 *994*	"Victrola the Eighteenth" - Upright	90
V-XX	1908	500	Production estimated (see page 91)	91
V-35	1924	45,000	Production estimated based on chart on page 8	92
V-50	1921	151,814	"Victrola No. 50" - Portable	94
V-80	1921	185,443 *75*	"Victrola No. 80" - Upright	95
V-90	1921	85,405	"Victrola No. 90" - Upright	96
V-100	1921	195,285 *49*	"Victrola No. 100" - Upright	97
V-105	1925	11,585 *3*	"Victrola No. 105" - Upright	98
V-107	1925	1,009 *13*	"Victrola No. 107" - Upright	99
V-110	1921	21,800	"Victrola No. 110" - Upright	100
V-111	1922	22,742 *1,277*	"Victrola No. 111" - Upright	101
V-120	1921	8,425 *919*	"Victrola No. 120" - Upright	102
V-125	1923	2,170 *120*	"Victrola No. 125" - Upright	103
V-130	1921	5,260 *595*	"Victrola No. 130" - Upright	104
V-210	1923	197,000	"Victrola No. 210" - Console	105
V-215*	1923	136,876 *167*	"Victrola No. 215" - Console	106
V-220	1923	23,246 *614*	"Victrola No. 210" - Console	107
V-230	1922	3,395 *820*	"Victrola No. 230" - Console	108
V-240	1922	65,821 *8*	"Victrola No. 240" - Console	109
V-260	1922	53,592 *2*	"Victrola No. 260" - Console	110
V-280	1922	12,730 *7*	"Victrola No. 280" - Console	111
V-300	1921	27,014 *2,006*	"Victrola No. 300" - Console	112
V-330	1922	3,620 *477*	"Victrola No. 330" - Console	113
V-350	1924	880 *159*	"Victrola No. 350" - Upright	114
V-360	1924	1,287 *229*	"Victrola No. 360" - Upright	115
V-370	1924	907 *161*	"Victrola No. 370" - Upright	116
V-400*	1923	12,863 *704*	"Victrola No. 400" - Console	117
V-405*	1923	26,000	"Victrola No. 405" - Console	118
V-410*	1923	7,359 *799*	"Victrola No. 410" - Console	119

Spring motor production is indicated in plain type, electric turntable production, if any, is shown in **bold italic** type. Where no production is shown, it indicates that the production is presently unknown.

VE" replaces "VV" when equiped with an electric turntable motor
 The "Special" editions of these models (equiped for radio) are identified by an "S" immediately preceding or following the numeral

Orthophonic Victrola Summary

ID Tag	First Year	Production	Comments	Page Number
Alhambra I	1926	2,000	"VV-7-1" - production estimated from VV-7-2	179
Alhambra II	1926	993	"VV-7-2" - Acoustically amplified console with Radiola 25	180
Borgia I	1926	1,456	"VV-9-3"- Acoustically amplified console with Radiola 28	200
Borgia II	1926	*3,000*	"VV-9-2"- Production estimated from "Borgia I" and VV-9-40	198
Colony	1925	19,993	"VV-4-5" - Orthophonic Victrola console	176
Consolette	1925	234,323 *4,935*	"VV-4-3" - Orthophonic Victrola console	173
Credenza	1925	47,922	"VV-8-1" - Orthophonic console with two or four front doors	194
Florenza	1926	3,911	"VV-9-1"- Acoustically amplified console with Radiola 25	197
Grenada	1925	78,608 *11,557*	"VV-4-4" - Orthophonic Victrola console	175
VV-1-1	1925	86,721	Table model	163
VV-1-2	1925	22,671	Table model	164
VV-1-4	1925	10,857	Similar in appearance to a VV-1-70 without a lid	
VV-1-5	1926	24,792	Suitcase portable	165
VV-1-6	1926	35,392	Suitcase portable	166
VV-1-40	1929		Same as a VV-1-4	
VV-1-70	1926	37,751	Orthophonic Victrola table model	167
VV-1-90	1927	22,348	Orthophonic Victrola table model	168
VV-2-1	1925	12	There are no known illustrations of this instrument	
VV-2-30	1927	37,021	Suitcase portable	169
VV-2-35	1928	74,735	Suitcase portable	170
VV-2-55	1928	333,720	Suitcase portable	171
VV-2-60	1927	165,310	Production estimated based on VV-2-30, 2-35, & 2-55	172
VV-4-1	1925	1,058 *27*	A small "treasure chest" on a stand	
VV-4-3	1925	234,323 *4,935*	"Consolette" - Orthophonic Victrola console	173
VV-4-4	1925	78,608 *11,557*	"Grenada" - Orthophonic Victrola console	175
VV-4-5	1925	19,993	"Colony" - Orthophonic Victrola console	176
VV-4-7	1926	64,953 *3,424*	Orthophonic Victrola console	
VV-4-20	1928	36,879 *396*	Orthophonic Victrola console	177
VV-4-40	1927	93,657 *4,259*	Orthophonic Victrola console	178
VV-5-1	1925	*14*	There are no known illustrations of this instrument	
VV-7-1	1926	2,000	"Alhambra I" - production estimated from VV-7-2	179
VV-7-2	1926	993	"Alhambra II" - Acoustically amplified console with Radiola 25	180
VV-7-3	1926	9,179 *4,021*	Acoustically amplified console with Radiola 20	182
VV-7-10	1927	5,403 *725*	Acoustically amplified console with Radiola 16	183
VV-7-11	1928	12,110 *14,323*	Acoustically amplified console with Radiola 18	184
VV-7-25	1927	4,073 *4,050*	Acoustically amplified console with Radiola 17	185
VV-7-30	1927	3,872 *182*	Acoustically amplified console with Radiola 20	188
VV-8-1	1925	47,922	"Credenza"- Orthophonic console with two or four front doors	194
VV-8-4	1926	18,913 *6,580*	Orthophonic Victrola console	188
VV-8-7	1926	2,075 *4*	Orthophonic Victrola made for school use	189
VV-8-8	1928	1,043	Orthophonic Victrola made for school use	191
VV-8-9	1928	5,497 *727*	Orthophonic Victrola console	192
VV-8-12	1927	21,883 *5,373*	Orthophonic Victrola console	193
VV-8-30	1927	10,740 *8,847*	"Credenza" - Orthophonic console with four front doors (see VV-8-1)	194
VV-8-35	1928	4,925 *5,104*	Orthophonic Victrola console	195
VE-8-60	1926	*3,442*	Acoustically and electrically amplified console	196
VV-9-1	1926	3,911	"Florenza"- Acoustically amplified console with Radiola 25	197
VV-9-2	1926	*3,000*	"Borgia II" - Production estimated from "Borgia I" and VV-9-40	198
VV-9-3	1926	1,456	"Borgia I"- Acoustically amplified console with Radiola 28	200
VV-9-15	1926	808 *1,747*	Acoustically amplified console with Radiola 28	201
VE-9-40	1926	*5,136*	Similar to the "Borgia II"	205
VE-10-35	1928	*3,222*	Acoustical console with second style record changer	210
VE-10-50	1927	*10,033*	Acoustical console with first style record changer	211
VE-11-25	1928	*3*	Coin-operated console with second style record changer	216
VE-14-1	1926	3,035	"Revere" - Acoustical Orthophonic horn points towards floor	226

Spring motor production, if any, is indicated in plain type, electric turntable production, if any, is shown in **bold italic** type. Where no production is shown, it indicates that the production is presently unknown.

"VE" replaces "VV" when equiped with an electric turntable motor

Electrola (Electrical Amplification) Summary

ID Tag	First Year	Production	Comments	Page Number
VV-7-26	1928	16,448	15.002 with PM speaker, 1,446 with dynamic speaker	187
VE-9-16	1928	*2,097*	Electrically amplified console with Radiola 18	202
VE-9-18	1928	*3,126*	Electrically amplified console with Radiola 64	203
VE-9-25	1927	*1,038*	Electrically amplified console with Radiola 28	204
VE-9-54	1928	*2,941*	Electrola with second style record changer and Radiola 64	207
RE-154	1930	*519*	Surplus VE-9-54 cabinets with the RE-45 chassis	
VE-9-55	1927	*2,046*	Electrola with first style record changer and Radiola 28	208
VE-9-56	1928	*251*	Electrola with second style record changer and Radiola 64	209
RE-156	1930	*245*	Surplus VE-9-56 cabinets with the RE-45 chassis	
VE-10-51	1927	*535*	Electrical console with first style record changer	212
VE-10-69	1928	*1,872*	Electrical console with second style record changer	214
VE-10-70	1927	*2,553*	Electrical console with first style record changer	215
VE-11-50	1928	*3*	11-25 + 11-50 production = 6 (individual not known)	216
VE-12-1	1926	*6,220*	"Cromwell"- Electrically amplified console phonograph	218
VE-12-2	1926	*1,620*	"Tuscany" - Electrically amplified console phonograph	219
VE-12-15	1928	*5,967*	Electrically amplified console phonograph	220
VE-12-25	1927	*2,194*	Electrically amplified console phonograph	221
VE-15-1	1926		"**Hyperion**" Electrical console with RCA Radiola 28	222
CD-20	1928		"Counter Demonstrator" for use in record stores.	

Spring motor production, if any, is indicated in plain type, electric turntable production, if any, is shown in **bold italic** type. Where no production is shown, it indicates that the production is presently unknown.

Radio Products Summary

ID Tag	First Year	Production	Comments	Page Number
VV-R-80	1922	50	Victor-designed four tube radio in Victrola # 80 Cabinet	
R-20	1927	6,382	RCA Radiola 20 only in a Victor cabinet with an Orthophonic horn	224
LS-1	1926		Loudspeaker Number 1	223

Sales by Class of Product
(may represent instruments made in prior years)
October 1, 1901 to December 31, 1929

Years	Outside Horn Victors	Table Top Victrolas	Original Upright Victrolas	Flat Top Victrolas	Portable Victrolas	Ortho-phonic Victrolas	Victrola Radiola Consoles	Electrolas	Radio Consoles	Misc.	Total
1901	7,570	—	—	—	—	—	—	—	—	—	7,570
1902	42,110	—	—	—	—	—	—	—	—	—	42,110
1903	40,601	—	—	—	—	—	—	—	—	—	40,601
1904	47,074	—	—	—	—	—	—	—	—	—	47,074
1905	65,591	—	—	—	—	—	—	—	—	—	65,591
1906	76,036	—	506	—	—	—	—	—	—	6,047	82,589
1907	98,368	—	3,559	—	—	—	—	—	—	5,505	107,432
1908	45,473	—	4,317	—	—	—	—	—	—	942	50,732
1909	56,147	—	11,764	—	—	—	—	—	—	320	68,231
1910	73,049	—	21,508	—	—	—	—	—	—	109	94,666
1911	31,106	51,805	41,956	—	—	—	—	—	—	60	124,927
1912	21,009	136,542	49,224	—	—	—	—	—	—	23	206,798
1913	18,435	116,561	115,342	—	—	—	—	—	—	1,571	251,909
1914	6,179	180,344	121,288	—	—	—	—	—	—	1,648	309,459
1915	3,949	185,466	188,725	—	—	—	—	—	—	1,356	379,496
1916	6,442	242,284	265,184	—	—	—	—	—	—	2,070	515,980
1917	6,623	278,971	284,712	—	—	—	—	—	—	2,706	573,012
1918	5,656	141,128	167,786	—	—	—	—	—	—	1,054	315,624
1919	9,185	219,203	243,691	—	—	—	—	—	—	2,523	474,602
1920	11,206	212,363	333,889	—	—	—	—	—	—	2,602	560,060
1921	1,768	37,563	243,581	12,321	24,645	—	—	—	—	982	320,860
1922	2,665	56,493	150,940	138,267	35,189	—	—	—	—	551	384,105
1923	3,105	74,444	90,958	208,688	25,572	—	—	—	—	813	403,580
1924	3,161	95,939	84,992	166,277	59,821	—	—	—	—	819	411,009
1925	2,190	79,751	36,960	53,082	47,678	42,446	—	—	—	147	262,274
1926	5,906	47,990	46	29	64,529	260,436	11	9	—	66	419,004
1927	—	59,447	—	—	92,366	228,895	31,680	8,322	6,321	486	426,973
1928	4	17,394	3	—	198,485	172,121	23,519	15,939	59	641	446,229
1929	—	4,355	3	—	166,255	31,346	46,329	11,193	212,775	268	533,283

THE EARLY YEARS

The Victor Talking Machine Company was incorporated in October of 1901 by a New Jersey manufacturer named Eldridge R. Johnson. The real beginning, however, of what was to become the world's largest manufacturer of records and record players can be traced back thirteen years earlier, into the previous century, when a German-born immigrant, Emile Berliner, demonstrated a disc playing machine at the Franklin Institute in Philadelphia. The concept of recording sounds and reproducing them at a later date was not new, as Thomas Edison had built his first phonograph in 1877. What was new about Berliner's approach was the technique he had developed to produce large numbers of copies from a single master record (such a process for cylinder records would elude Edison until 1901).

The disc records, therefore, could be sold more cheaply than the difficult-to-produce cylinders and gave Berliner's Gramophone an important competitive advantage over both Edison's Phonograph and Alexander Graham Bell's Graphophone.

The first Gramophones were simple hand-powered devices and while they were well received, Emile Berliner realized that, in order to achieve a broader market and to elevate his machine out of the toy category, he needed to develop a motor-driven version of his disc player. An electric-powered Gramophone was built in 1896, but the cost and nuisance of handling early batteries persuaded Berliner to seek an alternative motive power. The search for a suitable motor led him to a Camden, New Jersey machinist, the aforementioned Mr. Johnson. Not only did Eldridge Johnson make a silent and long-running spring motor for the Gramophone, by 1897 he had a contract to manufacture the entire machine. Sales of this machine grew at a very reassuring rate, and Eldridge Johnson found he had to invest substantial amounts of money into equipment and labor in order to meet the ever-increasing demand for Gramophones.

Unfortunately, Berliner's success was to bring him problems as well. Unscrupulous manufacturers began issuing unlicensed copies of the Gramophone and pirated copies of Berliner discs. Furthermore, in 1899 Berliner discovered that two of the top officials in the company responsible for the distribution of his Gramophones and records were also prominent in the operations of the Universal Talking Machine Company, manufacturers of the rival Zonophone. When Berliner sought to cut off their supply of Gramophones, the officials sued, as they had an exclusive contract to sell Berliner's Gramaphones in the United States. The court handed down a controversial ruling enjoining Berliner from selling Gramaphones in the U.S. to anyone except the former officers of the company.

Eldridge Johnson had to move quickly to protect his investment (in the order of $50,000 to $60,000) in his production facilities. He acquired the assets of the Berliner Gramophone Company (including the American copyright to a certain painting of a terrier listening to "His Master's Voice") and reorganized it as the Consolidated Talking Machine Company. A second injunction was sought by Berliner's former distributor to prevent this apparent continuation of Berliner's company, but the court ruled that Johnson could continue as long as he didn't use the word "Gramophone" in relation to his products. Johnson then, perhaps in celebration of this victory (or in anticipation of future success), named his machines "The Victor".

The first products of Johnson's Consolidated Talking Machine Company (reorganized the following year, 1901, as the Victor Talking Machine Company) were copies of the machine he had made for Berliner. Mr. Johnson was quick to introduce improvements in the design of his instruments and in the production of records. New models were introduced and discontinued as the product matured rapidly in the first decade of the new century.

As an example, Johnson was able to improve upon his original motor design (as seen on the types "A" and "B") for his model "C". The running time was increased and the winding crank was moved from its vertical position to the side of the case. This repositioning of the control had the advantage of allowing 10-inch records to be played without removing the crank. Improvements in the reproducer were also made at this early date, and were offered separately so that owners could update their machines for a relatively low cost.

Early Victor Monarch Special with 42 inch Horn and Stand

Various sizes of horns were also offered as accessories to modify the tone and volume of the recordings. Horns as long as 56 inches were provided for "use on the concert stage". While use of the larger horns on these early machines did dramatically increase their volume, they created several problems at the same time. The horn supports for the earliest Victors were designed to balance the original sized horn and provide the proper pressure of the needle against the record. As the horn grew larger, the balancing point had to be moved further from the center of the machine, requiring a special table or floor stand to hold the horn. While the weight of the needle against the record could be adjusted by moving the fulcrum of the horn, the mass could not. As a consequence, as the horn weight increased, so did its inertia. Since the disc grooves provided the force which moved the sound box-horn assembly (unlike Edison's Phonograph which had a separate feed screw for this purpose), the records wore out faster when used with a large horn.

1902 Victor IV with Rigid Arm

To overcome these problems, Johnson in 1902 introduced a new tone arm and horn assembly (which he called the "rigid arm") in which only the sound box and tone arm moved as the record played. Now the moving mass remained constant regardless of the horn size used. The horn mount was made substantial enough for even large horns, so that separate horn stands were no longer required.

While the first rigid tone arms had a constant diameter throughout their length, Johnson soon realized that if he provided a gradually increasing diameter in the arm, the effect would be the same as increasing the size of the horn. The patent covering the tapering tone arm, as it was known, was one of many important patents which allowed Victor to do business for many years with serious competition coming only from the Columbia Phonograph Company's disc Graphophone. Columbia had, in 1901, found itself in possession of the basic patent for the mass production of disc records when it hired a former Berliner employee by the name of Joe Jones. While some might argue that this patent rightfully belonged to Victor/Berliner since they developed the process, Eldridge Johnson respected Columbia's legal ability to defend their possession of the patent and took the simple expediency of entering into a cross licensing agreement with Columbia. This provided Columbia with access to the basic Berliner disc patent, but allowed both parties to devote their time to making phonographs instead of lawsuits.

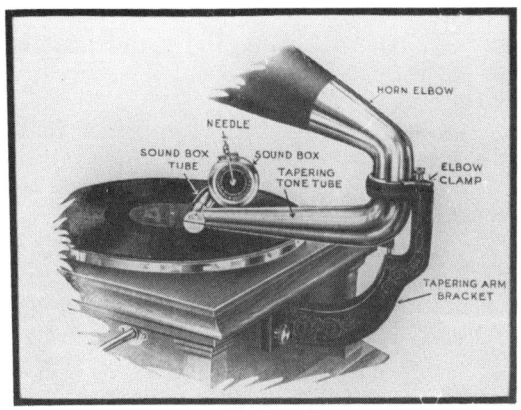

The Tapering Tone Arm

Victor was usually not this generous with its adversaries, and was quick to bring suit (sometimes a threat of a suit was enough) against anyone planning to market a disc playing machine. The Zonophone continued to be produced after Victor brought suit against the makers, the Universal Talking Machine Company, for its violations of Victor-owned patents, because (in light of Victor's claims against the company) Victor was able to negotiate the purchase of the assets of the Universal Talking Machine Company. Thus Eldridge Johnson obtained a line of phonographs to compete with the lower-priced Columbias while still maintaining the high quality which had characterized Victor machines to this point.

During his first few years in business, Johnson patented many designs for improvements to the sound box. The very first machines had used the Berliner reproducer design, but within the first year this had been replaced with a new design in which the mica diaphram was exposed on one side. This meant that the fragile membrane could be damaged more easily by careless handling, but apparently this was not a serious problem since an exposed diaphram was used in the sound box of nearly all subsequent Victors until the paper-thin aluminium diaphrams were introduced on the Orthophonic Victrolas in 1925.

Very early in the century, Eldridge Johnson introduced the first of the famous Roman numeral series of phonographs which would form the early backbone of his company. The Victor I through VI were similar in many important characteristics—particularly quality—and primarily offered the customer of that period a choice of size, finish, and power. The "Victor the First" and the "Victor the Sixth", as well as the others in between, shared such important features as the tapering tone arm, high quality solid wood cabinet (oak on the First and mahogany on the Sixth), powerful motors which could be wound as the machine played (one spring in the First, three springs in the Sixth), brightly plated controls and trim (nickel on the First and gold on the Sixth) and so forth. (The regal sounding titles which Victor gave to their machines in their early advertising are generally ignored by modern collectors, who seem to prefer a simpler nomenclature, such as "Victor Six", when referring to instruments in this series.)

Eldridge Johnson created the Roman numeral series of Victors by replacing the original "front-mount" tone arm of existing Victors with the new rigid or (after 1904) tapering tone arm (collectively refered to as "rear-mount" tone arms). Thus, as an example, the earliest Victor V's shared the cabinet and motor of the Type D, while a similar relationship existed between the Victor IV and Monarch Special, Victor III and Monarch, Victor II and Monarch Junior, and the Victor I and Type Z Victor. While the early catalogs clearly differentiate between the front-mount and rear-mount instruments by using a letter designation for the former and a Roman numeral designation for the latter, surviving instruments indicate that Victor was not this discriminating when labeling actual machines. Evidence shows that most, if not all Victors made prior to approximately 1907 used the letter designation on the ID plate, regardless of whether the instrument was equipped with a front or rear-mounted horn. Additionally, many instruments came with two sets of mounting holes and could accommodate either style of horn support. Where two sets of holes were provided, a plaque which covered the unused set (and explained its purpose) was affixed at the factory - thereby giving the dealer or the owner the option of exchanging one style for the other. Victor set the value of the rear-mount tone arm at $5 more than the front-mount arm, and maintained this differential for any of the dual-personality instruments regardless of their size. It should be noted that the designation "front-mount" or "rear-mount" is somewhat misleading since either horn support was attached to the same surface. The difference lay in the fact that the horns themselves pointed in different directions, and the bell of the horn was logically used to define the front of the instrument.

The Roman numeral Victors were each considered to be top grade instruments and even the smallest member of the series, the Victor the First, was priced at $25 - a respectible sum of money in those days. For the large group of Americans who could not justify an expense of this magnitude on a simple luxury, Victor provided an assortment of cheaper instruments. The very cheapest Victor ever was the Type P, which was actually given away free, although there was a catch. The Type P was provided in large quantities to concerns wishing to promote their product by offering a high grade talking machine as a premium (hence the designation "P"). The Type P was inexpensive to produce by virtue of its small single-spring motor, but impressive appearing thanks to moderately large oak case. A typical offer might have included the Victor P with a group of magazine subscriptions, set of dishes, or any number of other products.

Other low cost Victors available during the early part of the century were the Royal (1902-1903), the Type Z (1903-1908) and, after 1908, the Victor 0 (for zero, since it was one step below the Victor I). Each of these instruments was priced in the $15-$20 range, and was very popular. In 1909 Victor introduced the Victor Jr., the all time price leader in spring-powered Victors (if you disregard the Type P). At $10, this instrument was a "best buy", for it had all the traditional Victor quality, but simply on a smaller scale.

In 1905 Victor announced that it had acquired the American rights to manufacture a talking machine designed three years earlier by Sir Charles Parsons of England. Sir Charles' machine was unique in that it utilized an air compressor as a means to obtain greatly increased volume. The compressed air was used to amplify the needle movement through a special valved sound box. Because of the high price ($500), the Auxetophone, as it was called, was used primarily in hotels and restaurants where its cost could be offset by the elimination of the requisite band. Many Americans dined to the music provided by this curiosity, but history has lost whether they preferred the Auxetophone to the real musician.

In 1913 a new Victor aimed exclusively at educational institutions, which Victor had been courting for years, was introduced. The Victor XXV (later to be known as the Victrola XXV, or more commonly the "Schoolhouse Victor") was the last new outside horn talking machine design introduced by Victor. The instrument was a curious compromise, since it had the outside horn of a Victor, but was equipped with a lid and legs just like a Victrola. It marked an interesting acknowledgment by Victor, in light of its intended application, of the superior fidelity of the larger outside wooden horn as compared to the tiny horn used in all the Victrolas at that time. There was a price to pay for the added performance of the Victor XXV, however, and that was in convenience. Naturally, when the horn was in place on the XXV, the lid could not be closed, and when the lid was closed, a place to store the horn had to be found. Victor provided a solution the following year when the cabinet was enlarged and a hinge added to the shelf to allow room for horn storage under the motor. A new-style hinge permitted the lid to be removed and hung from the back of the case when not required to protect the mechanism from inquisitive little fingers.

Demand for outside horn Victors fell sharply after the introduction of the Victrolas, but Victors were still commonly available up until the United States' entry into World War I. The Auxetophone was removed from the price lists in 1918, as an example (although this probably represented the last of a stock of instruments manufactured years earlier), while the Victor Jr. and Victors 0 through V were still listed in the advertising as late as 1920 (and were probably available even after this date at many dealers). The Schoolhouse Victrola XXV was available until it was replaced by a special educational Orthophonic Victrola in 1926 (at which time all the remaining Victrola XXV's were exported to countries where they were still in demand).

the VICTOR

The $3.00 VICTOR
1901 $3.00

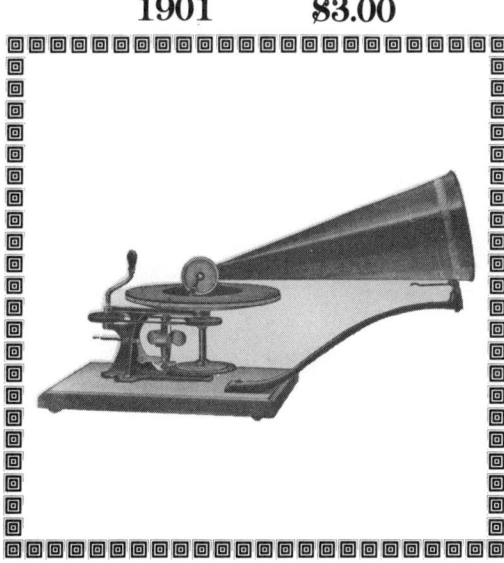

The $3.00 Victor was the lowest priced talking machine Victor ever made. A direct descendant of the first Berliner hand-powered disc playing machine, it was advertised as a children's toy. A governor similar to those on the higher priced Victors was used to provide an even rotational speed for the turntable. The "toy" sound box was unique to this instrument, and was of a simple, low cost design. The base board was oak, and the 10-inch horn was constructed of tin and painted black. The machine played only the 7-inch records, since the crank prevented the use of the larger 10-inch Monarch discs. The $3.00 Victor was supplied complete with a children's record containing six selections, and 100 needles.

Type A VICTOR
1901 $12.00

The Type A Victor was the lowest priced spring-powered talking machine offered by Victor in 1901. A continuation of a style manufactured by Eldridge Johnson for Berliner since 1898, the Type A was designed to meet the competition of Edison's $10.00 Gem. Most Type A Victors were sold with Johnson's "New Century" or "Standard" sound box, however the "Concert" sound box was available for $3.00 extra. The machine was designed to play only the 7-inch records on its 7-inch turntable, but since the crank was removable, 10-inch and the later 12-inch discs could be accommodated, although the latter would tax the capacity of the small spring motor. The 16-inch horn was constructed of tin, with a pewter bell and was painted black with a gold stripe. The cover for the motor was cast iron with an oxidized finish, as was the horn support. The base board and tone arm were made from oak, making this a very sturdy machine. A box of 200 needles was included with each machine.

Type B VICTOR
1901 $18.00

The Type B Victor was the improved version of the first talking machine Johnson built for Berliner in 1896, and is often referred to as the "Trademark Machine" since this is the style of Gramophone which Barraud included in his famous painting, "His Master's Voice", in 1899. It used the same spring motor and horn as the Type A Victor, but had a fancier oak cabinet. The tone arm was sturdier than the one on the Type A and incorporated a nickel-plated support to hold the arm in mid air while changing records. The turntable was 7 inches in diameter and utilized a screwdown clamp to hold the records secure under the heavy weight of the stylus, as did the other 1901 Victors. The Type B was normally supplied with the "Standard" sound box and the black 16-inch horn as shown, but these items could be exchanged for the "Concert" sound box ($3.00 extra) or any of the larger horns (such as the 30-inch horn and support at $5.00 extra). A box of 200 needles was also included with the purchase of the Type B Victor.

Type C VICTOR
1901 $25.00

In designing the Type C Victor, Eldridge Johnson improved upon his earlier motor design by moving the crank to the side of the cabinet and incorporating a mechanism which allowed the crank to remain stationary while the motor was running. The benefits of this design were that 10-inch records could be played on the 7-inch turntable without removing the crank, and that the machine could be wound while playing — a feat not possible with the Types A or B since their cranks revolved as the machine played. The cabinet was constructed of solid oak with ribbed corner columns — a design that would become popular with Mr. Johnson. The "Standard" sound box was normally supplied with the Type C, but the "Concert" was available for $3.00 extra (exchange). A 14-inch black steel and brass bell horn was usually supplied, along with a case of 200 needles.

Type D VICTOR
1903-1907 $55.00-$60.00

The Type D Victor became available in 1903 concurrent with the introduction of Victor's new 12-inch diameter records. The Type D was the first Victor to be equipped with a 12-inch turntable, and Victor tried to imply that the record's diameter should match that of the turntable for optimum results (curiously, they never introduced an instrument with a 14-inch turntable, even though they briefly made records in this large size). Early Victor catalogs illustrate this instrument with a tapering tone arm and label it as a Victor V, although specimens which survive contain the "D" designation on the ID plate. The fact that the ID plate carried the designation "D" would seem to imply that this phonograph was optionally available with a front mount tone arm, but available Victor literature does not support this assumption. The cabinet of Type D Victors manufactured from 1903 until late 1906 was similar in style, but larger than that of the Monarch Special. Made of top-grade quartersawed oak, the cabinet housed a three-spring motor. A "Concert" sound box was standard equipment, but the "Exhibition" sound box was available at the same price. In October of 1906, a new plainer cabinet was introduced for the Type D. The new cabinet offered simple, straight sides with plain corner columns, and most instruments with this later cabinet style carried the designation "V" rather than "D" on the ID plaque.

VICTOR MONARCH JUNIOR
1902-1905 $25.00-$27.50

The Monarch Junior (identified by an "E" on the ID Plate) was, as might be expected, a scaled-down version of Victor's popular Monarch. The same two-spring motor played five 7-inch or three 10-inch records on the 7-inch turntable. Like the larger Monarch, this instrument's case was constructed of high grade quartersawed oak. The motor was firmly mounted to the lid of the case and this assembly was hinged to allow easy access to the motor for oiling. The earlier machines were all equipped with the front-mounted style horn, but beginning in 1904, a mounting plate for a tapering tone arm support was incorporated into each machine. An instruction plaque normally covered the support's mounting holes, and when the front mount tone arm was replaced with the tapering tone arm support, a small dummy bracket was screwed into the former's mounting holes. "Concert" sound boxes were supplied with the early front mount machines, while a choice of "Concert" or "Exhibition" sound boxes was offered for the later Monarch Juniors.

VICTOR MONARCH
1901-1905 $35.00-$40.00

The Victor Monarch was supplied in several configurations over its short life span. Eldridge Johnson chose the name Monarch to indicate that this was the king of talking machines, as it was the largest and finest he had made up to that time. The machine had a 10-inch turntable to accommodate the new 10-inch Monarch disc records which played twice as long and cost twice as much as the older 7-inch Victor records. The case styling was modified in 1902 to incorporate the ribbed corner columns which graced many subsequent outside horn Victors. Beginning in 1903 the Monarch could be equipped with the new rear-mounted tone arm, for an additional $5. The front-mounted tone arms were usually equipped with a "Concert" sound box, while the later Monarchs generally came with the newer "Exhibition" sound box. Cabinets were solid quartersawed oak. The two-spring motor offered sufficient power to play three 10-inch records, and could be wound while the machine played. The standard horn (either front or rear mount) was 21 inches long and constructed of steel with a brass bell, although any of the larger horns was naturally available at extra cost.

VICTOR MONARCH SPECIAL
1902-1905 $45.00-$50.00

The Monarch Special replaced the De Luxe Monarch in the 1902 Victor lineup, and for a few brief months was Victor's finest talking machine. It was equipped with a new powerful three-spring motor for the 10-inch turntable and could play six 10-inch records with a single winding. The quartersawed oak cabinet was fancier and taller than that of the standard Monarch, and these differences accounted for the $10.00 price differential between the two machines. Like the Monarch, this machine was also sold with a rear-mounted horn and tapering tone arm beginning in 1904. The Victor catalog illustrations of this instrument with the tapering tone arm label the machine as the Victor IV, although it is thought that most ID plaques carried the "MS" designation. The earlier front-mount and rigid arm machines used a "Concert" sound box, while the tapering tone arm machines came with either the "Concert" or the "Exhibition" sound box.

VICTOR DE LUXE MONARCH
1901 $60.00

The Victor De Luxe Monarch was made only briefly during 1901 and was Eldridge Johnson's attempt to answer those people who thought that the talking machine was unrefined and did not belong in fine surroundings. When perched on top of its matching $90.00 record cabinet, the De Luxe Monarch was a striking example of the woodcarver's art and quite unlike anything offered by the competition. Technically, this instrument was identical to the $40.00 Monarch of the same period, and differed only in the oak cabinet. The motor was powered by two springs, which stored enough energy to play three of the new 10-inch records. The nickel-plated 10-inch turntable and "Concert" sound box were standard, and these items, like the motor and case, were the finest that Victor offered in 1901.

Type P VICTOR
1902-1906   Premium

The Type P Victor was unique in that it was not designed to be sold, but rather to be given away as a premium. The instruments were intended to be wholesaled in large quantities to any concern which wanted to mount a promotion wherein the phonograph could be given away as an inducement for the purchase of the product. Music stores might give away the Type P with the purchase of a minimum number of records, as an example, although frequently the purchased items were entirely unrelated to music.

The instrument itself was relatively large, with a 10-inch turntable and a simple oak case. The single-spring motor was usually mounted to the base board, in which case a hinged lid provided access for inspecting or oiling the motor, although the Type P Victor was also offered in a variation which utilized the motor and mounting plate of the Victor Royal. The horn support and other hardware had an "oxidized copper" finish which was obtained by copper plating the steel parts, then applying a black coating over the piece and buffing sections of this coating away to reveal the copper. The buffing was usually done diagonally across the piece, and gave it an attractive "tiger stripe" effect. A concert sound box and 18-inch steel horn with a brass bell were standard. Variations of the original design were identified on the ID plaque by the designation P-I or P-II.

VICTOR ROYAL
1902-1904 $15.00

The Royal was Victor's lowest priced talking machine during its production, and was very similar in appearance to Eldridge Johnson's first side-winding phonograph, the pre-Victor Style C Gramophone. In spite of the low price, the cabinet of the Royal was still constructed of fine quartersawed oak with oxidized metal corner braces. The single-spring motor required winding prior to playing each record, although an early brochure euphemistically stated that it had the power to play "nearly two 7-inch records on each winding." The turntable was 7 inches in diameter to match the size of the popular low cost discs made by Victor, and an "Exhibition Junior" or "Concert" sound box (initially $1.50 extra, but later offered as a no-cost option when the "Exhibition Junior" sound box was replaced by the larger "Exhibition" sound box) was normally supplied with the instrument. A 16-inch all-steel horn was standard.

Type Z VICTOR
1903-1908 $17.00-$20.00

In 1903 the Type Z replaced the Royal as the lowest cost ($20.00) talking machine in the Victor lineup. In July, 1905 a new Type Z utilizing the cabinet and motor of the Victor I was announced at the even lower price of $17.00. The new more powerful single-spring motor could play several of the new 8-inch size records per winding on its 8-inch turntable, and was an attractive alternative for those people who didn't care about the added feature of the tapering tone arm on the Victor I. These instruments were normally supplied with a "Concert" sound box and a small all-steel horn.

VICTOR JUNIOR
1909-1920　　　$10.00-$12.00

The small Victor Junior, introduced at $10 near the end of the new century's first decade, was Victor's lowest priced spring-driven phonograph ever. Significantly, it was also one of the last outside horn Victors to remain in production — surviving even World War I. The tiny cabinet was constructed of solid oak and all the metal controls were nickel-plated. The horn was painted dark red with gold stripes. A single-spring motor powered the 8-inch turntable, and the sound was delivered by a "Concert" or "Victor Junior" sound box. Because of shortages and inflation caused by World War I, the price was increased to $12.00 late in this instrument's life.

VICTOR O
1908-1920 $17.50-$20.00

In September of 1908, Victor introduced this instrument to replace their Type Z talking machine. The most obvious difference between the two was the 0's rear-mounted horn with tapering tone arm. The modest $.50 price increase put this instrument in the position of being the lowest priced Victor with a tapering tone arm. The cabinet had a mahogany finish, in contrast to the oak of most other Victors, and the hardware was all nickel-plated. A unique "Exhibition" sound box was normally furnished, and a single-spring motor powered the 8-inch turntable. Topping off the instrument was a handsome amber-colored steel horn with mahogany-colored stripes shaded at their edges to blend into the amber. The horn measured 16 inches in length (including elbow) and the bell was 14 inches in diameter.

Cabinet dimensions were 10 5/8 inches by 10 5/8 inches by 5 1/2 inches.

VICTOR I
1903-1920 $22.00-$30.00

Shortly after the turn of the century, Victor introduced a family of six talking machines that would form the foundation of the company's tremendous growth during the following decade. This instrument, the "Victor The First" as they called it, was the smallest of the six, but offered all of the important features which earned the company its fine reputation. Of foremost importance was the famous tapering tone arm which allowed ease of operation, flexibility of horn size, adjustable orientation of the horn, and superior tone quality. The solid oak cabinet contained a single-spring motor to power the 8-inch (increased to 10 inches in 1910) turntable, and the controls were all handsomely nickel-plated. A choice was offered the customer in the type of sound boxes ("Concert" or "Exhibition" at no extra cost) and horn style furnished. A black horn with a 9 1/2-inch diameter brass bell was standard on the earliest machines, but by the middle of the decade a larger flowered horn (painted black with gold stripes and a 17-inch diameter bell) was normally provided. Additionally, any of the larger horns, including the laminated oak horns, could be obtained by paying the difference in list price between the standard and optional horn.

As was Victor's custom, improvements were made from time to time. As an example, in September of 1909 shipments of an improved Victor I began. According to a press release of the time, the new instrument had a "stronger and better motor, better-designed cabinet, and a larger tapering arm." The price remained the same however, and dealers were admonished not to sell any of the improved machines before October 5, the official announcement date.

Cabinet dimensions were 12 inches by 12 inches by 5 7/8 inches.

VICTOR II
1902-1920 $30.00-$37.50

The "Victor The Second" was designed for those people who could afford a slightly nicer machine than the Victor I. Although in the later years the instruments appeared to be quite similar in design, the "Second" was about 1 1/2 inches deeper and wider than the "First". The very first Victor II's were built with the rigid (non-tapering) tone arm, but by 1904 the tapering arm had been substituted and this instrument was dubbed the "improved Victor II" (a subsequent price increase to $32.50 confirmed the improved status.) The cabinet was constructed of quartersawed oak and housed a single-spring motor. The 8-inch (later 10-inch) turntable and "Concert" or "Exhibition" sound box were nickel-plated. The ribbed corner columns were deleted when a restyled cabinet patterned after that of the Victor I was introduced in April, 1909. Although the instrument was initially available with only a "Concert" sound box and a steel horn with a 12 1/2-inch diameter brass bell, the choice was soon widened to include the "Exhibition" sound box and a black with gold stripe flower horn with a 19-inch diameter bell. As was the case with other Victors, larger horns were available at extra cost.

Cabinet dimensions for the later style were 13 5/8 inches wide by 13 5/8 inches deep by 6 1/2 inches high.

VICTOR III

1902-1920 $40.00-$45.00

The "Victor The Third" offered more than a mere cosmetic improvement over the Victor II. In addition to the extra decoration on the solid quartersawed oak cabinet, the Victor III boasted a double-spring motor capable of playing three 10-inch or five 7-inch records per winding, plus a 10-inch turntable. The cabinet and standard horn were larger than those normally supplied on a Victor II, as would be expected. The earliest Victor III's utilized the cabinet and motor of the Victor Monarch. Since Victor had established the value of the tapering tone arm at $5, the Victor III was always sold for $5 more than the front-mount Victor Monarch. A "Concert" or "Exhibition" sound box could be obtained with the instrument, as could a black steel horn with a 13 3/4-inch diameter brass bell, or a black flower horn with a 19-inch diameter bell. Larger horns, both in metal or oak, could be obtained at extra cost. A restyled cabinet was introduced in April, 1909 and its dimensions were 14 1/8 inches wide by 14 1/8 inches deep by 7 5/16 inches high.

VICTOR IV
1902-1920 $50.00-$57.50

The earliest "Victor The Fourths" were housed in the same highly ornamental quartersawed oak cabinet as the Victor Monarch Special, and possessed a triple-spring motor capable of playing six 10-inch or ten 7-inch records on a single winding. A tapering tone arm replaced the rigid arm in 1904, and in October of 1906 an entirely different looking Victor IV was introduced. In place of the fancy oak cabinet of its predecessor, the new Victor IV was equipped with a comparatively plain mahogany case. Inside, a newly designed double-spring motor replaced the older triple-spring motor. The change to a mahogany cabinet was made in order to offer those customers who preferred this wood's deep red tones and subdued grain pattern, an alternative to the expensive Victor VI. A matching mahogany horn was available at extra cost, but a steel horn with a 16 1/2-inch diameter brass bell or a black and gold flower horn with a 22 inch diameter bell was furnished as standard equipment. Also standard was a choice of a "Concert" or "Exhibition" sound box.

Dimensions of the mahogany cabinet were 14 inches wide by 14 inches deep by 7 3/32 inches high.

VICTOR V
1903-1920 $60.00-$67.50

The "Victor The Fifth" was introduced coincidentally with the 12-inch "Concert" records and was offered as the logical choice to play these new high-priced discs since the machine sported a 12-inch turntable. Catalog illustrations of the earliest style of Victor V show it to be identical to the oak Type D Victor (which was similar in appearance to the Monarch Special and Victor IV). In October of 1906, however, the Victor V received a larger and plainer cabinet (still made from solid quartersawed oak), but, unlike the Victor IV which was also redesigned at this time, the Victor V retained its triple-spring motor (Victor's best at this time). All exposed hardware was nickel-plated, and a choice of either the "Concert" or "Exhibition" sound boxes was offered as standard equipment. Although the earliest Victor V came with a steel horn with an 18 1/2-inch diameter brass bell, the later machines offered the additional choice of a black and gold flower horn with a 24-inch diameter bell. Larger horns, including the laminated oak horns, were available at extra cost.

Dimensions of the late style cabinet were 16 3/8 inches wide by 16 3/8 inches deep by 7 1/2 inches high.

VICTOR VI
1904-1915 $100.00-$105.00

The "Victor The Sixth" was designed to be the finest talking machine the company could make, and until the introduction of the Victor-Victrola and Auxetophone two years later, was their top-of-the-line instrument. The cabinet was fashioned out of solid mahogany - a more expensive and luxurious wood than oak at the time. All exposed hardware was gold-plated (a first on a Victor machine), and even the normally hidden motor parts were nickel-plated. The turntable rode on ball bearings and in 1908 incorporated a "yielding" shaft which prevented damage to the mechanism if the turntable were leaned upon. Early examples of the Victor VI were equipped with the gold-plated Victor No. 10 sound box which sold for $10.00 if purchased separately, and a special black papier-mache horn "having the appearance of polished hard rubber." In 1904, the price was reduced to an even $100.00, and the black horn was replaced by a standard 16.5 inch diameter brass bell horn with a painted wood-grain finish. After the Victor No. 10 sound box was discontinued, the "Concert" or "Exhibition" sound box (gold-plated, of course) was offered in its place. In October 1906, the Victor VI was equipped with a new style three-spring motor, and a slightly larger but identical-looking cabinet. These instruments came with a choice of the large laminated mahogany horn or a special solid brass flower horn with a 24-inch diameter bell. Cabinet dimensions of the later instruments were 16 inches wide by 16 inches deep by 7 25/32 inches high.

VICTOR XXV
1913-1925 $60.00-$115.00

Originally introduced in August 1913 as the Victor XXV at $60, this instrument is usually referred to as the "Schoolhouse Victor". The nickname was derived, logically enough, from the fact that this machine was expressly designed for use in educational institutions. Constructed of solid oak, the cabinet was a no-nonsense design (ugly, in other words) with four spindly legs supporting a plain rectangular box containing the vital mechanism. It is interesting to note that this instrument, designed to provide the best possible reproduction of records, came with an oak outside horn for amplification. In spite of the obvious nuisance of storing and attaching the awkward horn (in an environment full of mischievous youngsters), Victor opted to include this expensive amplifier with each Victor XXV. The earliest instruments came with the standard Victor No. 31 oak horn, but later machines featured a smooth-sided horn designed especially for the Victor XXV. Since this was basically a modestly priced machine, a double-spring motor was deemed to be sufficient, although a 12-inch diameter turntable was provided. A lockable lid, like that on the Victrolas, kept dust and unauthorized hands out of the mechanism. The Type A Victor XXV, announced in September 1914 at $67.50, incorporated several important design changes. The lid was made removable, so that it could be turned around and hung backwards from the rear of the cabinet. The shelf on the bottom was hinged so that the horn could be easily stored underneath when not in use. Less important changes included raising the turntable for easier access, and slightly increasing the size of the cabinet. Like other instruments of the period, this one received an "A" suffix on the model number to designate the new style motor in November 1917. At the same time, the price was raised to $75. The price was raised again in May 1918 (to $85), November 1918 (when a larger tone arm was introduced) and again in September 1919 when it reached the lofty plateau of $115. Also during 1917, the model designation of this instrument was mysteriously changed to Victrola XXV, (perhaps they ran out of "Victor" decals for the inside of the lid) and this instrument then became Victor's only outside horn talking machine ever to bear the famous "ola" suffix.

The early, smaller cabinet measured 40.25 inches high, by 18.6 inches wide and 23.9 inches deep.

AUXETOPHONE
1906-1918 $500.00

In May of 1906, Victor began the American production of a most unusual talking machine. The Auxetophone, as it was named by its English inventor, C. A. Parsons, used compressed air (supplied by a built-in compressor) to modulate a valve in the instrument's unique sound box. This arrangement permitted a significant increase in the amplitude of the air vibrating though the horn, hence resulting in a much louder reproduction of the record. The high price kept the instrument out of most front parlors, but it was quite popular with owners of hotels and restaurants, who used it to entertain guests during meals. Frequently, a small three-or four-piece live band would be used to back up the vocals of some of the popular Victor recording artists. The instrument in these establishments would pay for itself in a few months from the salaries saved, as it was normally expected that the finer eating establishments of the period would provide appropriate music with dinner.

The Auxetophone was first manufactured, beginning in 1904, by the Gramophone Company Ltd. of Great Britain, but Victor retained the exclusive American manufacturing rights, and during its long production run at Camden it never had any serious competition. In April 1909, a new lighter sound box and a new motor with an improved lubricating system were incorporated into the instrument. These changes might have been motivated by the observation of this instruments usual failure mode: fumes of the oil combusted within the compressor travelled through the tubing to the sound box, where they formed a crystaline deposit which in time caused the sound box to fail. These improvements were also offered to owners who wished to update their older machines, but other than this, the Auxetophone remained basically unchanged until its discontinuation in May 1918, exactly one dozen years from the date of its introduction.

Eldridge R. Johnson (President)
Leon F. Douglas (Chairman of the Board)   Louis F. Geissler (General Manager)

Victor's Top Officers at the 1915 Panama Pacific Exposition

DEVELOPMENT OF THE VICTROLA

In spite of all the progress Eldridge Johnson made in improving his talking machine and in spite of all of the decorative embellishments he added to it, there was still a large group of people who felt that the instrument was an eyesore with its ungainly horn and wouldn't permit one in their home. Eldridge Johnson recognized that this market existed and sought a way to entice it; and as early as 1903 sketches of the instrument which was to become the Victrola were circulating through the Camden facility. Ultimately he approached the respected Pooley Furniture Company of Philadelphia with a proposition to manufacture a cabinet to house a Victor mechanism with an unusual feature: the horn would be concealed within the cabinet! The new instrument, christened the Victor-Victrola, was introduced to a receptive public in August of 1906. The choice of the "ola" suffix was undoubtedly prompted by the success of the Aeolean Company's Pianola. That company's instrument became so popular that their copyrighted name became a generic term describing all makes of piano players. No doubt Johnson observed this and prophesied a similar fame for his new creation, and he could not have been more correct. Soon every manufacturer wanted to share in this success and the American public found themselves up to their neckolas in products bearing this famous appendage.

For his extra $100 (after all, the mechanism of the new Victrola was the same as that used in the Victor VI) the Victrola purchaser received a finely crafted cabinet which not only freed valuable countertop space, but also provided storage for all those bulky records and even a drawer to house needles, record cleaners, catalogs, or other accessories. Unfortunately, what the customer also received was a much smaller horn. Even though the sound emanating from the new Victrola was noticeably inferior to that from a large-horned Victor, the new machine became the talk of the town. To understand how the public must have reacted to this new invention, consider this text from an early Victrola brochure:

"Lift the lid and there is disclosed the turntable of a Victor, with all the devices for reproducing music, song or speech. But where is the horn? Perhaps you expect that from some corner of the room we must produce one and attach it as usual to the top of the cabinet.

"But you are mistaken, for there is no horn; the instrument is complete in itself. There it stands, ready to delight you, even as the regular types of Victors have done time and time again.

"Where is the record? Just here at hand, the door flies open and one of the albums of records is withdrawn and you are ready for an overture to your program.

"But stop, let us close the lid. What, shut in the music? No, not quite, but shut out all the sounds of operation. Here is a marvelous thing; you can test it for yourself. Lift the lid and play, then close it again and note the difference. Surely, the mechanical sounds are practically gone when the lid is down. But the music —

"Just open these doors and the melody pours forth. Don't you see we have simply reversed the ordinary practice. We take the sound as it were, by the hand, and lead it from the sound box above the record down through the tone tubes to a mahogany horn below rather than to a horn above, and modify the volume as we please by closing and opening, more or less, the doors. And we get by this new process, a mellow richness in the tones which comes nearer than ever to that goal of perfection which we seek in reproducing the voice or the musical instrument with all its color and feeling."

Eldridge Johnson knew that he had a winner on his hands and as soon as he could allocate the necessary floor space at the Camden plant one year later (the Victor factories were virtually continuously under expansion during the first fifth of this century), the cabinetmaking for the Victrola was transferred in house. At the same time (1907), the Victrola also received a numerical designation (the Sixteenth) in anticipation of the fact that this was only the first of a long new line of products in the Victor family tree.

In February of the following year, 1908, a second member of the Victrola family was introduced. The Victrola XX, as it was called, was essentially a Victrola XVI festooned with Louis XV gingerbread and fancy prominantly-grained "Laguna" mahogany. This style, at $300, was apparently not too popular, as the price was reduced by $50 in December of the same year to close out the remaining supply of 275 machines. These were sold by February 1909 when the style was officially discontinued.

The Victrola XVI was not to remain the only inside horn machine for long, for in July of 1909 a new baby Victrola, the XII, was announced. The family resemblance was unmistakable with the curved lid and concealed horn under the turntable, but this engaging youngster was designed to sit on a table top. This offspring also continued the dubious tradition of providing ever-decreasing horn dimensions. Fortunately for music lovers, this was the smallest horn ever to appear on any non-portable Victrola, and a trend towards larger horns became apparent as more models were added to the line.

September 10, 1910 must have been a day of celebration for Victrola lovers, as three new concealed horn instruments were born. The models X and XI introduced that day were table top models, similar in appearance to the baby Victrola they replaced, while the new Victrola XIV was a shorter cousin of the popular XVI. These new machines were designed to meet the competition provided by Columbia, which had placed a $150 floor model and $75 table model enclosed-horn phonograph on the market a few months earlier. The $75 Victrola X provided all of the features of the discontinued $125 Victrola XII, but in a smaller, plainer cabinet, with a less powerful motor. For an extra $25, the Victrola XI offered all of the features of the Victrola X, plus rounded cabinet corners and gold plating. Topping off the new Victrolas was the $150 Victrola XIV. This machine sported a simple, but gracefully proportioned, floor cabinet with ample storage racks for records and offered an interesting alternative to the Victrola XVI. Unlike the Victrola XVI, which displayed features somewhat reminiscent of the Louis XV school of furniture design, the model XIV with its slender curved legs was in the Queen Anne style.

Moorish Marquetry   Vernis-Martin

Art Case Victrola XVI's

For those people who could not find what they wanted in these standard styles, some custom made-to-order Victrolas were also available. Other concerns for years had made special cabinets for Victor mechanisms, and continued to do so for the enclosed horn mechanisms as well. Victor also offered custom cabinets for the wealthy few who could afford them. The premier example at this time was the $750 mother-of-pearl inlaid Moorish Marquetry cabinet which Victor commissioned to be made in Morocco. This particular style was offered for three or four years beginning in 1909, but because of the advanced price, only a very few were manufactured. For those of more limited means, Victor catalogued a $400 Victrola XVI to which an artist carefully applied oil paintings on the front and sides (plus inside the doors and lid) of a standard cabinet. This was usually referred to as the Louis XV cabinet by the trade, or the Vernis-Martin design by Victor in honor of the French cabinet makers (Martin) who popularized the style during that monarch's reign. These cabinets were never popular with dealers because of the extreme delicacy of the finish, and many were reportedly returned to the factory when new because of checking of the varnish (or vernis in French). The simple act of leaving a crated instrument on the doorstep for an hour or so during the cold of the winter before bringing it inside a warm building was enough to damage the finish seriously (and also an excellent way to break motor springs). Despite these difficulties, the Vernis-Martin style was Victor's only true period art style Victrola available until 1917, when several new cabinet styles were introduced.

**A Japanese Lacquer Victrola X
custom made for the residence of John Wanamaker**

The phonograph price war gained momentum in April 1911 when the $50 Victrola IX was announced, but Victor saved its biggest attack for September when the $40 Victrola VIII, $25 Victrola VI and $15 Victrola IV were introduced. At that time no one else had a concealed horn machine which could match the value offered by the model IV Victrola. For $15 the prospective buyer received all the expected Victor features such as a nickel-plated Exhibition sound box and tapering tone arm, a solid oak cabinet of the traditional Victor quality and a single-spring motor ingeniously concealed within the horn to take maximum advantage of the small case. The front louvers were angled in such a way as to hide the motor from view and front doors were provided to modify the volume as in all previous Victrolas.

The next step up was the Victrola VI with a larger oak case (mahogany would be offered later), a two-spring motor and, initially, the same ten-inch turntable as supplied on the

Victrola IV. In this price range the buyer did not receive a lid to contain the surface noise of the record while it played as in previous Victrolas — this feature required the expenditure of a minimum of $40 for a machine such as the new Victrola VIII. This new instrument was essentially a slightly smaller version of the popular Victrola IX, but at four-fifths of the cost. Like the styles IV and VI, the new VIII was initially available only in oak.

During the early part of this century, oak was a popular wood noted for its durability and moderately low cost. When "quartersawed" as Victor usually used it, it became particularly attractive. Quartersawing of the log yielded less usable lumber than if the tree had been cut conventionally, but produced a very attractive and predominant grain pattern sometimes referred to as "tiger-stripe". Consequently, quartersawed oak was the premium grade of this wood, and was enormously popular during the first quarter of this century for use in medium-priced furniture. Victor offered several finishes in this serviceable wood. The smaller Victrolas were generally available in a choice of high or low gloss golden finish, while the oak style XVI was available in no less than eight different colors!

Mahogany and walnut were the usual choices for the more expensive pieces, however, particularly when done in imitation of some of the better period furniture. The desire to match the wood grains, coupled with the added expense of these woods meant that larger cabinets were usually manufactured by gluing a thin veneer of the desired wood (actually, it was usually a double veneer) over an oak or other hardwood core. The most expensive wood cataloged by Victor was Circassian walnut, which cost a whopping $50 extra on the larger Victrolas. This wood has an unusually prominent swirl pattern in its grain, and is found primarily in the Mediterranean area. Today this rare wood finds its best known use in Rolls Royce automobiles, where a single tree is rationed to provide material for the entire year's production of dashboards.

By the close of 1911 the Victrola line had fairly well stabilized with an offering of eight different models, and it was to remain at this size for the next four years. However, this is not to say that there were not changes in store for the individual machines. Victor continued to "improve the breed" by changing cabinet styling and offering mechanical improvements during this period. First on the agenda, in

August of 1912, was a restyling of the models XVI, XIV, XI, and X. The Sixteenth lost its "L" shaped doors and received a larger horn in exchange. The Fourteenth was changed from a pseudo-Queen Anne style to a shrunken copy of the Victrola XVI, while the Tenth and Eleventh became floor models.

The Eleventh was the more traditional looking of the two new floor models, resembling a still smaller version of the Victrola XVI. In the change, however, the Eleventh lost its gold plating and deluxe trim, but since it retained its $100 price tag, perhaps this was a fair exchange. It must have seemed more than fair to the public, as this machine became Victor's best selling floor model in later years.

The most unusual member of this new group of four machines was the new Victrola X which became a floor model by the simple expediency of adding four legs and a shelf! A set of record albums to sit on this shelf added $10 to the price, but it was still Victor's cheapest floor model. This ungainly skeleton apparently was not well received, for only eight months later dealers were advised to sell off their remaining stock of the open sided X, because an enclosed version would be forthcoming soon. When the new X's became available in August of 1913, dealers were authorized to reduce the price (discreetly) of the older style to $60. Some dealers, however, were actually indiscreet enough to advertise this bargain price, and in doing so incurred the wrath of Camden.

Victor traditionally did not feel that the image of price cutting had any place in relation to an item of such prestige as theirs. For years they vigorously prosecuted any and all dealers who would dare to sell a Victor product at less than the price established by the factory. It was not until 1917, when the Supreme Court ruled against Victor, that the company relaxed its strict dealer licensing agreements. As a result of the ruling, Victor accepted a consent decree prohibiting price maintenance and dealer exclusivity. From this time onward, the Victor price list was only a guide, and dealers could not be forced to refrain from offering discounts. Additionally, Victor could no longer force its dealers to maintain a service department (often not a profit center), and many customers were required to send their Victrolas to Camden for repair.

In August of 1913 Victor also announced that the automatic brake (actually it was only semi-automatic) which it had been putting on its models XI, XIV and XVI since March would be sold separately for older machines at $2 in nickel or $3 in gold finish. A rod protruding downward from the tone arm was used to trigger the brake. As the arm traversed the final (silent) grooves of the record, the protruding rod contacted a pre-set lever which operated the brake, thereby shutting off the motor. Unfortunately, there was no industry standard for ending records, requiring that the brake actuation point be manually set for the various types of records. It was not until the middle of the 1920's, when Victor incorporated an eccentric groove at the end of each record, that a reliable "non-set" automatic brake became possible.

In 1914 some new finishes were added to the choices offered new Victrola purchasers. English brown mahogany was offered as an alternative to the traditional red mahogany, and fumed oak was made an option for the styles X and XI.

For some years a public preference trend towards the larger Victrolas had been slowly taking place. The sales of the $15 and $25 machines had started off at a fantastic pace, but Victor officials were surprised and gratified to note that a large number of these owners wanted to upgrade their music systems and were purchasing the larger Victrolas in ever-increasing numbers. Victor reasoned that now perhaps there was a market for a new machine with a cabinet superior to that of the venerable XVI. Thus was born the Victrola XVIII in May of 1915. This $300 beauty had the basic shape shared by all of the others in the line-up, but with added embellishments: the front and sides were each gracefully curved and contained fancy moldings to outline the specially selected wood grains, resulting in a particularly handsome cabinet. When equipped with the new $50 electric motor introduced at the beginning of the year and with walnut veneer, the price soared to $400, the same as the model XVI with the Vernis-Martin treatment. This must have been more than the traffic could bear, for nineteen months later Victor retreated somewhat and replaced this $300 jewel with the slightly less pretentious Victrola XVII at $250.

This was only a temporary move, however, as Victor had something more spectacular than the XVIII in mind for all those affluent art lovers looking to decorate their homes.

Following the trends set earlier by Columbia, and most notably, Aeolean, Victor unleashed an assortment of 46 (46!) different and distinct period model Victrolas in October of 1917. The period cases were offered in variations of the following basic styles: William and Mary, Sheraton, Gothic, Jacobean, Chippendale, Hepplewhite, Empire, Adam, Queen Anne, Louis XV, Louis XVI and Chinese Chippendale. Special catalogs (receiving a very limited distribution) were issued which showed each of these styles in a suitable surrounding, so that the prospective purchaser could see just how well it would harmonize with his or her new castle. Prices started at $300 and did not stop until they reached $900 ($950 with the electric motor), although most styles were priced around $500. Needless to say, these instruments were available on special order only, and took "considerable time" to manufacture. All of these instruments were unmistakably Victrolas, and bore the familiar shape so carefully adhered to by the company over the years. Even though the public had demonstrated a desire for the shorter and wider console cabinets offered by Aeolean, Columbia, Edison and others, Eldridge Johnson stubbornly refused to market a machine that "didn't look like a Victrola". One fear, the speculation went, was that if a person had a wide flat top on his talking machine, he would use it for holding all sorts of non-musical items such as vases, clocks, statues and the like, thus complicating access for casual record playing and consequently reducing the demand for new records. Brunswick had solved this problem by providing access to their turntable from the front of the cabinet on some models, but Victor refused to make any compromises until 1920, when, begrudgingly one assumes, a line of "wide" cabinets was added to the Period catalog.

In any event, these new art styles were designed more to return prestige to the Victor line than for the direct purpose of increasing company sales. The spotlight had been stolen from Victor in recent years by some of the spectacular cabinets which had been heavily advertised by others in the best periodicals of the day. The Victrola XVI looked positively poverty-stricken compared to the $3000 one-of-a-kind Gothic style phonograph displayed by Edison, or the seemingly infinite variety of period cabinets in the $1000 to $2000 range shown by Columbia and Aeolean. Although sales of these instruments were insignificant by Victor standards, the company could not afford to have the public think that the finest machines came from East Orange or New York.

The bread-and-butter instruments were not forgotten in the celebration of the new period pieces, however. Victor simultaneously announced that most of the smaller machines would now be equipped with an improved spring motor, and that an "A" would suffix the numerical designation of instruments so equipped. This gave the company a convenient excuse to raise the prices of these machines, as the war had created severe shortages (and consequently higher prices) of several critical materials, most notably steel. Prices were increased from six to thirty percent, with the biggest increases on the smaller instruments. Two more price increases followed: one in May 1918, and again in September 1919. Hardest hit was the schoolhouse Victrola XXV which saw its price nearly double to $115 in just five years.

Victor had devoted a significant portion of its manufacturing facility to the war effort making rifles and other armament. More than patriotism was involved in this gesture, as the U.S. Government tied delivery of war-rationed raw materials to Victor's acceptance of military contracts. Victor's metal department made small rifle fittings, while the cabinet factory made stocks for the American version of the British Enfield rifle and constructed wooden fabric-covered wings for larger airplanes. When they returned these areas to talking machine production at the war's end, they discovered that the other phonograph manufacturers had made significant inroads into their business. Dealers who had formerly handled only Victor products had been forced by the shortage of Victrolas to sell other brands as well in order to meet the public's strong demand for record players. In 1918, Victor's consumer production dropped to 55% of the previous year's record due primarily to their government contracts, and this set an ominous tone for the following years. Production rose slowly after the war, but failed to equal the pre-war total. It was clear to the Victor policy makers and dealers alike that a substantial number of sales were being lost because of the now obsolete cabinet styles contained in the Victor catalog. The public was buying phonographs that looked like end tables, desks, buffet tables, pianos, grandfather clocks, or even lamps, and was bored with the "Victorian"-looking Victrolas. Eldridge Johnson finally capitulated by offering a low and wide cabinet for the new model No. 300 Victrola in late summer of 1921. He was none too soon either, for 1921 Victrola sales were a disaster-the equal of those during the war, however this time the shortfall could not be blamed on the national defense.

Johnson managed to maintain the family resemblance of the new No. 300 by giving it the curved top surfaces and domed lid of the upright Victrolas. These also served to thwart attempts to use the top of the machine for storage of foreign objects, but resulted in a shape that only a mother (preferably a mother camel) could love.

Nevertheless, sales of Victrolas did improve as more console-style cabinets numbered in the 200 and 300 series were introduced. Also, several new upright-style instruments were added to the line to augment the older designs. Victor modernized the design of the upright style by changing the proportions of the cabinet slightly. The horn opening became larger in relation to the rest of the cabinet and the overall effect was somewhat more purposeful looking than the older styles. The "modern" style Victrola uprights were offered alongside the traditional designs, giving the buyer a choice of two almost identical instruments in nearly every price range.

By 1923 fully 21 different floor models were illustrated in the Victrola catalog and the console styles were outselling the uprights by more than two-to-one. By this time, nearly all of the Roman numeral designations had given way to Arabic numerals, to emphasize the modern nature of the designs. Now even the period cabinets were available in virtually any configuration imaginable, designed to the personal specifications of the customer by Victor's Art Department at costs of up to $1500. While phonograph sales were still not approaching the pre-war level, Victor management was predicting a rosy future.

Unfortunately, this was not to be the case, as the conservative leadership again failed to heed a threatening cloud now appearing in a different quarter of the horizon, and this time their inattention almost proved fatal. Had Johnson and his staff been more alert to the public's growing infatuation with radio, they might have aligned themselves with one of the fledgling radio companies and become positioned in the forefront of the new opportunity. Instead, believing that nothing could replace records as the prime musical entertainment medium, for a time they preferred to try to ignore this electronic upstart and treat it as a passing diversion. In early 1921, David Sarnoff, the young guiding genius behind the newly created Radio Corporation of America, demonstrated a radio-phonograph combination to Victor officials at his home, yet Eldridge Johnson remained unmoved. To be fair, there was a limited effort at Victor to develop a radio receiver "worthy of the name" during this period, but the only apparent result was the production of twenty instruments of a type known as the VV-R-80. The model number would indicate that these were radio receivers installed in Victrola No. 80 cabinets, although this is purely speculative. Such an instrument might not have been much different than the one any radio fan could have constructed with the aid of several popular accessories designed specifically for the purpose of adapting a phonograph to play radio programs through its horn. Victor continued to hope for a reversal of the sales trend as the radio fad continued to steal Victrola sales, but by Christmas of 1924, the situation became devastating. The fall months had always accounted for the greatest number of Victor's sales as Americans rewarded themselves or their families for a prosperous year by placing a new Victrola under the tree. Spring and Summer production at the factory was scheduled in anticipation of the demand the following fall, but the public was buying radios for Christmas in 1924, not Victrolas. For the first time in recent memory there were great numbers of unsold instruments crowding the storerooms of the dealers, the distributors and the factory alike.

In 1925, in an effort to cater to the demand for radio receivers, four instruments in the standard Victrola line were modified to accept "any standard make" of radio receiver. By adding a second lid to the left of the turntable in these instruments, Victor created a space which could accommodate a radio chassis. In true Victor fashion, the blank panel under the lid contained a disclaimer in the form of a brass plaque warning that "Any radio apparatus installed in this cabinet was not made or installed by the Victor Talking Machine Company." While these instruments (identified by the addition of a "S", for Special, to the model number) were normally supplied with albums, batteries could be mounted in place of the record albums, allowing all the equipment to be self-contained within the console. These instruments were known as the "Radio-Adaptable Victrolas" by the dealers, and were heavily promoted as the answer to housing a radio receiver which might soon be obsolete. Money spent on a fancy Victrola cabinet would not be wasted, dealers advertised, because "a Victrola will always remain in style". As will be seen, this was a promise which the great Victor company could not keep.

Lightweight Portable Victrola
custom made for the Airship Shenandoah

The Radio Adaptable Victrola

How Victrolas Were Made

A Tour of the 1917 Victor Factory

The plant which was to become Camden's largest employer began as a tiny machine shop at 108 N. Front Street. Known originally as the Standard Machine Shop, it was one of several such small businesses in the area which specialized in the repair of home appliances and farm equipment, or the occasional construction of models of inventions which were required to be submitted with the application for a patent. Eldridge Johnson worked for the owner, Captain Andrew Scull, on and off for several years. Mr. Johnson excelled at this work, and was soon offered a partnership in the concern (a dubious honor, considering that on good weeks young Eldridge was able to draw a salary of only ten or twelve dollars.) It soon became apparent that the income of the shop could not be relied upon to support two owners, so Capt. Scull and Mr. Johnson faced the question as to which of them should leave. Capt. Scull agreed to sell his interest in the shop to Eldridge Johnson in October 1894, and for the next few years, Eldridge struggled to keep the business alive. Years later, he never forgot the long hard years of apprenticeship he invested in his small business before he was to taste success. Decades after it ceased to function as a work area, the original machine shop could be seen standing as a monument to perseverance and hard work in the shadow of the giant Victor factory.

Following the incorporation of the Victor Talking Machine Company in 1901, the company embarked on a lengthy and ambitious building program. Dollars were poured back into the factory as fast as they were made, and soon it seemed that no part of Camden was safe from the expansion. Perfectly sound buildings were bought and torn down to make room for further Victor floor space. By 1917 the company was a model of modern, efficient manufacturing methods. Operations were arranged to flow from one floor to another, and from one building to the adjacent one. Covered bridges connected certain operations in different buildings so that the absolute minimum amount of energy was expended in transporting a Victrola through the manufacturing process. The company was self-sufficient even to the point of generating its own electricity.

**Eldridge Johnson's original machine shop
as preserved on the Victor property**

Victor urged its dealers to visit the factory for a tour, because no amount of linguistic over-kill could relay to the novice the magnitude of the company's facilities. Many dealers (and tourists as well) took advantage of Victor's invitation and received an eye-opening excursion through the genesis of a Victrola. A lucky visitor in 1917 might have started his tour by seeing one of the world's largest and most valuable lumber yards in one corner of the company's property.

Prior to 1907, when the company completed its first cabinet factory, Victor's use of raw lumber was minimal. As the factory expanded, the company came to rely less and less on outside vendors and hence had much tighter control on both the quality and cost of the product it produced. Such independence required a heavy investment, and at any one time the Victor lumber yard contained stocks of oak, mahogany, walnut and other fine woods worth many hundreds of thousands of dollars.

Each piece of lumber was individually inspected as it arrived in the yard, prior to storage. As it was needed, the wood was removed to the kilns to prepare it for use in the cabinet factory.

The cabinet factory! If there was anywhere a more striking example of the wonders wrought by the American Industrial Revolution, it would have been difficult to imagine. From raw lumber to gleaming furniture, there was not a wasted motion or lost process in the entire building. Of the eight thousand employees at the Victor plant, fully five thousand of them were employed in the construction of the cabinets for which the company was justifiably renowned. To house this immense work force, Victor erected, at the corner of Market and Delaware Avenue, a six story building which occupied nearly a full third of a square city block and contained 12.8 acres of floor space.

A cabinet began its life as the raw wood cores and veneers were sandwiched to make the strong composite board used in cabinet construction. Hot animal-hide glue (piped to all parts of the cabinet factory from two huge 150 gallon vats) was applied by large steel rollers which spread an even coating on both surfaces of the "cross bands" used in the material's contruction. The glue-saturated cross bands functioned to bond the veneer to each side of the core wood. Care was taken to orient the grain of the core orthogonal to that of the cross bands to assure maximum strength and resistance to warping. A power press clamped the assemblage together until the glue had set. From here, the wood progressed to a large dry kiln for tempering, before being transported to the millwork department on the second floor.

Victor had good reason to be proud of the ornamentation adorning the larger Victrolas, for, unlike some phonograph brands (such as Brunswick) which utilized numerous molded appliques just glued to the cabinet, all of the carving embellishing Victrola cabinets was done by hand. To be sure, automatic carvers were used to rough legs and corner posts to shape, but the final decoration was always applied by the hand of a skilled "old-world" craftsman with the traditional carving tools. In order to convey an idea of the magnitude of work which passed through the second floor milling department, Victor boasted that this one floor produced *seven to fifteen tons* of sawdust *everyday..*

The various pieces which were to become a handsome new Victrola cabinet finally met on the third floor where they first received a thorough sanding by both hand and machine. Faster than words can describe, the various cabinet pieces were brought to one spot where experienced workers quickly applied the hot glue, and pressed the pieces into position. A man with a talented mallet nudged any obstinate pieces into their proper places before a three-minute stint in a press allowed the glue time to set. A Victrola XI cabinet could be assembled by this seasoned team in only one minute, and even the larger Victrola XIV required only three minutes to assemble (exclusive of the time in the press).

On the fifth floor, the cabinets began to acquire their final color. The process began by way of a swift plunge into a tank of the appropriate stain. While the stain was applied in an instant, the drying of it was allowed to occupy a full twelve hours in Victor's special zinc-clad drying kilns.

Following this thorough drying, the porous mahogany grain was filled by a most unlikely substance -seaweed. Seaweed was used not only because it was economical, but more importantly, because it was soft enough not to scratch the wood. The dryed seaweed was rubbed across the stained cabinet, filling the grain and polishing the surface.

Following a light sanding, the cabinet received its first coat of shellac to form a base for the varnish which was to come later. An elaborate spraying system was installed at the factory in 1915 to replace the earlier brush application of shellac and varnish, so all subsequent instruments benefited from the even, smooth application afforded by the spray process. The cabinet received, in total, a sanding, a coat of shellac, a second sanding, a second coat of shellac, a visit to the kiln, and finally three coats of varnish (each separated by a twenty-four hour drying in the kiln). This procedure was followed until 1925, when lacquer replaced varnish as the protective coating on the new Orthophonic Victrolas.

Fumed oak instruments followed a different route as the raw, unfinished cabinet was first placed in a steam bath while surrounded by a six-foot-deep trough of diluted ammonia. The steam opened the pores, while the ammonia fumes produced the dulled color characteristic of this technique. Instead of varnish, these oak instruments received a wax finish.

Prior to final assembly, the varnished cabinets received a combination hand and machine rubdown with pumice and water.

In an obscure corner of the sixth floor a small but dedicated group of craftsmen sat gilding the Vernis-Martin cabinets of the top-of-the-line Victrola. A painter of forty-plus years of experience applied the elaborate Watteau pictures to the sides of the instruments.

As the completed cabinets crossed the enclosed bridge con-

The bridge connecting the Cabinet Factory to the final assemby area

necting the cabinet factory to the assembly building, each one received a scrutinous inspection, and any found to be imperfect were sent back to be redone.

While the cabinets were being fabricated, countless operators elsewhere in the factory labored to produce the metal parts essential to the operation of the instruments. As Eldridge Johnson originally began as a machinist, it was here that he exercised his greatest influence in the production process. Great automatic machines turned out parts by the hundreds and thousands. Winding cranks, as an example, could be made without human intervention - all the operator had to do was to assure a supply of raw materials and to stand back. Automatic screw machines turned out screws of every conceivable size, and even hinges were made in Victor's own stamping department.

Taper tubes were made by the most modern of methods. Straight brass tubes, nine inches long and one and one-quarter inches in diameter (closed at one end), were first bent to a right angle in 15 seconds by forcing a watery solution at a pressure of 5000 pounds per square inch into the tube as it lay in a mold of the proper shape. The patented taper was obtained by three separate drawing processes separated by annealings at temperatures of 1300 degrees Fahrenheit.

Turntables were fabricated even more quickly. Long sheets of steel were fed into an immense stamping machine which, in a single stroke, produced seven twelve-inch-plus discs. The following press turned over the edge of each disc, and a similar

Polishing and buffing Taper Tubes

final press finished the rough forming by stiffening the turntable with a center die. After being turned on a lathe (to smooth and polish the edges), the turntables received their nickel or gold plating before progressing to a workbench where a young lady swiftly and deftly applied and cut the green felt cover common to all models.

Upstairs, in the enameling room, quantities of taper-tube supports received the customary two coats of black enamel (separated by a three and one-half hour baking). The fine gold pin striping was entirely applied by hand, after which the piece was varnished to protect the finish.

Bachelors living in Camden might have thought that all of the young ladies simply vanished during the day, swallowed by some unseen force. They would have been wrong, for not only was the force not unseen, it was virtually impossible to miss! It was, of course, Victor, for the company had discovered early in its history that women were more adept in the handling of delicate governor and sound-box parts than were men. Consequently, these sections of the factory were almost exclusively occupied by women.

The sound box assembly line must have appeared to have come straight out of the Ford Motor Company, for the same principles formulated by Henry Ford were in evidence here. Each girl had but a single operation to perform before passing the sound box on to the next station. At the end of the conveyor chain, the boxes were required to pass a simple but

Final Sound Box assembly and test

revealing test -they had to perform for the trained ear of the inspector by playing a record on a Victrola XVI.

In other corners of the factory, an army of skilled hands was assembling motors, record albums, instruction manuals and every other item required to complete the product. All these components met the finished cabinet at the final assembly area, where they were carefully assembled into row upon row of glistening new Victrolas. A barrage of inspections followed and, if and when the instrument passed all tests, it was then sent to the immense shipping department where it could be forwarded without delay to the distributers who, it seemed, could usually not get enough to satisfy all the dealers' requests.

The woodworking equipment contained in the 5.5 acre Victor shipping department would have been the envy of most furniture factories! Down each aisle the visitor could see countless custom automatic boring machines, saws, nailing machines and the like. Victor had reduced to a science the art of shipping a Victrola to a dealer and having it arrive in the same perfect condition as when it left the factory.

While the smaller instruments could be shipped simply packed in excelsior, the heavy floor model Victrolas required a very sturdy package. Prior to shipping, all movable pieces, such as the motor, turntable, sound box and record albums, were individually wrapped to prevent marring. The rear and/or bottom of the Victrola cabinet was drilled to receive the bolts

Assembling Victrola IX's

Assembling Victrola XIV's

which would secure the instrument to its new temporary shelter. A carefully designed frame surrounded the cabinet and spaced the instrument away from the walls of the packing crate. Natural cork, coated with paraffin wax, separated the frame of the container from the newly finished cabinet and prevented damage to the varnish. When thus prepared, the completely packed Victrola was inserted into its packing case, and the latter was secured with screws (instead of nails, to facilitate removal). This elaborate procedure was designed to protect the instrument from the hazards of shipping while still being light enough to keep the shipping charges reasonable. Victor approved the case design after inspecting instruments which were dropped from loading dock height onto concrete slabs, and observing that no damage had occured.

The boxed Victrola made its way, by a series of gravity conveyors and elevators, to the trackside loading dock from which boxcars full of new Victrolas were shuttled to the nearby Pennsylvania Railroad tracks by Victor's electric switch engine. Shipments going forward via boat line were trucked to Philadelphia in ample time to be loaded prior to sailing. For many years, the company ran a special train to New York City on Christmas Eve carrying Victrolas to fill last minute holiday orders, because while the Victor factories might have been pre-eminent in the industry, they were still not always adequate to meet the heavy seasonal demand for instruments.

the VICTROLA

VICTROLA IV
1911-1926 $15.00-$25.00

The first "Victrola The Fourth" was shipped from the Camden factory on September 1, 1911 and was Victor's response to the low cost, concealed-horn phonographs that Columbia had been so successfully promoting the previous year. At $15.00, it undercut even Columbia's lowest-priced machine and was, of course, an instant best seller. The earliest style cabinet was solid oak and the single-spring motor actually sat in the center of the horn. The closely spaced slats covering the horn opening were so angled as to conceal the motor from view. This design minimized the required cabinet size and was one factor in the instrument's initial low cost. Through the years improvements were made and the price inched higher. In September 1917, a new motor design was used which resulted in the "Victrola IV-A" designation and forced a $2.50 price increase. The material shortages and inflation of World War I caused the price to jump to $20.00 in October 1917, $22.50 in May 1918, and $25.00 in September 1919. The cabinet styling was modified in November 1918, and the "A" designation was dropped from the nameplate after this time. The motor of the later-style Victrola IV's was completely enclosed, and the standard widely spaced slots were incorporated into the horn opening. All Victrola IV's were shipped with a nickel-plated "Exhibition" sound box and a 10-inch turntable, and were offered in a glossy or dull golden finish.

VICTROLA VI
1911-1926 $25.00 - $35.00

Shipments of the first Victrola VI's were made on October 16, 1911, just 1.5 months after the first of the popular Victrola IV's. The Victrola VI was very similar in concept and design to the Victrola IV, but offered a double-spring motor and a larger oak cabinet. The premium for this added luxury was $10.00 - a price differential which was maintained throughout all of the price increases of the late teens. In May of 1913, the Victrola VI was remodeled with a "suspended horn amplifying chamber" (the front of the horn was not attached to the case, but rather floated within the cabinet) and a 12-inch turntable to replace the former 10-inch diameter turntable. The new style motor caused a change in designation (to VI-A) and price (to $27.50) in September 1917. Further price increases were announced in October 1917 ($30.00), May 1918 ($32.50), and September 1919 ($35.00). In November 1918 the "A" suffix was dropped when the cabinet was redesigned to include a removable motor board (formerly, the entire top was hinged) and for the first time, the cabinet was available in mahogany. All Victrola VI's were equipped with an Exhibition sound box and nickel-plated hardware. Cabinet dimensions on the earliest style (circa 1912) were 15 5/16 inches wide, by 16 3/8 inches deep, by 8 1/8 inches high. In later years, the cabinet grew taller to a final size of 15.5 inches wide, 16.5 inches deep, and 8.75 inches high.

VICTROLA VIII
1911-1924 $40.00-$50.00

The Victrola VIII, when introduced in September 1911, became the lowest priced Victrola equipped with a lid. This machine shared many of the features of the initial Victrola VI, such as a double-spring motor, Exhibition sound box, 10-inch turntable, nickel-plated hardware and oak cabinet, but through the years additional features, such as an automatic speed indicator and semi-automatic brake (introduced in October 1917) and Victrola No. 2 sound box (1921), were added to the Victrola VIII which were not added to the smaller machine. The newly designed motor of September 1917 resulted in a designation change to VIII-A and a price hike to $45.00, but the "A" suffix was rescinded and the price was increased to $50.00 the following year.

Dimensions of the earliest cabinets were 12.5 inches high, by 15.25 inches wide, by 18.9 inches deep. By the end of production, the cabinet had grown to 13.5 inches high, by 15.5 inches wide, by 19.25 inches deep.

VICTROLA IX
1911-1926 $50.00-$75.00

The Victrola IX was added to the Victor line in May 1911 to augment the higher priced Victrola X introduced the previous year. The cabinet of the "Victrola the Ninth" was plainer than that of the "Victrola the Tenth" and available in red mahogany as well as golden oak. In April 1914 a "fumed" oak finish was added to the choices and in October 1914 an "English brown" mahogany finish was made available. The Victrola IX-A of September 1917 offered the newly designed double-spring motor plus an automatic speed indicator, semi-automatic brake and redesigned tapering tone arm. The new price was $57.50, but that increased to $60.00 in May 1918, $70.00 in September 1919 and $75.00 in 1921. The "A" designation was dropped after 1918. A Victrola No. 2 sound box replaced the older style Exhibition sound box in 1921. The 12-inch turntable and other hardware were all nickel-plated.

Cabinet dimensions when first introduced were 16 inches wide, by 20.2 inches deep, by 13.75 inches high. The cabinet was subsequently enlarged to 17 inches wide, 21.5 inches deep, and 14.75 inches high.

VICTROLA X
1910-1921 $75.00-$110.00

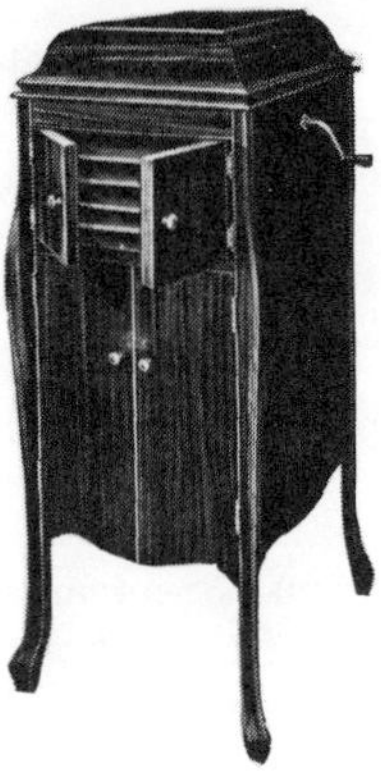

The Victrola X was one of two machines that Victor introduced in September 1910 to replace the discontinued Victrola XII. At $75.00 it was $50.00 less than the XII, the first tabletop Victrola, and was available in either mahogany or oak. Its configuration remained unchanged until August 15, 1912 when the first examples of a new style X were shipped. By adding four legs and a shelf to the old table-top cabinet, Victor transformed this phonograph into a floor model. The price was held at $75.00, but an additional $10 would equip the machine with a shelf full of record albums. This styling apparently did not catch the public's fancy, as in March 1913 Victor quietly told its dealers to sell off their remaining stocks of these open sided Victrola X's since in July they would begin to ship a new style Victrola X with enclosed sides. When the new "Victrola the Tenth's" were in the stores, Victor authorized its dealers to sell any remaining open sided machines at $60.00 to clear them out. Like the original style X, the new floor model was available in red mahogany or golden oak, and came with a double-spring motor (although the earliest examples had single-spring motors), Exhibition sound box and nickel-plated hardware. The newly introduced semi-automatic brake was standard on the enclosed style Victrola X and vertical slats were provided for record storage. In April, 1914, Victor announced that a fumed oak finish would be available for this machine, and the following month they replaced the vertical slats with horizontal shelves spaced to hold record albums. English brown mahogany was announced in October of that year, and when a new style motor was introduced in October 1917 the price was raised to $85.00 and the model designation was changed to "X-A". The price was increased again in May 1918 ($90.00) and once more in September 1919 ($110.00), when the "A" designation was dropped.

Dimensions of the table top model were 18.5 inches wide, by 22.5 inches deep, by 15.5 inches high.

VICTROLA XI
1910-1921 $100.00-$130.00

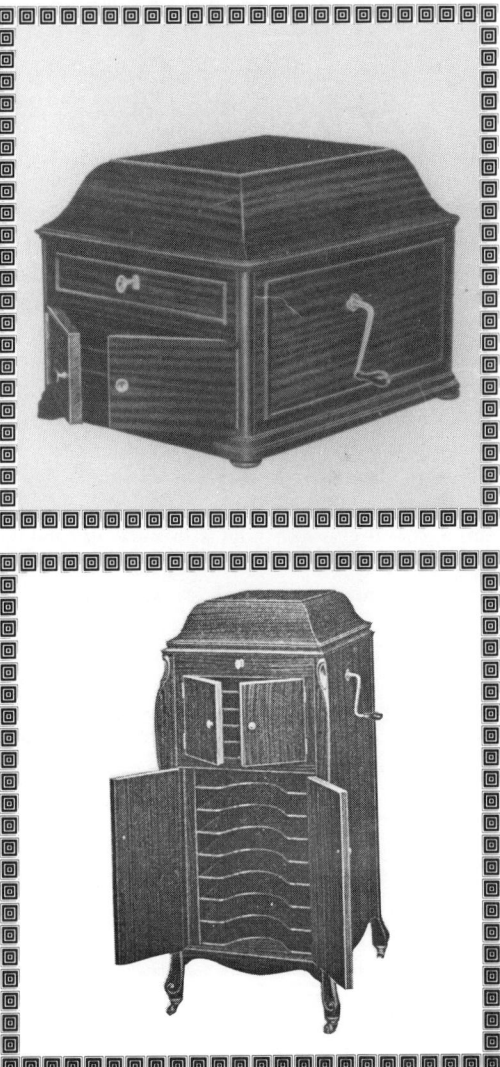

The Victrola XI was the second of the two table-top Victrolas which were introduced in September of 1910 to replace the discontinued Victrola XII. Like the Victrola XII, this instrument had a gold-plated Exhibition sound box, an attractive mahogany cabinet (oak was available as well) and a nickel-plated motor. The $25.00 price reduction was achieved by reducing the motor's power by one third, but in most other respects the new instrument was very similar to the older one. One important improvement was the enlargement in the size of the horn opening which provided increased volume and response. Victor apparently decided that even this reduced price was too much for a table-top instrument, so after the introduction of two lower priced Victrolas (the VIII and IX), both the Victrola X and XI were converted to floor models. The first of the new style Victrola XI's left the factory on August 15, 1912 in time for their debut on the showroom floors September 15. Since the price was maintained at $100.00, some of the deluxe features of the original style were deleted to compensate for the added woodwork. The nickel plating was removed from the motor and deposited instead on the interior hardware. The small moldings were also deleted, but the public seemed to approve of the exchange as they soon made this the most popular of all the floor model Victrolas. In March of the following year the semi-automatic brake was added to the Victrola XI's standard equipment and in May of 1914 the cabinet was enlarged slightly to incorporate horizontal shelves for record albums in place of the previous vertical slats. Fumed oak and English brown mahogany were added to the available finishes in April and October 1914 respectively. The new motor design incorporated in October 1917 caused the price to jump to $110.00 and the designation to be changed to Victrola XI-A. Further price increases in May 1918 and September 1919 (when the "A' was dropped) raised the price to $115.00 and finally to $130.00.

Dimensions of the earliest table top version of the Victrola XI were 17.6 inches wide, by 21.9 inches deep, by 15.5 inches high. The later floor model cabinet measured 43 inches high, by 20 inches wide, by 23.5 inches deep.

VICTROLA XII
1909-1910 $125.00

In July of 1909 Victor introduced a new style of talking machine. The Victrola XII, as it was known, was quite literally a cross between a Victor VI, their best outside horn machine, and the Victrola XVI, at the time the only other concealed horn phonograph in the Victor lineup. The mechanical components of these three machines were all identical: each was powered by Victor's best three-spring nickel-plated motor, which was capable of playing eight 10-inch records per winding; each had the 12-inch "yielding" turntable; and each had all of its major controls gold plated. The Victrola XII, like the Victor VI, was available only in mahogany, as this wood was very fashionable in the better homes of the period and appeared particularly luxurious when contrasted with the gold plating of the metal hardware. As was the case with the Victor VI, the Victrola XII could be obtained with either a Concert or Exhibition sound box, although the latter was usually supplied. In an effort to compensate for the very small horn opening in the Victrola XII, Victor added a set of horizontal slats in the opening which the company claimed acted as sounding boards for additional amplification of the sound waves. It is significant to note that Victor made the horn opening larger in all subsequent Victrolas, as this machine did not fare well in a listening comparison with the less expensive Victor VI, although the XII's closable lid did help to reduce the record's surface noise. In January of 1910, a bit of carving was added below the lid, and some small molding graced the front and sides of the cabinet to relieve the plain appearance of the original design. By September 10 of the same year however, production of the Victrola XII had been halted and two new, less expensive instruments (Victrolas X and XI) were introduced in its place.

Cabinet dimensions were 15.875 inches high, by 17.875 inches wide by 21.9375 inches deep.

VICTROLA XIV
1910-1921 $150.00-$200.00

In September 1910, Victor introduced a second floor model Victrola to complement the popular Victrola XVI. The Victrola XIV was smaller and less expensive than the XVI, but had the same technical specifications: a nickel-plated triple-spring motor and gold-plated hardware. The cabinet, available in oak or mahogany, was decidedly different looking however -the doors covering the horn ran the full width of the front and the body of the cabinet sat high on four curved legs. A sliding shelf was provided under the horn for ease in sorting records, and numbered vertical slats were used to file records in the bottom of the cabinet.

On August 15, 1912 the first examples of a new style Victrola XIV were shipped from the factory. The unique styling that had previously characterized this instrument was gone and it now simply looked like a shrunken Victrola XVI (also restyled at this time). Thirteen record albums were now supplied with the machine, replacing the previous slats. Refinements continued to be made to this instrument: in March 1913 the semi-automatic brake was added and in October 1914 English brown mahogany finish was made available. The machine was modified in May 1917 to incorporate a larger tone arm and a "more artistic cabinet" (although the change was very subtle). The triple-spring motor was later superceded by a four-spring motor. A flurry of price increases followed - the list price was changed to $165.00 in October of 1917, $175.00 in May 1918, and finally an even $200.00 in September 1919.

Dimensions of the first cabinet style were 22.5 inches wide, by 23.6 inches deep, by 46.9 inches high. The revised cabinet measured 47 inches high, by 22.25 inches wide, by 24 inches deep making it nearly identical to the earlier size.

VICTOR-VICTROLA
1906-1907 $200.00

In August of 1906, Eldridge Johnson introduced the most significant new product to come from his Camden workshop since his spring-driven Gramophone a decade earlier. This product was the Victor-Victrola and it previewed a radically new style of phonograph that would come to dominate the industry only a few years later. Eldridge Johnson had been wrestling with the problem of getting his talking machines accepted into society for many years. It seemed that no matter how fancy he made the cabinet, it was still regarded as a simple, ugly toy in a large number of the elegant households of this country.

The Victor-Victrola was Mr. Johnson's solution for making his product not only socially acceptable, but even socially desirable. With the help of a respected Philadelphia cabinet making firm - the Pooley Furniture Co. - he constructed an instrument which would both ornament any room and conceal its true identity when not in use. The awkward and often criticized horn was incorporated into the body of the cabinet, along with ample storage for a large collection of records. A drawer at the bottom could hold a lifetime supply of needles or record catalogs. The finest components were used in the construction of the Victor-Victrola, and its $200.00 price tag reflected this fact. The motor, sound box and turntable were all the same as used in the Victor VI: nickel-plated with three springs, gold-plated Exhibition or Concert and 12 inches in diameter, respectively. The tone arm was a new design, turning downward, instead of upward, to mate with the horn. Since there was no grill over the horn opening, the entire inside of the horn was visible when the "tone modifying doors" (the first volume control) were open. The horn, like the rest of the cabinet, was mahogany with a red finish applied. The record albums were covered in a matching maroon cloth, and all exposed metalwork was finished in gold. The result was a striking piece of furniture which furthered the acceptance of the talking machine as a serious cultural asset exactly as Eldridge Johnson hoped it would.

The cabinet of the Victor-Victrola (identified as the model VTLA on the ID plaque) was made in three distinct styles. The earliest style had flat sides with a hint of Louis XV molding on the corners. The flat lid sat atop a curiously curved bezel which surrounded the turntable. A pair of doors covered the horn opening and provided a new means of controlling the volume. From under the horn, a shelf could be pulled for the purpose of supporting a record album while the operator removed a selection for playing. When the concert had concluded, the operator returned the record album to its storage space in the cabinet, probably unaware of the revolution in musical entertainment his actions represented.

A short time after the unveiling of the first cabinet style, a second Victrola was introduced. It differed markedly in appearance from the original style, but was identical in operation and name. As on the first style, the sides and top of this new Victor-Victrola were completely flat. Instead of the modestly curved corners of the first style, this new instrument had plain corners, but substituted carving under the lid. The lid itself closed nearly flush with the top molding of the set, and the only means of opening the lid was by using the key as a knob. Pity the poor owner who lost his key!

After some study and use of these two instruments, the men at Victor must have realized that each of the Victrola cabinets had a serious operational shortcoming: access to the turntable was difficult through the high, flat lid. They improved the turntable accessibility markedly when they introduced, in 1907, a third style Victor-Victrola (still identified as the model VTLA) with a deeply domed lid. As the original style of Victrola cabinets had proved to be the more popular, this third cabinet retained nearly all of its styling features.

By this time, the acceptance of the Victrola seemed assured, (it was a modest sales success at first, but encouraging nonetheless), but Victor's lack of differentiation between styles was becoming confusing. Following the format they had established for the outside-horn Victors, it was only natural to give this instrument a numerical designation. The number sixteen was chosen, probably by simply adding a digit to the best machine in the outside-horn line-up. Thus was born one of the best known instruments in the company's catalog, the Victrola the Sixteenth.

The Victor-Victrola cabinet measured 48 inches high, by 20 inches wide, by 22 inches deep.

VICTROLA XVI

1907-1921 $200.00-$750.00

By the summer of 1907, Victor was able to begin the manufacture of Victrola cabinets in its Camden plant and no longer required the services of the Pooley Furniture Co. In August, exactly one year after the introduction of the revolutionary Pooley-built Victor-Victrola, the new Victor-built Victrola the Sixteenth was announced. The new instrument was nearly identical to the last cabinet style offered under the designation "VTLA". Changes made when the Victrola the Sixteenth replaced the Victor-Victrola included a subtle reshaping of the front doors, plus the elimination of the separate turntable mounting board used in the earlier Victor-Victrola. The new numeric notation allowed the company the option of expanding the line without causing undue confusion in the future.

Until its deletion in 1910, a carved panel decorated the area beneath the lid. Initially the instrument was available only in light or dark shades of solid mahogany, but in November of 1908 Circassian Walnut (a beautifully grained wood which cost $50.00 extra) and oak veneers were offered. The standard oak finish was what Victor termed "dull weathered", but "antique", "golden", "early English", "Flemish", "fumed", "driftwood", or "gun metal" finishes were available on special order. In 1910 a fourth finish became available. The Vernis-Martin Victrola XVI sold for $400.00 and was a standard cabinet which had delicate scenes hand painted on the front doors, lid and sides. Special molding outlined the paintings and added to the Louis XV character of the cabinet. A more expensive art style cabinet was also available for this instrument for several years beginning in 1909, but in very limited numbers. The Moorish Marquetry Victrola was built in Morocco to special order and carried a price of $750.00. It featured fancy inlays of mother-of-pearl and rare woods in a style characteristic of that part of Africa. It was not shown in the standard Victor catalogs, but was occasionally stocked by some of the more elite Victor agencies such as John Wanamaker in Philadelphia. Also not shown, but available on special order were Victrola XVI's with non-standard finishes such as ebony or rare wood veneers.

In September 1912, a restyled Victrola XVI was introduced. The L-shaped doors of the older style were replaced by more conventional looking doors -those covering the horn opening ran the full width of the cabinet and revealed the now familiar "sounding board" slats when opened. Gone too were the drawer and the sliding tray that had been features of the earlier-style cabinet. The semi-automatic brake was incorporated in March 1913, and English brown mahogany finish was made available in October of the following year. An electrified version of this instrument (known as the Victrola XVI Electric) was introduced shortly before Christmas, 1914. Since electricity by this time was common in the better homes of the cities, an electric turntable motor was a reasonable luxury for many potential customers. The Victrola Electric's cabinet was similar to that of a regular Victrola XVI, except that a pair of doors at the rear of the cabinet could be opened to reveal a bank of three large selectable resistors which were used to convert the customer's line voltage (110-220 VAC or VDC) to that required by the motor. Record storage was accessible through the front doors as before and was not impaired by this addition. After February 1916, a switchable lamp was also included under the lid for ease of operation in darkened rooms. The electrification option cost an additional $50.00, and these new instruments carried the ID plate nomenclature VE-XVI instead of VV-XVI. A new set of serial numbers was initiated for the Victrola XVI Electrics as they were not officially considered Victrola XVI's. By 1917, the war-induced shortages caused several price increases in this instrument. The first increase to the basic mahogany or oak Victrola XVI (the Vernis-Martin cabinet had just been discontinued) was a modest $15.00 in October. A $10.00 and $25.00 increase followed in May 1918 and September 1919 making the final list price for a standard VV-XVI $250.00. The walnut and electric motor options were increased to $62.50 each for this machine making the top-of-the-line walnut VE-XVI $375.00.

Dimensions of the earliest configuration of the cabinet were 21 inches wide, by 22 inches deep, by 47 inches high. The 1912 style cabinet measured 23.75 inches wide, by 25.2 inches deep, by 49 inches high.

VICTROLA XVII
1916-1921 $250.00-$615.00

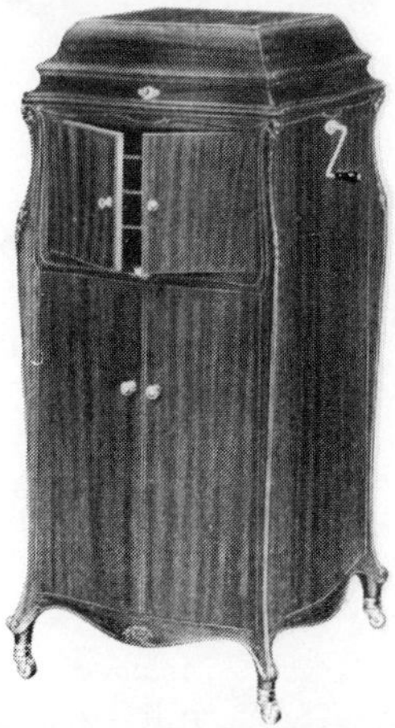

In December 1916 Victor introduced the Victrola XVII; an instrument destined to replace the elegant Victrola XVIII and become the most expensive Victrola in the catalog. With an initial list price of $250 ($300 with electric motor) this instrument was $50 more than the standard Victrola XVI. Victor had overestimated the market for high priced instruments when they introduced the XVIII, and the Victrola XVII was designed to be a compromise between the Victrolas XVI and XVIII. The cabinet also was a compromise, since it retained the swell front and sides of the style XVIII, but gave up some of the ornamental molding on the doors and sides. The Victrola XVII used a three-spring motor (later with four springs) with nickel plating and sported gold plating on the visible controls such as the automatic speed indicator and Exhibition sound box (later replaced by the Victor No. 2 sound box). Sixteen record albums were included, providing storage for 160 discs. The cabinet was available in either mahogany or quartersawed oak veneer at the same price, but walnut veneer cost $50 extra. In October 1917 the first of the price increases raised the cost of this instrument $15. In May 1918 and September 1919, the price rose by $10 and $25 respectively. The costs of the walnut and electric options were increased to $65 each. In December 1919, Victor announced the availability of the Victrola XVII with Japanese lacquer decorations. This instrument carried a list price of $550.00 with a spring motor and $615.00 with the electric motor.

The large cabinet measured 46.75 inches high, by 22.5 inches wide, by 24.5 inches deep.

VICTROLA XVIII
1915-1916 $300.00-$400.00

In the ten years since the introduction of the Victrola, the company executives had noted with pleasure the gradual shift in public preference towards the more expensive offerings in their product line. Since the demise of the Victrola XX in 1909, the Victrola XVI, which sold for $200, was (except for special order instruments) the top-of-the-line. In June of 1915, Victor acknowledged the apparent demand for expensive phonographs by introducing the Victrola XVIII. The extra $100 which this machine commanded over a Victrola XVI bought a smaller cabinet with swell front and sides and Louis XV-style moldings highlighting the carefully selected mahogany or walnut (either American or Circassian at the same price of $50 extra) veneers. Motive power was provided by Victor's best nickel-plated three-spring or electric (again $50 extra) motor, and naturally the Exhibition sound box, semi-automatic brake, speed indicator and 12-inch turntable were all gold-plated. A cabinet full of sixteen record albums was provided with the instrument, but the price for this package of elegance was more than the market would bear. The production of the Victrola XVIII was quietly discontinued after the 1916 Christmas season to be replaced with the plainer and less expensive Victrola XVII. For a few months both the Victrola XVII and the Victrola XVIII were available simultaneously, until stocks of the previously produced Victrola XVIII's could be sold. This elegant cabinet measured 48 inches high, by 23.25 inches wide, by 25.25 inches deep.

VICTROLA XX
1908-1909 $250.00-$300.00

Flushed by the initial success of the Victrola XVI, Eldridge Johnson decided to double the number of inside horn phonographs offered by his company. He did this on February 15, 1908 by announcing that a new Victrola, the Twentieth, would be placed on sale in Victor showrooms March 1st. This new instrument was essentially a Victrola XVI with highly figured Laguna mahogany (which, according to Victor literature, "possesses even richer figure than the celebrated San Domingo variety") applied to form "V" patterns on the front doors, and gilded Louis XV style gingerbread ornamenting the cabinet. The Victrola XX shared the nickel-plated three-spring motor, gold-plated Exhibition sound box and yielding 12-inch turntable with the Victor VI and Victrola XVI. Included with each instrument were ten record albums holding fifteen records each (60 twelve-inch and 90 ten-inch records). The instrument originally carried a $300 price tag, but this was reduced to $250 in December when Victor advised their dealers to order quickly, as only 275 of these machines remained in stock, and no more new ones would be built. The remaining stock of Victrola XX's was sold by February 1909 when it was officially discontinued.

Cabinet dimensions were 21 inches wide, by 22 inches deep, by 47.5 inches high.

VICTROLA No. 35

1924 - 1925 $30.00 - $35.00

The Victrola No. 35 was a significant instrument for Victor not because it had impressive appearance or performance, but because it represented the most durable of all Victrola forms. While this was not the first truly portable Victrola (the Victrola No. 50 deserves that distinction), it did symbolize the final style of the acoustical phonograph. Even though the sensational Orthophonic Victrola (which was yet to be introduced at the time the Victrola No. 35 was placed on the market) can be considered the swan song for the Victrola, technology was slowest at finding a better alternative for music at the beach or mountains than was offered by the type of instrument which would become known as the "suitcase Victrola". Fabric covered wooden or metal boxes housing a small phonograph mechanism such as that found in the Victrola No. 35 remained popular through the second world war, long after electrical amplification had banished the last upright acoustical Victrola from America's front parlors. Indeed, the last of these "suitcase" instruments to come off of the Camden assembly line was not much different than the one under examination here.

The black fabric covering a wooden frame (no longer a prime hardwood such as mahogany or oak, as seen on the Victrola No. 50), built-in needle case and storage for ten 10-inch records of the Victrola No. 35 were specifications common to a trunkful of subsequent instruments whose main claim to fame was ease of portability, convenience, and independance from electricity.

The small suitcase style cabinet of the Victrola No. 35 measured 6.75 inches high, by 12.25 inches wide, by 17 inches deep.

VICTROLA No. 50
1921-1925 $50.00

Although several companies, including Victor, had for years sold custom suitcases for protecting small talking machines while traveling, the Victrola No. 50 was Victor's first talking machine designed specifically to be portable. The most obvious departures from the traditional design were the boxy shape with the latching lid, the removable carrying handle, and the nickel-plated corner protectors. Inside was Victor's small single-spring motor (the same as used in the Victrola IV), the newly introduced Victrola No. 2 sound box, and a ten-inch turntable. All of the hardware was nickel-plated, and the cabinet came in a choice of mahogany or oak. The horn was located behind the turntable and faced upward, relying upon the open lid to deflect the sound towards the front of the instrument. The earliest instruments had their cranks facing forward, but in 1925 the design was modified to permit a side entry for the crank. Six 10-inch records were storable inside the case, as was a supply of needles.

Dimensions were 9 inches high, by 12 inches wide and 18 inches deep.

VICTROLA No. 80
1921-1925 $100.00-$110.00

Introduced in the Spring of 1921, the Victrola No. 80 became Victor's least expensive upright style instrument. It offered a slightly more stylish and deluxe cabinet than the former price leader, the Victrola X. Features included a 12-inch turntable, nickel-plated Victrola No. 2 sound box, semi-automatic brake, automatic speed indicator and a double-spring motor. The cabinet was available in a choice of mahogany, oak or walnut veneers. In 1924, the price of the Victrola No. 80 was increased to $110.00, although it still remained the lowest priced upright Victrola.

Dimensions were 40.5 inches high by 20 inches wide by 22 inches deep.

VICTROLA No. 90
1921-1924 $125.00

The Victrola No. 90 was Victor's replacement for the very popular style XI, at a slightly reduced price. Like the Victrola XI, it came with a double-spring motor, 12-inch turntable, nickle-plated Victrola No. 2 sound box, semi-automatic brake and automatic speed indicator. The cabinet was offered in a choice of oak, mahogany or American walnut veneers.

Dimensions were 41 inches high by 20 inches wide by 22 inches deep.

VICTROLA No. 100
1921-1925 $150.00

The Victrola No. 100 was a modernization of the type of machine which had sold so well in the previous years. This model was equipped with a 12-inch turntable, nickel-plated Victrola No. 2 sound box, semi-automatic brake and automatic speed indicator. The cabinet was offered in a choice of mahogany, oak or American walnut veneers. Actual hand carving graced the slender columns on each side of the horn. Shelves were provided for record album storage. In the Fall of 1924, the cabinet of the Victrola No. 100 was restyled to accomodate a larger tone chamber, and air supports for the lid.

Dimensions were 42.5 inches high by 21.25 inches wide by 22.75 inches deep.

VICTROLA No. 105
1923-1925 $180.00

The style 105 Victrola offered a subtle variation on the cabinet styling seen on previous Victrolas. The horn opening was proportionally larger than in the past, giving the machine a more "modern" appearance. A 12-inch turntable, nickel-plated Victrola No. 2 sound box, semi-automatic brake, automatic speed indicator, double-spring motor and locking lid were standard equipment, as was a set of record albums. The cabinet was available in a choice of oak; mahogany or American walnut veneers with hand carving on the corner posts.

Dimensions were 44.5 inches high by 21.5 inches wide by 24.25 inches deep.

VICTROLA No. 107
1925 $200.00-$240.00

The medium priced and short-lived style 107 Victrola offered several deluxe features. As an example, this was the lowest priced Victrola which offered the four-spring motor (Victor's best) as standard equipment, or the optional electric motor at $40 additional. The cabinet, styled with Regency influence, was something of a departure from the standard Victrola. Available in mahogany only, the cabinet featured an air-supported lid for "hands-off" closing. Gold plating highlighted the controls, and the overall effect was impressive.

The cabinet measured 44.25 inches high, by 24 inches wide, by 23.75 inches deep.

VICTROLA No. 110
1921-1924 $225.00

The spitting image of the Victrola XIV, the Victrola No. 110 at $225 offered Victor's finest four-spring motor in addition to the usual 12-inch turntable, nickel-plated Victrola No. 2 sound box, semi-automatic brake and automatic speed indicator. A locking lid and record albums were standard. The cabinet was available in a choice of oak, mahogany or American walnut veneers.

Dimensions were 47 inches high by 22.25 inches wide by 23.75 inches deep.

VICTROLA No. 111
1923-1925 $225.00-$265.00

The Victrola No. 111 was designed to update the classic Victrola styling. Introduced in the summer of 1923 at the same price as the Victrola No. 110 and No. 120, this instrument offered a slightly smaller and differently proportioned cabinet with a larger horn opening. At the time of its introduction, this was also the least expensive upright style Victrola available with an electric motor drive for the turntable. Although normally supplied with a four-spring motor, it could be equipped with the electric motor for a mere $40 extra. Inside, gold plating highlighted the 12-inch turntable, Victrola No. 2 sound box, semi-automatic brake and automatic speed indicator. On the outside, genuine hand carving decorated the corner posts. Record albums and a locking lid were also included. The cabinet was initially available in a choice of mahogany or American walnut veneers, but oak was added when the Victrola No. 110 was discontinued in 1925.

Dimensions were 45.75 inches high by 22.5 inches wide by 24.75 inches deep.

VICTROLA No. 120
1921-1924 $225.00-$265.00

In the year of 1921, the famous Victrola XVI was renamed the Victrola No. 120 in keeping with Victor's new nomenclature. At the same time, the price was reduced by $25. These two measures, it was hoped, would help create a much needed increase of traffic in Victor salesrooms. Standard equipment included record albums, a gold-plated 12-inch turntable, lid lock, casters, Victrola No. 2 sound box, semi-automatic brake and automatic speed indicator. As in the case of the Victrola No. 111, the style No. 120's standard spring motor could be replaced by the electric motor for $40 extra. Unlike the No. 111, however, which could be obtained in walnut or mahogany, the Victrola No. 120 offered the option of oak veneer in addition to the popular mahogany finish.

Dimensions were 49 inches high by 23 inches wide by 24.75 inches deep.

VICTROLA No. 125
1923-1925 $275.00-$365.00

The Victrolas No. 125 and No. 130 were the most deluxe of the the upright style instruments offered by Victor in 1923 (with the exception of the custom art case styles). The Victrola No. 125 offered a larger horn opening than previous Victrolas, but did not lose the characteristic Victor styling. The standard four-spring motor could be replaced with an electric version for an additional $40. Like all of the better Victrolas, this machine was equipped with a gold-plated 12-inch turntable, locking lid, Victrola No. 2 sound box, semi-automatic brake and automatic speed indicator. The cabinet, with its swell front and sides, was finished in mahogany or walnut, but unlike the lower priced Victrolas of the period, this instrument's American walnut veneer cost $50 extra. Record albums were included at no extra cost, however.

Dimensions were 46.25 inches high by 22.75 inches wide by 25 inches deep.

VICTROLA No. 130
1921-1924 $275.00-$415.00

Announced late in 1921, the Victrola No. 130 was in reality a renamed Victrola XVII. Originally priced at $350, the No. 130 was reduced to $275 in 1923 to stimulate sales. The four-spring motor was standard, but an electric motor was available for an additional $40 (reduced from the 1921 price of $65). Also standard were a gold plated 12-inch turntable, locking lid, casters, Victrola No. 2 sound box, semi-automatic brake and automatic speed indicator. The cabinet was available in a choice of oak or mahogany veneers, and was supplied with record albums.

Dimensions were 46.75 inches high by 22.5 inches wide by 24.5 inches deep.

VICTROLA No. 210
1923-1925 $100.00-$110.00

In 1923, Victor finally produced the machine Victor dealers had been pleading for for years. The Victrola No. 210 was the low cost, flat top, console-styled phonograph that would bring the customers back to Victor showrooms. The competition had been selling phonographs of this style in ever increasing numbers since World War I, and Victor sales had declined alarmingly because they offered no similar instrument. This small but attractive cabinet was initially available in mahogany or American walnut and oak was added as a choice in 1925. Contained under its one-piece lid were a 12-inch turntable, nickel-plated Victrola No. 2 sound box, double-spring motor, semi-automatic brake, automatic speed indicator, and a flat panel with the ostensible purpose of holding a record or two during use. Victor was quick to point out, however, that a small radio chassis could be inserted into this panel and published pictures showing this adaptation. If desired, the record rack behind the two left doors could be removed for record album storage and in fact this was done by Victor beginning in 1925, when the price advanced $10.

Dimensions were 33.25 inches high by 29 inches wide by 20.5 inches deep.

VICTROLA No. 215
1923-1925 $150.00

Introduced in the spring of 1923, the Victrola No. 215 was another in the series of flat-topped console-styled instruments which departed so drastically from the traditional Victrola look. Under the right half of the split lid (the left half was fixed in place) was a 12-inch turntable, nickel-plated Victrola No. 2 sound box, semi-automatic brake, double-spring motor and automatic speed indicator. The mahogany or walnut cabinet contained a handy drawer for storage of instructions, needle tins, or record catalogs, plus a full set of record albums behind the left pair of doors. In 1925 a special edition of this instrument (referred to as the Victrola No. 215 S) containing provisions for mounting a radio chassis of any standard make was introduced at $160. The radio controls could be mounted in a blank panel provided for this purpose under the left lid of the cabinet. The chassis and batteries then occupied the space formerly used by the drawer and the record albums.

Dimensions were 34 inches high by 32.75 inches wide by 21.25 inches deep.

VICTROLA No. 220
1923-1925 $200.00-$240.00

Introduced early in 1923, the Victrola No. 220 was difficult to distinguish from its slightly smaller cousin, the Victrola No. 215. The most obvious differences, other than price, were the gold plating on the interior hardware, and hand carving on the corner posts. The technical specifications were otherwise similar: 12-inch turntable, Victrola No. 2 sound box, record albums, double-spring motor, semi-automatic brake and automatic speed indicator. As on other Victrolas in this price range, an electric motor could be substituted for the spring motor for an additional $40.

Dimensions were 34.75 inches high by 36.75 inches wide by 22.75 inches deep.

VICTROLA No. 230
1922-1925 $375.00-$480.00

The Victrola No. 230 was Victor's most expensive standard instrument when introduced in 1922 (the custom art case models cost up to $1500, but were available only on special order). The large flat-topped cabinet had bowed front and side surfaces (like the Victrolas No. 125 and No. 130) which were expensive to manufacture and contributed to the high price of the Victrola No. 230. The gold-plated 12-inch turntable was centered under the one piece lid and was driven by either Victor's best four-spring motor or the optional ($40 extra) electric motor. The instrument was furnished with special record albums, a Victrola No. 2 sound box, semi-automatic brake and automatic speed indicator. The cabinet was normally finished in mahogany, but American walnut was available for $65 extra, giving the buyer the choice of up to $105 in options.

Dimensions were 36.75 inches high by 39.25 inches wide by 24.5 inches deep.

VICTROLA No. 240
1922-1925 $115.00

The Victrola No. 240 was the smallest instrument in the so-called "humpbacked" series. It's nickname was derived from the outline of the characteristic Victrola lid set atop its wide body. Although it may have been externally odd, it was internally identical with similarly priced Victrolas. It contained a 12-inch turntable, nickel-plated Victrola No. 2 sound box, double-spring motor, semi-automatic brake and automatic speed indicator. Record albums were included in the low price. The cabinet was available in a choice of oak, mahogany or walnut veneers.

Dimensions were 34.75 inches high by 29.25 inches wide by 21 inches deep.

VICTROLA No. 260
1922-1925 $150.00-$160.00

The Victrola No. 260, introduced in early 1922 for $160, was reduced in price by $10 the following year in order to be more competitive with the multitude of different machines on the post-war market. This low console phonograph was equipped with a nickel-plated Victrola No. 2 sound box, semi-automatic brake, automatic speed indicator, 12-inch turntable, record albums and double-spring motor. The cabinet was finished in a choice of mahogany or walnut veneer, with the additional choice of oak made available in 1925. Air dashpots for automatic closing of the lid were made standard in 1925.

Dimensions of the instrument were 35.25 inches high, by 33.75 inches wide and 21 inches deep.

VICTROLA No. 280
1922-1924 $200.00-$265.00

When it was introduced early in 1922, the Victrola No. 280 was the lowest priced "humpback" style Victrola offered with an electric motor option. Initially, the standard double spring motor could be replaced by the electric motor for an additional $65, but this option was dropped the following year. Other features of this instrument were a gold-plated Victrola No. 2 sound box, semi-automatic brake, automatic speed indicator, 12-inch turntable and record albums. The cabinet was finished in a choice of mahogany or walnut veneer.

Dimensions of the instrument were 35.25 inches high, by 34 inches wide and 22.75 inches deep.

VICTROLA No. 300
1921-1925 $250.00-$315.00

The Victrola No. 300 was Eldridge Johnson's answer to the many requests he had received from his dealers for a more modern-appearing horizontal style Victrola. This instrument, with its odd Victrola lid creating a humped silhouette, was probably not what the dealers had in mind, but Victor's sales did improve after its July 1921 introduction. Mr. Johnson managed to create a machine that looked like no other, as had been his goal with the first Victrola in 1906. Under the traditional Victrola lid, this offering contained a gold-plated Victrola No. 2 sound box, semi-automatic brake, automatic speed indicator, 12-inch turntable, lid lock, record albums and four-spring motor. An electric motor was available for $65 extra (later reduced to $40). The record albums, instead of being stored under the horn as in previous Victrolas, were kept behind locking doors on each side of the horn. The cabinet was offered in a choice of mahogany, oak or walnut veneer.

Dimensions of the instrument were 37.25 inches high, by 38.25 inches wide and 23.5 inches deep.

VICTROLA No. 330
1922-1925 $350.00-$480.00

The Victrola No. 330, introduced in the spring of 1922, was Victor's finest model in the so-called "humpback" series. With fancy bowed front and side panels, the cabinet was a good example of Victor's furniture craftsmanship. As with other high-priced Victrolas, this model was available with an electric motor drive ($65 extra in 1922, $40 extra thereafter) for the gold-plated 12-inch turntable. A four-spring motor was standard, as was a Victrola No. 2 sound box, semi-automatic brake, automatic speed indicator and a set of record albums. The cabinet was usually supplied with mahogany veneer, but American walnut was available for $65 extra.

Dimensions of the instrument were 38.5 inches high, by 39.25 inches wide and 24.5 inches deep.

VICTROLA No. 350
1924-1925 $235.00-$275.00

In 1924, Victor added three upright style Victrolas to their line in a effort to "dress up" the catalog. Each of these Victrolas, the models 350, 360 and 370, was very similar in styling to a horizontally-styled phonograph introduced into the Victor line the previous year. The Victrola No. 350, as an example, was designed with "influences of Sheraton, Hepplewhite and Adams", and matched the lines, if not the silhouette of the Victrola No. 400. Like other Victrolas in its price range, the No. 350 offered an air-supported lid, Victrola No. 2 sound box, gold plating on the exposed controls, an optional electric motor and a full complement of record albums. Mahogany was the only wood offered for the cabinet.

The cabinet measured 41.5 inches high, by 21.5 inches wide, by 23.25 inches deep.

VICTROLA No. 360
1924-1925 $235.00-$275.00

The Victrola No. 360 was a short-lived instrument, introduced in time to take advantage of the 1924 Christmas trade (what there was of it for Victor). It can best be described as having a semi-period style case (Victor called it early English in character) with an almost flat lid and stretchers between the legs. Available only in walnut (with an electric motor optional at $40) the No. 360 Victrola offered the usual deluxe Victor features such as a gold-plated Victrola No. 2 sound box, semi-automatic brake, automatic speed indicator, 12-inch turntable, air dashpots in the lid support, record albums and four-spring motor. The same English styling was available in the horizontal Victrola No. 405.

The cabinet measured 44.25 inches high, by 21.5 inches wide, by 23 inches deep.

VICTROLA No. 370
1924-1925 $275.00-$315.00

Introduced in the fall of 1924, the unusual looking Victrola No. 370 was produced for less than one year. This upright style phonograph had none of the familiar Louis XV touches of previous Victrolas, and along with the Victrolas No. 350 and No. 360, formed a marked departure from traditional upright Victrola styling. The distinctive ball-and-claw feet, reeded corner posts and raised panels and medallions on the doors were shared by one of Victor's more artistic horizontal style Victrolas, the No. 410. Victor termed this cabinet style American Colonial, and the design of a machine such as this is indicative of Victor's realization that the products which had served the company well in previous years were now archaic and outdated. Sales of the older style Victrolas were alarmingly low in 1924, and this machine illustrates the erosion of Eldridge Johnson's resistance to depart from the proven formulas of the past, and offers an insight into the climate which made Victor receptive to the propositions of Bell Laboratories in 1925. The Victrola No. 370 was available only in mahogany, with an electric motor as the only option at $40. Normally, the machine was equipped with a four-spring motor, gold-plated Victrola No. 2 sound box, semi-automatic brake, automatic speed indicator, 12-inch turntable and record albums. The lid featured an air dashpot for automatic closing. The cabinet measured 44.25 inches high, by 23 inches wide, by 24.25 inches deep.

VICTROLA No. 400
1923-1925 $250.00-$305.00

The Victrola No. 400 was one of three similar period style instruments introduced as the 400 series in the summer of 1923. The cabinet was constructed with highly figured mahogany veneer arranged to form two "V" patterns on the four front doors. A handy storage drawer was provided on the left above the record compartment. The phonographic equipment included a four-spring motor (electric optional at $40), a gold-plated Victrola No. 2 sound box, semi-automatic brake, automatic speed indicator and 12-inch turntable. Records albums were included, unless the special edition instrument was ordered. The 1925 Victrola No. 400S cost $265 and contained provisions for mounting any standard radio receiver in the left half of the cabinet. The area formerly allocated to record albums and the drawer was used to house the radio chassis and its batteries. The lid was restrained in its fall by air dashpots on the supports.

Dimensions of the instrument were 35 inches high, by 37.5 inches wide and 21 inches deep.

VICTROLA No. 405
1923-1925 $250.00-$305.00

The beautiful cabinet of the Victrola No. 405 was veneered in three shades of walnut, and rivaled the styling of some of Victor's more expensive custom period pieces. Although normally equipped with a four-spring motor, the electric motor was available for $40 extra. Gold plating ornamented the Victrola No. 2 sound box, semi-automatic brake, automatic speed indicator and 12-inch turntable. A drawer and record albums were included in the model 405, but not in the 405 S (for special) introduced in 1925. The $265 Victrola No. 405 S had a two piece lid, with the left lid covering a blank walnut panel supplied for the mounting of any standard radio chassis of the period. Newly designed lid supports incorporated air damping for hands-off lid closing.

Dimensions of the instrument were 35 inches high, by 37.5 inches wide and 21 inches deep.

VICTROLA No. 410
1923-1925 $300.00-$355.00

The most expensive member of the 400 series triumvirate was the Victrola No. 410 introduced in 1923. The Georgian or Queen Anne mahogany cabinet featured a small drawer above the left two doors for storage of record catalogs and similar items. In 1925, a special version (the 410S) was offered which provided accommodation for a standard radio receiver in the left half of the cabinet and cost an extra $15. The same styling was also used on an upright Victrola (the No. 370) introduced in 1924. Like the other Victrolas in its price range, the No. 410 contained a four-spring motor (unless the $40 electric motor was specified), a gold-plated Victrola No. 2 sound box, semi-automatic brake, automatic speed indicator, 12-inch turntable, and record albums. A pneumatic lid support provided automatic closing.

Dimensions of the instrument were 35 inches high, by 38.25 inches wide and 22.5 inches deep.

Period Victrolas 1917-1925

Since the introduction of the first Victrola in 1906, Victor could claim to catalog a style of talking machine to grace any home. Special models were available from nearly the beginning. Elaborately decorated Vernis-Martin cabinets sought to attract the carriage trade and were sold for many years in both the Victrola XVI and later the Victrola XVIII styles. Yet, somehow, there was a void in the offering. By itself, the Louis XV-influenced styling of the Victrola line was insufficient to satisfy the new American desire to imitate the grand style of old Royal Europe.

Victor acted to remedy this shortcoming by introducing in the fall of 1917 an assortment of Victrolas with cabinets crafted in the style of the best European artisans. Twelve different periods were represented by the new cabinet styles, and variations in wood, trim and finish increased the choices to a total of 46. This was a remarkably varied selection, especially considering the very limited distribution these instruments were to have.

Victor was keenly aware that these period Victrolas could never account for many sales, and frankly told its dealers so. Still, the company tried to persuade the larger dealers to carry one or two in stock at all times to illustrate their quality of detail and construction to those customers in every city who might be a prospect for an uncommon talking machine.

No one passing a store window displaying one of these period Victrolas would mistake the instrument for anything other than a product of the giant Camden factory, for in silhouette, the shape was unmistakeably Victor.

In 1920, however, Victor did something unexpected. It introduced to the period catalog a radically different cabinet configuration. The very boxy console style cabinet (referred to by Victor as the "wide" style) was covered by Design Patent # 54,928 and was totally without peer in the industry. Such a statement, by the way, was not necessarily a compliment. By placing the traditional Victrola lid atop a very angular cabinet, Victor designers believed they had the basis for a varied line of period styles. The judicious application of an ogee curve here, a medallion there, or a change in the legs could, Victor thought, turn this new shape into a true work of art reflecting the craftsmanship of the period it purported to represent. In practice, all of the wide style cabinets looked essentially alike, and although the cabinets were beautifully made, it took a generous person to proclaim the result as graceful or attractive. The wide cabinets did serve a supplemental purpose however, and that was to introduce to the market place the basic horizontal shape which would appear in the regular Victrola line in 1921. Presumably, public and dealer reaction to the wide period cabinets was influential in the design of the Victrola No. 300 and the subsequent smaller Victrolas of the same style.

The upright period cabinets were retained in the line after 1920, although certain subtle modifications had been made to several of the styles. By now the choice of cabinets in the period style was tremendous; a curious condition considering that most Victrola customers did not even know they existed. Not that it would have made much difference - at prices averaging between $500 and $700, these instruments were out of the price range of all but a very few families.

Victor could claim to offer such a wide variety of style by virtue of the fact that each cabinet was a special order item. Unlike an instrument from the regular Victrola line which could generally be shipped from stock, any period Victrola was manufactured only upon receipt of a firm order. Victor confirmed that it was in the custom cabinet business in 1922 when it announced that the Victor Art Department stood ready to work with the customer to design a cabinet in any configuration imaginable, at prices ranging up to $1500. Ads in the most exclusive magazines illustrated suggested treatments for the custom cabinets. In an effort to bolster the disappointing Victrola market in 1923, Victor even dropped three period-like cabinets (Victrolas No. 400, 405 and 410) into the regular Victrola line. These attractive cabinets were known as the Art Victrolas and were very popular, considering their high price.

With the introduction of the Orthophonic Victrolas in 1925, every standard console cabinet received a period designation. Most styles were Mediterranean or English in ancestry, with new Italian and Spanish influences prominent in the selection.

the PERIOD VICTROLA

Gothic

The Gothic period began somewhere in the early Middle Ages and came to height during the years 1200-1500. It followed the Romanesque and gave way to the Renaissance. The first and most obvious sign of Gothic style is the pointed arch. In later Gothic, especially in domestic architecture, a flat arch was developed, particularly for constructive reasons. These beautiful forms passed to the cabinet maker by direct inheritance. The Gothic Victrola console exhibited a number of Gothic decorative features, including several forms of the flat arch. Varied forms of tracing and the quatrefoil were also introduced into the cabinet. The moldings, corbels and side columns were deeply and strongly carved in the true Gothic spirit. Traditional Gothic furniture was constructed of oak and protected by handrubbing with beeswax and oil. Victor modernized the wax finish by using the same procedure it had developed for other waxed oak Victrolas. The mountings were finished in antique wrought iron.

Louis XV

The reign of Louis XV in France (1715-1774) was a period of gaiety and frivolity. Curved free forms, S-shapes and asymmetry became the dominant line of forms in this period. Lacquered and painted furniture added to the effect of this "age of the boudoir", and Mme de Pompadour was a guiding influence of this period. The Martin brothers perfected the technique of applying a varnish finish to furniture during this period, initially in imitation of Chinese and Japanese lacquer work. This painted finish, refered to as Vernis-Martin in honor of the brothers, remained very popular and was introduced into the standard Victrola line in 1910, seven years prior to the introduction of the Period Victrola line. Most of the standard Victrolas, in fact, were influenced by the Louis XV Period, although only the Victrolas XVII and XVIII contained the curved sides usually associated with the finer Louis XV pieces. Even these elegant instruments had sides curved in only the horizontal plane. The Period style Louis XV Victrola however, had Bombe sides which were curved in both the horizontal and vertical planes, making a very striking instrument. Craftsmanship such as displayed on this period cabinet reflected the true artistry of the Victor cabinet factory.

Louis XVI

The Louis XVI style can partly be ascribed to the delicate and refined taste of Marie Antoinette, queen of the unfortunate Louis XVI. But it was a reaction, too, against the ornate taste of the Louis XV style, in which decoration reached a degree of development in France beyond anything since Gothic times. The cabinetry art of Louis XV could, as a rule, be identified at a glance, since its decorations were largely curvilinear. With the reign of Louis XVI, the pendulum swung back, and straight, severe lines ruled again. The Louis XVI Victrola was faithful to this tradition. The straight lines were highlighted by chaste bands of "fasces". These were derived from the Roman fasces, symbolic of the authority of magistrates, which were bundles of rods bound by crossed bands of ribbons. Where the plain sunken corner posts joined the related panelings of the cabinet body, square rosettes were introduced. The instrument was typically finished in mahogany with antique gold hardware.

Empire

The Empire or Napoleonic Period in France (1804-1820) represented a great classic revival style of architecture, art and decoration. It was a period which combined the grandeur and martial symbols of Rome with Ancient Egyptian motifs and the elements of Greek architecture. The furniture of the period was massive, architectural in concept, and lavishly trimmed in bronze and brass on rosewood, mahogany, and ebony. The single style of Empire Victrola shown in the Victor Period catalog was finished in mahogany (always a favorite wood at Victor) with brass or gold-plated decorations on the side, doors, and corner posts.

Jacobean

The period in English architecture and art from 1603 to 1649 (extending over the reigns of both James I and Charles I) was known as the Jacobean Period. It represented a merging of the designs and motifs of English Tudor with the Renaissance in England. Ornamentation of Jacobean furniture was often in the form of bands of molding applied in geometric patterns to create a paneled effect. Jacobean furniture was thus suited to the styles of the great medieval halls of seventeenth century England, and so was shown in such an environment in the Victor Period catalog. The Jacobean Victrola was crafted of oak, as this was the most popular choice of woods for furniture during the Jacobean Period (mahogany and walnut would gain favor in the eighteenth century). The "Jacobean # 2 Victrola" illustrated above was offered only in fumed oak for a price of $600.

William and Mary

Named for the period encompassed by the reign of William of Orange and his bride, Mary, on the British throne, the William and Mary style (1689-1702) represented a transitional style - a blend of Dutch, Flemish and French sources. The chief characteristics of this period involve the subtle contrast of straight and curved lines. The upright and console Victrolas both evidenced this trend as the formal, almost severe, lines of the body broke into rich and graceful curves of the turned legs and the under braces. The upright style Victrola was finished to show the natural grain of the wood (oak, mahogany or walnut would each be appropriate), while the larger instrument was panelled in marquetry with burl walnut and mahogany. The mountings were either antique gold or silver.

Queen Anne

The reign of Queen Anne was a brief one, yet it ushered in the beginning of the great period of English cabinet design. The Queen Anne period, for example, first signaled the appearance of the "cabriole" leg, which afterwards became so characteristic of Chippendale's work. The art of lacquering furniture - an inheritance from China and Japan - reached a fine degree of development during this reign. The upright model Victrola was finished in resplendent black lacquer, with polychrome "chinoiserie" decorations, and its interior was lined with vermilion. The door knobs were of white metal, in the form of lotus blossoms. The wide model, devoid of lacquer, had few embellishments. It relied instead on basic proportions and subtle beading to appeal to prospective purchasers. The delicate pear-drop knobs and other hardware were finished in antique gold.

Chippendale

Although Thomas Chippendale (1705-1779) copied extensively from styles of earlier periods, he managed to make his furniture distinctively his. He united English and Dutch solidity of construction with French grace and Chinese fantasy. He was the first in England to use mahogany in large quantities, as walnut had previously been the favored selection. Chippendale's work was characterized by splendid vigorous carving with deep undercutting and rich detail. The stongly curved "cabriole" leg with ball and claw feet (as seen on the Chippendale Victrola) was also a recognizable signature. The Chippendale Victrola had the typical moldings and carvings of the finest original pieces. The finish was a very deep alkanet red, and appeared almost black from a distance. The mounts, including the door knobs, keyhole escutcheons and the like, were appropriate in design and heavily gold-plated.

Chinese Chippendale

The term Chinese Chippendale refers to a period in Thomas Chippendale's work, in the mid-18th century, when he was greatly influenced by chinoiserie, Chinese motifs, and the work of Sir William Chambers. True to this period, colorful lacquer-work highlighted the cabinet of the striking Chinese Chippendale Victrola. In place of the curved cabriole legs seen on the Chippendale Victrolas, this instrument was supported by a very angular set of legs typical of the finest Chinese furniture.

Hepplewhite

George Hepplewhite was an 18th century English furniture designer who worked in the classical style. His work was characterized by lightness of construction, elegant curvilinear forms, and perfection of workmanship. As an example, his chairs used heartshaped and shieldshaped backs, carved with wheat ears, fern leaves, honeysuckle, swags, and Prince of Wales feathers. He designed Japanned furniture with fruit and flowers on a black background, as well as satinwood and inlaid pieces. The Hepplewhite Victrola displayed many of these characteristics. Colorful inlays, both curved and geometric, were used to highlight the traditional Victrola shape. While only a single style was illustrated, the Hepplewhite Victrola was one of the most elegant of all the Period Victrolas, and was a tribute to the skill of the Victor staff.

Adam

Robert, John, James and William Adams were four brothers in search of harmony between household architecture and its furnishings. As architects, they gained fame by designing the famous Adelphi Terrace in London in 1768. The Adam Victrola exemplified the quiet charm of the period it represented. Particular attention was paid to such details as the panelled corner posts, recessed tapering legs, and the characteristic medallions in the amplifying doors. Other touches were delicate cock-beadings at the joints of the doors, the classical urns at the tops of the corner posts and the dainty pendants beneath them. As with most of the other period Victrolas, mountings were especially created for the style and finished in antique gold. The Adam Victrola was furnished in mahogany, as it was during the influence of the Adams that mahogany first came into recognition as one of the most popular of all cabinet woods.

Sheraton

Thomas Sheraton (1750-1806) was the last of the four great names in Georgian English cabinet design, surviving his contemporaries Thomas Chippendale, George Hepplewhite, and the brothers Adam. Sheraton's designs were noted for refinement and delicacy. They were distinguished by a predilection for straight lines and flat surfaces almost unheard of in his own time. Sheraton used the only type of decoration suitable to flat surfaces - that is, painted decorations or wooden inlays. Victrolas were produced with either style of decoration. In the inlaid model, the doors were panelled in finely-proportioned low relief. The painted Victrolas were given a dainty pastel background for the colorful decorations. The hardware in either case was antique gold.

Illustrations of custom cabinets designed by the Victor Art Department in 1922.

THE ORTHOPHONIC ERA

By Christmas season of 1924, Victor knew that they had very serious problems. Their sales of Victrolas were lower than at any time in the previous decade, and the management was unable to reverse the trend in spite of their largest-ever advertising budget, or restyled cabinets. The salvation for the Victor Talking Machine Company was to come from a most interesting source, and in fact had been in development for more than a decade.

The Bell Telephone Laboratories, working to improve their understanding of wave transmission, had discovered that the same laws that governed the propagation of electrical energy, were also valid for mechanical energy. Prior to World War I, Bell had abandoned the trial-and-error method of designing telephone transmission equipment, and developed instead a series of mathematical formulae which described the behavior of the system. They could design on paper what had previously taken scientists repetitive and laborous experimentation to achieve. The theoretical methods which they developed for the design of electrical lines were adapted to the design of the vibrating parts of the mechanical system such as the telephone's transmitter and receiver. Bell scientists discovered that the electrical terms in their equations each had a mechanical equivalent. For example, mechanical displacement was analogous to electrical charge, displacement velocity replaced current, voltage became force, mass replaced inductance, elasticity was substituted for the reciprocal of capacity, and mechanical resistance (frictional loss) was analogous to electrical resistance.

By observing these changes in nomenclature, Bell engineers were able to describe a mechanical system for the transmission of sound which was optimized around the energy available to the system. It became little more than an engineering exercise to formulate the design of a phonograph which guaranteed matched impedances throughout.

Concurrent with the development of the theories of mechanical impedance, Bell engineers, through their Western Electric Division, were working on a system to record phonograph records electrically. The net result of this study was a disc record which contained not only a greater range of frequencies, but more total energy as well. These two developments, when combined, resulted in a recorded performance so far superior to what had previously been available as to totally astound all who heard it. The new phonograph and record combination was capable of reproducing five and one-half octaves, compared to the three octaves of the older style talking machines.

Men from Bell approached those at Camden with an offer to sell these discoveries, but rumors of their work had preceded them, so some of the impact they hoped to achieve had been lost. Victor, aided by their intelligence reports, had constructed a talking machine with a coiled metal exponential horn and a sound box scrounged from a previous experiment, and while it did not measure up to the one which their visitors brought with them, it did serve to steal some of the thunder from the telephone men's demonstration. Its only real purpose, however, was to boost moral among the Victor engineers, as Victor needed Bell's patents in order to produce the machine.

As obvious as it must have appeared to all concerned that Victor needed these inventions for its own survival, the company still managed to procrastinate long enough to lose the opportunity to secure exclusive rights to their use. It wound up, instead, sharing the license with the Columbia Phonograph Company; but, after all, half of the pie was still better than none.

On January 27, 1925 J.P.Maxfield, of Bell Laboritories, set up a studio at Camden for the demonstration of electrical recording. In February, numerous test recordings were made, many of them made both electrically and acoustically for comparison. One of these electrical test recordings, made on February 26, 1925 by "Eight Famous Victor Artists", was so good that it was issued (as Victor Black Seal No. 35753), thus becoming the earliest recording made by this magical new method to be released by Victor. By March 11, one of the regular recording rooms at Camden had been permanently converted to electrical recording and on that day pianist Olga Samaroff made five takes, and formally ushered in the era of electrical recording. The remaining recording rooms were gradually converted, and on July 31, the last acoustical recording was made at Camden. The only clue given to the public concerning the revolution taking place, was the inclusion of a small "VE" stamped into records made the new way, (the "Orthophonic Recording" label did not appear until the Fall of 1926) although many must have noticed that the latest recordings had an unaccustomed loudness and stridency when played on their existing Victrolas. With the recording process taken care of, Victor addressed the problem of what to do with the tremendous remaining stock of old-style Victrolas. In June of 1925, the company announced its plans for new instruments to its dealers, in an effort to soften the blow of what it would soon ask them to do. The company knew that it had to sell all the remining old-style Victrolas before the new models were introduced, if it expected to sell them at all. It reluctantly told its dealers of the only plan it could devise which could do, in only a few months time, what continuous advertising since Christmas of 1924 could not do. It would ask its dealers to take a loss on all the instruments which they still carried in stock (and the company would do the same with all those it still held). The resultant half-price sale of Victrolas was a tremendous success. From the sale's beginning in August, until the introduction of the new instruments in November, nearly all of the older instruments were sold. Dealers reduced their losses by buying additional instruments from the factory (at half price), and cleared their floors for the introduction of the new Orthophonic Victrolas (as they were to be called). Beginning with teaser advertisements in major periodicals in October, the public was gradually prepared for one of the industry's greatest campaigns.

November 2, 1925 was officially proclaimed "Victor Day", and every dealer in the country staged countless demonstrations comparing carefully selected new recordings on the top-of-the-line Credenza model Orthophonic Victrola to older recordings on the older instrument (if the dealer had managed not to sell every last one, that is). Newspaper accounts of the day reveal that it was a remarkable, unqualified success. Long lines formed in front of many dealers as the public crammed the stores, straining to see the new Victrolas. Dealers sold out in a matter of days, in many cases, and waited anxiously to replenish their stock. The new recordings sold very well too, and dealers enjoyed their best Christmas in memory. The shortage of instruments guaranteed that the demand carried over past the traditional holiday season, and most of 1926 must have seemed like Christmas to the Victor dealer. To say that the Orthophonic Victrola created a sensation is an understatement at best, as the volume and fidelity produced by a good Orthophonic recording on one of the larger Victrolas is startling, even today.

The newspaper advertisements claimed that the instrument was "NEW! in everything but name", and were not far from being correct. The only major component which was carried over from the older styles was the spring motor. The cabinets

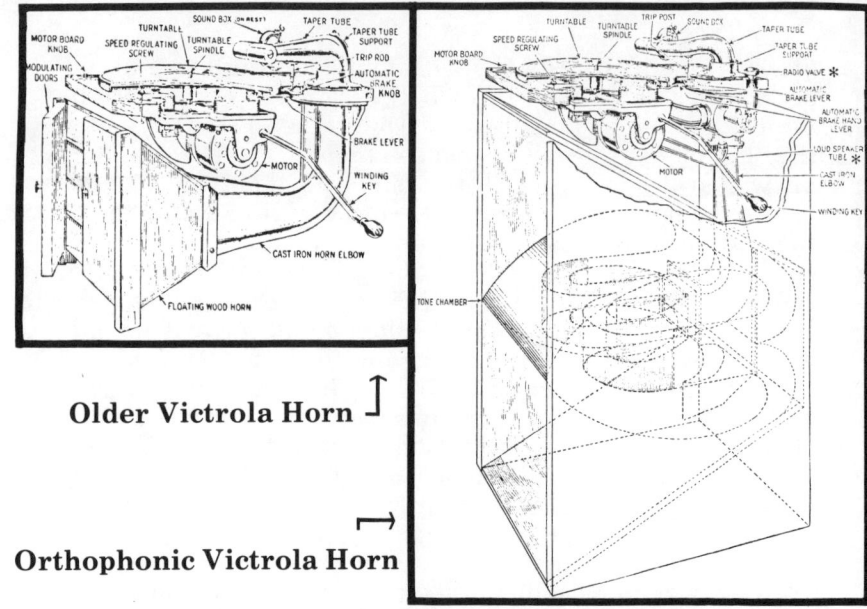

Older Victrola Horn ⌐

⟶
Orthophonic Victrola Horn

were completely different in appearance. Not only were the designs new, even the finish was new. Where the older instruments had been given a highly polished varnish finish, the new Orthophonic Victrolas were clothed in a coat of satin lacquer. Victor hired a new advertising agency, and completely revamped the style of its catalogs in an effort to emphasize the change. John Q. Public would have had to have spent the year in a cave not to know that there was something new in talking machines from Camden.

Naturally, the Orthophonic sound box was unlike any used on previous Victor products. A pleated aluminum diaphram replaced the formerly universally-used mica disc as the active element. The stylus assembly was set in ball bearings to increase needle response. Internally, the motive power was unchanged. The wind-up and extra-cost universal motor were the same as those used previously, with the Credenza receiving Victor's best four-spring power plant as standard equipment. A new, lower cost, AC-only induction electric motor was now also available on several models.

Three smaller Victrolas were also in the initial Orthophonic line up: the Granada at $150, the Colony at $110, with the Consolette bringing up the rear at $85. Each of these machines shared all of the important Orthophonic features of the Credenza, with the exception of the horn size. None had as large a horn as the premier model—with the consequence that the sound quality, particularly at the lowest frequencies, was inferior (a six-foot horn, as used in the largest Victrola, would reproduce a note of half the frequency of the lowest note reproducible by the horn in the smallest Victrola). Nevertheless, any one of them was capable of blasting the cobwebs off any ordinary talking machine, so sales were reassuringly brisk.

Victor experimented with building larger Orthophonic horns and actually constructed a 40-foot long (folded) horn at the Camden plant to test the exponential horn theory. According to their calculations, 35 feet were all that were necessary to reproduce the lowest note of a bass viol. Even though the horn was folded, the mouth measured a whopping ten by fourteen feet! This was clearly not practical for the average living room. Commercial applications frequently have more room, however, and Victor did produce several specialized instruments for hotels and theaters. Some early sound movies were reproduced through large Orthophonic horns, and Victor produced a monstrous Orthophonic Victrola with a 20 foot long folded horn and supplemental electrical amplification for use in auditoriums and hotels.

Auditorium Orthophonic Victrola

Concurrent with the introduction of the new Victrolas in 1925, Victor finally capitulated and admitted that radio was not just a passing fad. An even half-dozen radio phonograph combinations were announced, all using components supplied by the Radio Corporation of America. RCA had been set up following World War I to control the key early radio patents and act as a distributor for the consumer products of

Westinghouse Electric and General Electric. Headed by the young David Sarnoff (who had gained instant fame in 1912 by monitoring the wireless reports transmitted by the rescue ship Carpathia regarding the sinking of the great ocean liner Titanic), RCA quickly became synonymous with the latest in electronic technology, and was an ideal ally for Victor.

Three of RCA's most popular receivers were offered in various forms in conjunction with the Orthophonic Victrola. The least expensive combinations used the five-tube Radiola 20, a battery powered set with a TRF (tuned radio frequency) circuit. This radio was sold in a table top cabinet by RCA for $115, speaker and tubes extra, and was one of their most popular models. When incorporated into a Victor cabinet, the chassis was modified to mount horizontally adjacent to the turntable. The batteries, consisting of three 45 volt cells, six 1.5 volt cells and one 22.5 volt cell with a 4.5 volt tap, were contained under the radio chassis, in a compartment accessible through doors in the front of the cabinet. Typically, the battery sizes were chosen to give about one year's service, so the owner could look forward to spending $20 or so per year to keep his radio humming (for increased hum, the owner could spend even more and install an AC-powered battery eliminator such as the one made by Philco especially for Victrola-Radiolas). The speakers provided for these sets were the same as used in early radio horns, except that they were physically modified to interface with the Orthophonic horn of the phonograph. A lever or knob-operated valve near the turntable allowed the vibrations from the Victrola sound box or the radio speaker to be channeled through the horn for amplification.

The Radiola 25 with a six-tube superhetrodyne circuit was similarly installed in the medium priced sets, while the prestigious eight-tube Radiola 28 was reserved for the top of the line. Both of these sets contained an RCA development fittingly christened the "catacomb": an assembly in which the most delicate components were sealed against the ravages of climate. A hot tar-like substance was used to encapsulate these parts in an impregnable tomb which to this day defies all but the most dedicated electronic technicians to repair. In the 1920's, the repairman simply replaced a malfunctioning catacomb with a new one from stock (a concept widely used later because of the high value placed upon the repairman's time), but this luxury is not available to most collectors today. When working, however, these sets are capable of a fine performance as they were considered the state of the art in 1926. Both of these receivers, like the Radiola 20, were designed to be run off of a bulky set of batteries, but by 1926 RCA had made available an optional "lighting socket power package" that eliminated the need for batteries. The price for this convenience was high however; the cost for an RCA Radiola 28 with the AC package was between $525 and $840 depending on the cabinet. Despite the high tariff, this was the set that those with the wherewithal to afford it wanted, and in 1926 there was plenty of wherewithal going around.

Victor took notice of this and dutifully offered this combination in their most expensive instrument, the Borgia II which could be obtained in exchange for a crisp $1000 bill. The Borgia II resembled two Orthophonic Credenzas sitting side by side. Instead of a second turntable under the left lid however, a Radiola 28 AC control panel with its controls neatly gold plated in the finest Victor tradition awaited the proud owner. Hidden from view was a rotatable loop antenna, saving the owner the nuisance of stringing a wire across his attic or yard. An unfamiliar sight greeted the uninitiated on the Victrola side of the instrument, for instead of a single sound box on the end of the tone arm, this machine had two! The second sound box was an electrical pick-up which worked much like the familar acoustical sound box, with the exception that it converted the musical information in the record's grooves to electrical energy rather than mechanical energy. This enabled the operator to use the radio's electronic amplifier for the reproduction of his record collection, and offered him a degree of control over the volume not previously possible on purely acoustical phonographs.

Interestingly, these first electrically amplified phonographs could produce music only moderately louder than could the Orthophonic Victrolas, plus they had the ability to incorporate some interesting new forms of distortion into the reproduction. In spite of these shortcomings and the high price penalty (usually about double the cost of a comparable acoustical Victrola) the new Electrola-Victrola combinations sold well, and soon Victor introduced an electric-only phonograph (the Electrola) to compete with the Brunswick Panatrope. Internally, both instruments were identical since they each owed their origin to RCA, but Brunswick had managed to stage a *demonstration* of their Panatrope first and is therefore commonly given the credit for designing the first all-electric phonograph. Some authorities suggest that Victor was the first to *sell* a cone-speaker-equipped phonograph, but in reality, RCA deserves the ultimate credit, since it sold the electrical components to both Victor and Brunswick.

The Electrolas used a cone speaker to deliver the amplified sound to the listener. Ultimately, phonographs similar in concept to these new Electrolas would come to dominate the home entertainment industry and displace for all time the type of talking machine which had made possible the expansion of the Victor plant from its humble one-room beginnings.

These developments must have been unsettling to the aging Eldridge Johnson. He had built Victor into the world's largest producer of musical instruments by following a carefully defined path using a highly refined formula. He understood everything there was to know about marketing Victrolas and records. Now, overnight, the rules had changed and he was treading on new ground. While it is true that Victor sales were outstanding in 1926, it is probably not surprising to learn that Mr. Johnson (in ill health) was entertaining an offer to sell his interest in Victor. In December of 1926 an agreement was reached and on January 6, 1927 Eldridge Johnson turned control of his company over to a New York banking syndicate consisting of the banking houses of J & W Seligman and Speyer and Company.

The company continued to prosper, despite the absence of its founder, and 1927 saw the introduction of several new phonographs, including four with Victor's first-ever record changer. Inventors had been trying for years to sell an automatic record-changing phonograph of one design or another, but without the backing and marketing skill of a major company such as Victor, their efforts had met with little success. The 1916 Gabelola, a $600 home version of John Gabel's coin-operated Entertainer, probably deserves the credit for being the first widely available disc-changing home phonograph, but it was not until Victor introduced the Automatic Orthophonic for the same price a decade later that the record changer reached a mass market. Because of the bulky changer mechanism, this machine was housed in a huge (by previous standards) cabinet. At nearly five feet wide, this front-loading Victrola was quite unlike anything previously made in Camden and dominated the average living room. If you wanted automatic record changing, but the model 10-50 Automatic Orthophonic with its acoustical

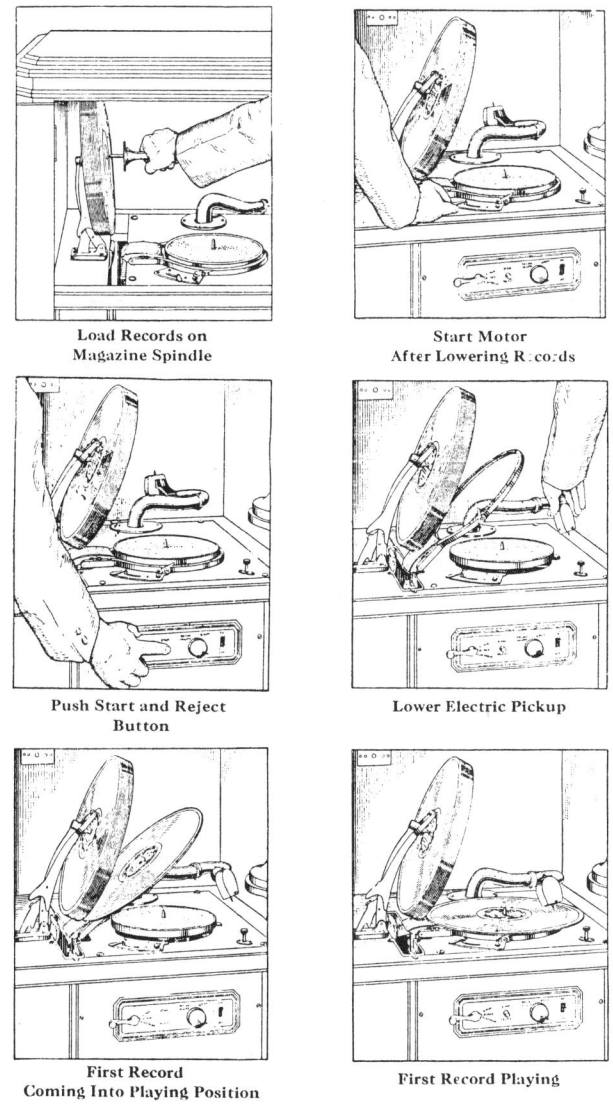

RECORD CHANGER OPERATION

amplification was not satisfactory, the models 10-51 and 10-70 offered the same changer in conjunction with electrical amplification. If radio was a must, then the only choice was the model 9-55 Automatic Electrola-Radiola. Even at the stratospheric price of $1550, the ornately carved 9-55 found several thousand customers, far more than had ever bought any one of the similarly priced period style pre-Orthophonic Victrolas.

In retrospect, the operation of Victor's first record changer seems odd and unnecessarily complicated, but it must be remembered that in 1927 it was unique—there simply was no standard to follow. For example, it was known that for the optimum needle-to-record angle to be maintained, only one record could be permitted on the turntable at any given time. This, of course, required that each record be removed from the turntable after it had been played—a luxury of design seldom found in modern record changers. Many subsequent record changer designs followed the guidelines set by this first Victor product, until the Depression economy forced a simplification of the requirements and adaptation of the cheaper drop-type designs in the middle thirties.

To play a program of recordings on one of the new automatic Victors, one assembled as many as a dozen 10-inch or 12-inch records (but not both intermixed) into one of the new style partitionless record albums provided with the instrument. A special "Record Loader" was slipped through the center hole of each record and lifted to the overhead spindle which held the selections prior to their use. As a ring surrounding the turntable was brought upwards to meet the bottommost record on the spindle, it automatically deposited the last record played into a drawer in the lower part of the cabinet. In this way, the only record on the turntable was the one being played. At the conclusion of the program, the entire stack was removed from the drawer and returned either to the spindle (upside down, in order to hear the flip sides) or to the record album.

If the operation sounds clumsy, it was, but it did have one redeeming feature: it worked! The instrument's one Achilles' heel, and the reason for its poor reputation today, did not usually make its presence known until the instrument had served a long and useful life. Nine of the key components in the changer had been cast in pot metal which, typically, did not age gracefully. Most of these parts today are seriously swollen, cracked or broken and must be recast from a more inert material before the changer will function again.

The pot metal was discontinued when Victor introduced a redesigned changer mechanism in the fall of 1928. The new design had the advantage of accepting 10-inch and 12-inch records intermixed and took up considerably less room in the cabinet. It held the program of up to twelve records in a tray rather than on a spindle, and was thus easier to load than its predecessor (and could be loaded while playing). A repeat control was added, allowing the owner to hear his favorite records again and again. The finished record was ejected simply by lifting it at the rear and allowing the clockwise rotation of the turntable literally to fling it to the left and into a receptacle. This technique was not as gentle as the older, more complicated system and occasionally record damage was known to occur.

This changer, unlike the one which had preceded it, was available in an assortment of six models, including a strictly acoustical Victrola, the model 10-35, at the bargain price of $365. This, however, was to be the Victrola's last glorious stand, for its days were clearly numbered. The public was showing a strong desire for electrically amplified phonographs, and prices were coming down as the increased demand and advanced technology coupled to lower production costs. The Victrola's fate was officially sealed in early 1929 when the banking syndicate sold control of the Camden giant to the Radio Corporation of America—a company with a demonstrated bias toward vacuum tubes.

On March 15, 1929, RCA (as a partner with General Electric and Westinghouse Electric) concluded its $150 million purchase of the Victor Talking Machine Company. The two new companies emerging from this pact were the Radio-Victor Corporation of America (which was formed to handle the sales and distribution of Radiolas and Phonographs, just as RCA had done for Radiolas in the past) and the Audio Vision Appliance Company (which gave control of the enormous Victor factories to GE and Westinghouse for the manufacture of the sets distributed by Radio-Victor.) David Sarnoff had traveled to Europe in February of 1929 secure in the belief that the Victor factories, which he had been coveting for RCA for nearly ten years, were now his. He was understandably enraged when, upon returning to America, he discovered that he still did not control the manufacturing facilities he felt were so vital to the growth of RCA. Fortunately for him, in spite of the fact that the new management was already in place, the organization required the formal approval of RCA's Board of Directors to become official. This was something which Sarnoff was not about to allow. His persuasive arguments (coupled with his threat to quit) convinced the other principals in the new combine to throw out the original agreement, and form a new division of the assets giving RCA the giant Victor plants.

In the fateful month of October, 1929, the agreements were formalized and the new RCA-Victor Company embarked upon the enormous program which would propel the company to the forefront of technological leadership in the years and decades ahead. Other events of that month changed the economic picture significantly, and the entire recording industry suffered greatly in the years immediately following The Crash as the public simply stopped buying records and record players. The recovery was slow and painful, but with the efforts and skills of many talented individuals, the company, aided by a new line of instruments (including a very popular Victor-designed radio, introduced almost coincidentally with the change in managment), achieved goals which would have seemed impossible to anyone studying the crude first products at the turn of the century.

the ORTHOPHONIC VICTROLA ELECTROLA and RADIOLA COMBINATIONS

One-One
1925-1929 $17.50

The successor to the famous Victrola IV, this machine sported a redesigned mahogany cabinet without doors (and therefore without volume control). Equipped with a single-spring motor and Exhibition sound box, this was the cheapest Victrola available at the time. The single-spring motor could play two 10-inch or one 12-inch record on a single winding. Other features were a 10-inch turntable and nickel-plated controls. This instrument did not offer Orthophonic reproduction of recordings.

This same instrument was available with the cabinet painted white and decorated with children's scenes for an extra $.50. This children's version was known as the model 1-2 Victrola.

Dimensions of the instrument were 6.5 inches high, by 12.5 inches wide and 13.75 inches deep.

One-Two
1925-1929 $18.00

This machine was identical in construction to the Victrola 1-1, except that the cabinet had brightly colored decorations on a white enamel background. This phonograph was intended for use by children and did not offer Orthophonic reproduction of records. Like the Victrola 1-1, this machine featured a single-spring motor, Exhibition sound box, 10-inch turntable and nickel-plated hardware.

Dimensions of the instrument were 6.5 inches high, by 12.5 inches wide and 13.75 inches deep.

One-Five
1926 $35.00

If the Victrola 1-6 seemed too small for a customer's needs, this portable Victrola might have been more suitable. At sixteen and one half pounds, it outweighed the smaller instrument and undoubtedly outperformed it as well. The fabric-covered case contained a flexible carrying handle and sported nickel-plated trim. The same single-spring motor and Victrola No. 4 sound box used in the smaller Victrola 1-6 were found here as well, but this phonograph used an upward pointing rear-mounted horn which reflected the sound off the open lid and theoretically reproduced lower frequencies.

The closed cabinet measured 6.5 inches high, 12.75 inches wide, and 15.75 inches deep.

One-Six
1926 $25.00

This thirteen and one-quarter pound portable Victrola replaced the short-lived Victrola No. 35 at the beginning of Victor's Orthophonic era. Although this instrument did not offer Orthophonic reproduction of the new electrically recorded discs, it did use the newly developed Victrola No. 4 sound box in place of the Victrola No. 2 sound box (obviously twice as good) used on the earlier instrument. The Victrola No. 4 sound box was designed to provide a somewhat flatter frequency response than could have been offered by the older sound box when playing the new recordings. The metal case was finished with a black crackle paint, highlighted with nickel-plated trim, and contained a flexible carrying handle. A spring held six records against the turntable when the lid was closed. Unlike the Victrola 1-5 which cost $10 more, this instrument had a front-pointing horn protected by a fabric grill cloth. It was claimed that the motor would run the machine for five minutes per winding.

The cabinet was 7.75 inches high, 11.25 inches wide, and 14 inches deep.

One-Seventy
1926-1929 $50.00

This table top Victrola was priced at $50 and offered an attractive looking wooden cabinet to those people who could not afford an Orthophonic Victrola. It contained a double-spring motor which ran for eight minutes on one winding. Nickel-plated hardware and the Victrola No. 4 sound box were featured. This machine did not have the automatic stop of the more expensive Victrolas. The cabinet was mahogany veneered with maple trim and a blended finish.

Dimensions of the instrument were 12.5 inches high, by 17.5 inches wide and 14.5 inches deep.

One-Ninety
1927-1929 $75.00

The Victrola 1-90 was the least expensive stationary Orthophonic offered by Victor. It contained the same double-spring motor as the Victrola 1-70, but in a larger cabinet. The hardware was nickel-plated and housed in a mahogany veneered cabinet with a blended (light and dark stain) finish. An automatic brake stopped the motor at the end of any record equipped with an eccentric groove.

Dimensions of the instrument were 13.5 inches high, by 19.5 inches wide and 18.5 inches deep.

Two-Thirty
1927-1928 $25.00

The Victrola 2-30 was a portable 17-pound instrument for people who wanted to take their music with them. The wooden framework was covered with a black fabric on the outside, and a bright red material on the inside. It was equipped with nickel-plated fittings, a Victrola No. 4 sound box and a spring clamp to hold six 10-inch records against the turntable while the case was closed.

Dimensions of the instrument were 7.75 inches high, by 11.75 inches wide and 14 inches deep.

Two-Thirty-Five
1929 $25.00

This 23-pound portable Victrola was built with a metal case covered with a padded black fabric on the outside. The inside was finished with a golden brown crinkle paint which harmonized with the gold-colored hardware. An Orthophonic sound box and single-spring motor highlighted the technical specifications.

Dimensions of the instrument were 7 inches high, by 16.5 inches wide and 14.5 inches deep.

Two-Fifty-Five
1929 $35.00

This portable Victrola was constructed on a steel frame, with a padded blue or brown covering. The record container in the lid held 10 ten-inch records. The 24-pound instrument sported an Orthophonic sound box and automatic brake, but was otherwise little different from the standard portable Victrolas which preceded it.

Dimensions of the instrument were 7.5 inches high, by 16 inches wide and 14.5 inches deep.

Two-Sixty
1927-1928 $40.00

Introduced in May 1927, this was Victor's most deluxe portable Victrola of the period. Gold-finished hardware highlighted the 22-pound instrument which was available in a choice of dark blue fabric with a leather figured texture, or brown fabric with a sharkskin texture. A Victrola No. 4 sound box and a motor which ran eight minutes on a single winding highlighted the technical specifications. A new style record storage container with a capacity for 12 ten-inch records was incorporated. A spring clip secured the crank next to the turntable when traveling.

Dimensions of the instrument were 7 inches high, by 16.5 inches wide and 13.5 inches deep.

CONSOLETTE (Four-Three)
1925-1928 $85.00-$150.00

As one of the four original Orthophonic Victrolas, the Consolette gave an entirely new definition to the upright Victrola. It bore no relationship in styling or performance to the instrument it replaced (the Victrola No. 80 was previously closest in price). In spite of its low cost, the Consolette easily outperformed even the most expensive of the older Victrolas, and consequently sold very well. In 1927, Victor converted to a system of identifying its instruments by numbers instead of names, so the Consolette became the Orthophonic Victrola 4-3 and the price was increased $10 to $95. Standard motive power was provided by the two-spring motor, with the induction (AC only) and the universal (AC-DC) motors optional at $35 and $55, respectively. The turntable was under the top lid, while two front doors concealed the speaker. Two record albums, storing ten records each, were provided with the instrument. The mahogany cabinet was designed in the Hepplewhite/Sheraton/Colonial style (Victor apparently wasn't sure which), and was modestly ornamented with small trim pieces of maple veneer. Nickel-plated hardware included the automatic brake, while spring supports held up the lid. Dimensions of the instrument were 36.5 inches high, by 19 inches wide and 19.5 inches deep.

COLONY
1925-1926 $110.00

The Colony Orthophonic Victrola was designed to offer, at a small advance in price, a slightly more luxurious instrument than the bottom of the line Consolette. In reality, the public seemed to be more willing to spend slightly more still and purchase the larger Granada model. Noting this, Victor discontinued the Colony after only one year of production, preferring instead to concentrate on the larger and more profitable instruments such as the Orthophonic Victrola 8-12, which was introduced at the same time that the Colony was dropped from the line.

The Colony possessed all of the standard Orthophonic features such as nickel-plated hardware, automatic brake and double-spring motor. The cabinet was veneered in mahogany and given a brown finish which was designed to harmonize with all styles of furniture.

Cabinet dimensions were 34 inches high, 28 inches wide and 20.5 inches deep.

GRANADA (Four-Four)
1925-1928 $150.00-$215.00

Officially introduced in time for the 1925 Christmas season, the Granada was second only to the famed Credenza in price and performance among the new Orthophonic Victrolas. The Spanish style cabinet was long and low, proportions which were relatively new to the men at Camden, and the lid covering the turntable was centered in the top of the case. Immediately underneath the lid was a pair of doors which covered the opening of the large horn. At each side of the horn was a door which covered the record storage area. The standard Victrola features such as nickel-plated hardware, automatic record brake and spring-supported lid were included, as was album storage for 60 records. The usual double-spring motor could be replaced with either of the electric motors at an extra cost of $35 (for the AC-only motor) or $55 (for the universal motor). In 1927, the name of the instrument was changed to the Orthophonic Victrola 4-4, but its other important features were retained. The nickel plating was replaced by an "antique bronze" finish on the hardware in later production, to bring the look more into line with the fashions of the times. The cabinet measured 34 inches high, by 34 inches wide, by 21.5 deep.

Four-Seven

1926-1928 $125.00-$180.00

The Orthophonic Victrola 4-7 was a slightly larger alternative to the Victrola 4-3, and offered turned legs and ribbed columns in the Italian Renaissance style. The cabinet, like that on most low cost models of this period, was mahogany veneer with a blended finish. Nickel plating graced the interior hardware. Spring-balanced lid supports and an automatic brake were included, as were three record albums stored horizontally under the horn. The double-spring motor ran ten minutes on a single winding, but the induction (AC only) and the universal (AC-DC) motors were optional at $35 and $55, respectively.

Dimensions of the instrument were 38 inches high, by 21.75 inches wide and 18.75 inches deep.

Four-Twenty
1928-1929 $135.00

This medium sized Victrola was typical of the style of instrument bought by a very large number of Americans in the middle and late twenties. It offered all of the features which the public thought to be important, such as the famous Orthophonic sound box and exponential horn. The double-spring motor supplied the power to play several records on a single winding and a small storage area was supplied to the left of the turntable for the containment of a single record album. The plain dark brown mahogany console featured two doors over the speaker grill to allow the volume to be modified as in all previous Victrolas, but in spite of the somewhat unpretentious appearance, this little phonograph was capable of extracting a remarkable performance from a good electrical recording, and gave serious competition to the expensive electrically amplified phonographs so much in vogue in 1928.

The cabinet measured 25.5 inches wide, 18 inches deep, and 36.5 inches high.

Four-Forty
1926-1928 $165.00-$220.00

As one of the shortest styles of Orthophonic Victrolas, the model 4-40 was popular with those who preferred the console-style cabinet. The mahogany cabinet had raised panels of highly figured veneer, giving an artistic overall effect. The standard spring motor could be replaced with the induction (AC only) or the universal (AC-DC) motors for $35 and $55, respectively. The cabinet provided storage for six record albums and contained nickel-plated or (later) antique bronze-finished hardware. The lid supports were spring-balanced for ease of operation, and the automatic brake shut the machine off at the end of any record equipped with an eccentric groove.

The cabinet measured 37.75 inches high, by 37 inches wide, by 20 inches deep.

ALHAMBRA I (Seven-One)
1925-1926 $350.00

This popular instrument became one of Victor's very first Victrola-Radiola combinations. Here, in a single cabinet, lay the future of home entertainment. The Orthophonic Victrola on the right side of the cabinet was similar in most respects to the Colony Orthophonic Victrola. The horn was the same size as that used in the Colony, as an example, and the other mechanical components (double-spring motor, Orthophonic sound box, etc.) were the same as well. On the left side of the cabinet sat something new for a Victor product: a built-in radio! Through an agreement with RCA, Victor was able (as was Brunswick) to incorporate the Radiola in their phonographs and chose, in this instance, the Radiola 20, a modern and very popular receiver. The combination was a natural one. In addition to offering the convenience of having two forms of home entertainment in one central location, the alliance of the Victrola and Radiola allowed the economies of a shared cabinet and acoustical amplifier (horn). The public was quick to see the logic of such an idea, and radio-phonograph combinations became common in America's living rooms within a few years. The mechanism was contained in a Spanish-style cabinet made of mahogany veneers with maple overlays which measured 33.25 inches high by 35.5 inches wide by 23.5 inches deep.

ALHAMBRA II (Seven-Two)
1925-1926 $425.00

Victor had long ago learned the value in having a full line of instruments priced for every budget. The Alhambra II fit nicely into the basic Victor marketing philosophy by offering a slightly nicer product than the Alhambra I for a few ($75) dollars more. Instead of using the Radiola 20 chassis, the Alhambra II used the more deluxe Radiola 25 chassis. Whereas the Radiola 20 had a five-tube tuned radio frequency (TRF) circuit, the Radiola 25 used a six-tube Superhetrodyne circuit (an exclusive with RCA at the time). A Superhetrodyne radio was, in 1925, a costly and prestigious item, for it offered performance superior to the other radio circuits of the day. As a consequence, the combination of an Orthophonic Victrola and a Superhetrodyne Radiola made an unbeatable instrument. Those who heard the Radiola played through an Orthophonic horn declared it notably better than any other method of radio reproduction. Cone speakers of that period had very limited response to the higher (above 600 Hz) frequencies, while the typical horn radio speaker had a useful range of only 300 to 2500 Hz. An Orthophonic Victrola horn, because of its large size and fundamentally correct shape, had superior performance to either a cone or a regular radio horn. Radio fanciers lamented the fact that they could not buy a Victrola horn separately to use with their existing radio receiver. Their only alternative was to buy a Victrola-Radiola, such as the Alhambra II, if they wished to hear radio at its 1926 best.

The Alhambra II, like the less expensive Alhambra I, was designed to use an outside antenna, but for those to whom this represented an inconvenience, provision was made for adding to the cabinet (with "minor alterations", according to the catalog) a loop antenna. As the chassis of the Radiola 20 and the Radiola 25, as well as their required battery packs, were similar in size, the overall dimensions of the two Alhambras were identical. Victor used this technique of offering different electronics in similar cabinets until it could accumulate some experience in determining public buying habits, as it was now experimenting in a foreign field. The data gathered during this first year of radio-phonograph production were put to use when Victor introduced a smaller, refined line of instruments the following year.

The mechanism was contained in a Spanish-style cabinet, made of mahogany veneers with maple overlays, which measured 33.25 inches high by 35.5 inches wide by 23.5 inches deep.

Seven-Three
1927-1928 $325.00-$430.00

The Orthophonic Victrola-Radiola 7-3 was, like its brother the 7-30, the lowest priced of the early phonograph-radio combinations built by Victor and was similar to the 1926 Alhambra I Victrola-Radiola. The introductory price of $375, including tubes, was soon reduced by $50. The radio was RCA's Radiola 20, a very popular tuned-radio-frequency (TRF) receiver which used four UX-199 and one UX-120 tube. Power was provided by three 45 volt (which were combined to give 45v, 90v, and 135v), one 22.5 volt, one 4.5 and six 1.5 volt batteries. Access to the battery compartment was provided by a removable panel behind the left two front doors. Above these doors, the split lid could be lifted to uncover the radio controls. The radio tubes were exposed to view on these early sets as electronics were still something of a novelty. Four record albums were stored behind the front doors. Under the right half of the lid was the standard Victor turntable with its gold-plated controls. The double-spring motor could be replaced with either the induction (AC only) or the universal (AC-DC) motor for $35 or $55, respectively. A lever at the right front corner of the turntable compartment operated a valve under the tone arm to direct vibrations from the sound box or the radio speaker to the Orthophonic horn. A separate jack was provided for an external speaker, if desired. The lids were held open by a friction-type brace, and an automatic brake stopped Orthophonic recordings at their conclusion.

Seven-Ten
1927-1928 $275.00-$330.00

The model 7-10 was what could be termed a second generation radio-phonograph combination. For radio reception, the set used RCA's newly introduced Radiola 16, a battery-powered chassis utilizing five UX-201-A and one UX-112-A tubes (the RCA designation for this chassis was AR 1058.) A single tuning dial was employed for the first time in a Victor combination, simplifying radio operation significantly. Radio reproduction was through the Orthophonic horn, as on previous designs, and a lever-operated valve was used to connect the horn to either the radio speaker or the Victrola sound box. Because of developing economies in the production of radio receivers, this set could be priced lower than combinations with similar performance of only a year previous, such as the 7-3. As in the case of the 7-3 and others, the standard double-spring motor could be replaced with either the induction (AC only) or universal (AC-DC) electric motor for an extra $35 or $55, respectively. The cabinet was mahogany veneered with trim in the Adam style.

Cabinet dimensions were 40.5 inches high, by 24 inches wide and 21.75 inches deep.

Seven-Eleven
1928 $250.00-$285.00

The Orthophonic Victrola-Radiola 7-11 was one of the last acoustical radio-phonographs introduced by Victor. By this time, interest was high in the electrically amplified Victrolas, and spring-powered acoustically amplified instruments were simply not exciting. Interestingly, even though the phonograph was acoustically amplified and spring wound, the radio was powered from the wall. The radio used was RCA's Radiola 18, a TRF circuit using one UY-227, one UX-171-A and four UX-226 tubes. As was the practice by 1928, the tubes were included in the purchase price of the set. A single-tube Socket Power Unit, the SPU-30, was used to supply the necessary voltages to operate the receiver. The unusual Victrola horn was formed of sheet metal, and incorporated a mount for the turntable motor. The sound was channeled around and under the turntable, towards the horn opening near the rear of the cabinet. The turntable compartment acted as an extension of the horn, thus allowing the front doors to double as the volume control for the phonograph. The radio receiver had its own cone speaker and volume control knob. An electric motor was optional at $35. The cabinet of the 7-11 was designed in the 18th Century English style, and sported antique brass fittings, gold lacquered controls and four record albums. The walnut or mahogany cabinet was 53.75 inches high, 29.75 inches wide and 17 inches deep.

Seven-Twenty-Five
1927-1928 $385.00-$420.00

The model 7-25 incorporated the Radiola 17 chassis, RCA's first "popular priced" AC receiver. The radio used seven tubes, four UX-226, one UY-227, one UX-171-A and one UX-280, in a TRF (tuned radio frequency) circuit. A single dial which simplified tuning was accessible through the two front doors. The radio and Victrola shared the Orthophonic horn for amplification, and a lever-operated valve permitted instantaneous change from one to the other. Only the induction electric motor was available as an option ($35), since the radio required alternating current for operation. The Italian-style cabinet was veneered in walnut, with a blended antique finish. The hardware was oxidized bronze in color, and the lid covering the turntable was spring balanced.

Cabinet dimensions were 41.25 inches high, by 24.75 inches wide and 23.25 inches deep.

Seven-Twenty-Six
1928-1929 $425.00-$475.00

This radio-phonograph combination offered an interesting option: for an additional $50, the buyer could elect to have the RCA model 100-A cone speaker replaced by an electro-dynamic cone speaker (these latter instruments are identified by having a serial number higher than 12000). Given the low cost of cone speakers today, this differential appears unwarranted, but the technology was in its infancy at the time and even at the higher price of $475, this instrument was one of the lower cost, totally electric radio-phonograph consoles available. The chief difference in these two speakers lay in their method of generating the magnetic field required for the modulation of the cone. The 100-A speaker used a permanent magnet to generate the field, which offered the advantage of being low cost and totally passive. The dynamic speaker contained an electromagnet capable of producing higher magnetic fields than the permanent magnets of the day. The advantage here was louder reproduction of music and better low frequency response. The penalty in using an electromagnet was increased complexity, cost and power consumption. In its standard configuration, the 54 inch high by 29.75 inch wide by 16.5 inch deep model 7-26 offered an electrical pickup which shared the amplifier of RCA's Radiola 18 with Socket Power Unit SPU-34 for record playing. Separate volume controls were used for the radio and Victrola. A built-in antenna plate was claimed to be sufficient to pull in local broadcasts, but for reception of distant stations a separate antenna was required.

Seven-Thirty
1926-1928 $325.00-$380.00

The combination Victrola-Radiola 7-30 was identical in construction to the model 7-3. Only slight variations in trim distinguished one from the other. RCA's Radiola 20 chassis was contained on the left side of this cabinet, with the battery storage provided below. The battery compartment was roomy, as this five-tube set required three 45 volt, one 22.5 volt, one 4.5 volt (usually provided by a tap on the 22.5 volt battery) and six 1.5 volt batteries for operation. Because of the space requirements of the batteries, only four record albums could be stored within the cabinet: two horizontally filed below the batteries behind the left two front doors, and two similarly positioned beneath the Orthophonic horn behind the right two front doors. A lever-operated valve permitted either the radio or the Victrola to speak through the horn. Interior hardware was gold plated on both the Radiola and Victrola controls, lending a rich look to the instrument. The cabinet was Spanish styled with mahogany veneer and a blended finish. The standard double-spring motor could be replaced with either the induction (AC only) or universal (AC-DC) electric motor for an extra $35 or $55, respectively.

Cabinet dimensions were 38.25 inches high, by 40.25 inches wide and 20 inches deep.

Eight-Four
1926-1927 $235.00-$290.00

The Victrola 8-4 was a medium priced instrument included in Victor's early line of Orthophonics. The Italian Renaissance cabinet was offered in mahogany or walnut veneer with a blended finish. Naturally, as would be expected in an instrument in this price range, the AC and universal motors were optional replacements (at $35 and $55 respectively) for the standard four-spring motor. Six record albums were provided and together had the capacity to store sixty records. Features such as a twelve-inch turntable, automatic brake and gold-plated controls were standard.

The cabinet measured 45 inches high, 28.75 inches wide, and 22.75 inches deep.

Eight-Seven
1926-1927

The Orthophonic Victrola 8-7 was introduced in 1926, but its heritage dates from 1911 when Victor established its Educational Department under Mrs. Francis Elliott Clark. Victor shrewdly realized that it could mold minds at an early age by providing special programs and equipment for schools. Even if the student could not immediately influence the purchase of a Victrola, he might be favorably disposed to buy one for himself when he was old enough. At first, there were no machines in the Victor catalog which were especially designed for schoolroom use. The Victor V with the wooden horn was what Mrs. Clark recommended because it had the best sound quality of any Victor (the Victor VI, after all, was simply a gilded Victor V - all of the critical specifications were identical). In 1913 Victor introduced the Victor XXV, an instrument with the audio performance of a Victor V, but in a cabinet more suited to the educational environment. The price of the Victor XXV, $60, even matched that of the Victor V. This was accomplished not by great manufacturing economies, but by reducing the dealer's margin of profit. Not surprisingly, dealers were reluctant to push the early Victor XXV's, until Victor increased the list price to $67.50 in 1914, at which price the instrument returned what the dealer thought to be a fair profit. The outside-horn Victor XXV continued to be sold throughout the heyday of the Victrola because it still remained the finest-sounding of all Victor phonographs. In 1926, however, there was no way it could compete with the new Orthophonic Victrolas, so it was clear that the Educational Department deserved a new "schoolhouse Victrola". The 8-7 was exactly what the market called for -a simple, portable record player with a large Orthophonic horn. The cabinet was very plain (Victor described it as being in the "Italian Primitive" style), was made of sturdy oak and was just as ugly as the Victor XXV it replaced. Victor designed certain new features into the 8-7 which gave the instrument an even greater adaptability to the requirements of school life. The fact that the horn was enclosed was naturally an asset, but Victor went further by placing large rubber tires at the rear of the instrument to facilitate movement to and from the classroom, or out to the playing field. A large shelf unfolded from the rear to create a handy storage area for records, while a steel handle aided in moving the instrument. In 1928, Victor replaced the 8-7 with the Orthophonic Victrola 8-8. The 8-8 shared the important technical specifications of the 8-7, but was housed in a larger and more attractive cabinet.

Eight-Eight
1928-1929 $195.00

The Victrola 8-8 was the second replacement for the Victrola XXV, the famous outside horn schoolhouse phonograph. By utilizing the new Orthophonic horn and sound box, Victor developed a superior-sounding instrument that was, at the same time, better suited for the educational environment. Large rubber-tired wheels and casters gave this machine a portability which the older model lacked, while the Orthophonic horn gave both added convenience (since the horn was built in) and louder reproduction of the records. A full-width steel handle was attached to the back of the case for ease of guidance, and a large dropping shelf could hold records or catalogs during the performance. A spring-powered motor was standard, as this instument was designed to be used both indoors and outdoors. The cabinet was veneered in oak with a "Baronial" finish, and highlighted with blue painted panels at the top and bottom of the doors. Space for two twelve-inch record albums was provided under the horn. As on the Victrola XXV, the lid on this Schoolhouse Victrola could be locked. Victor offered the 8-8 at a 25% discount off list price to schools. This policy was adopted to encourage the use of the 8-8 in the schools, while still encouraging private parties who wanted an oak Orthophonic Victrola to buy the home version, known as the Orthophonic Victrola 8-9. The cabinet measured 44 inches high, by 25.25 inches wide, by 21.5 inches deep.

Eight-Nine
1928-1929 $175.00-$230.00

The Victrola 8-9 was, for all practical purposes, the new schoolhouse Victrola 8-8 without wheels. Both instruments shared the same oak veneered cabinet, but the home version Victrola 8-9 was given some extra embellishments. Additional front and side panels received blue painted inserts, while the molding was highlighted in gold. Since this instrument, unlike the 8-8, was not intended to be used out of doors, 115 VAC or universal electric motors were offered as an option at $35 or $55 each, depending on the customer's electrical service. Normally, the machine came with a double-spring motor, automatic brake, five albums, twelve-inch turntable and gold-finished hardware. Small carved appliques graced the corners and covered the keyhole area (no lock was provided on the home version) of the cabinet. Attractive carved feet replaced the wheels of the 8-8, making this instrument a stand-out in the 1929 Victor catalog.

Cabinet dimensions were 45.75 inches high, 26.25 inches wide, and 20.25 inches deep.

Eight-Twelve
1927-1928 $235.00-$290.00

For the person to whom the Credenza seemed too large, the model 8-12 Orthophonic Victrola offered a pleasant alternative. Using the medium-sized Orthophonic horn, this instrument managed to look impressive, while actually being slightly smaller and less expensive than the top-of-the-line Victrolas. The four-spring motor powered the turntable for twenty minutes on a single winding, although the two electric motor options (induction at $35 and universal at $55) were available on this machine as well. Eight record albums were included with this model and stored on either side of the horn. The French Renaissance style cabinet was finished in walnut veneer, with a blended antique finish. The lid supports were spring assisted.

Cabinet dimensions were 45 inches high, by 30.5 inches wide and 18.5 inches deep.

CREDENZA (Eight-Thirty)
1925-1928 $275.00 - $405.00

First shown in November of 1925, the Credenza (later called the 8-30) is probably the most famous of all the Orthophonic Victrolas. This machine contained the largest horn Victor made, and was always chosen to demonstrate the Orthophonic principles. Originally priced at $275, the price was increased to $300 in January 1926. Induction (AC) and universal (AC-DC) motors were available at $35 and $55 extra respectively. The Italian Renaissance style cabinet came with a choice of walnut or mahogany veneer. A tooled leather front panel was available on the walnut cabinet for $50 extra. The four-spring motor ran the 12-inch turntable 20 minutes on one winding. The instrument was supplied with eight record albums storing a total of eighty records. Air dashpots lowered the lid, and the earliest models had two large front doors, while the later examples provided separate doors for the record storage compartments.

The six-foot long folded horn (measured from the sound box to the grill cloth) provided the finest reproduction of recordings of any of the new acoustical Victrolas. Early owners of this instrument who also owned radios regretted the fact that they could not utilize the wonderful amplifier of their Victrola to improve the quality of their radio reproduction. Victor responded to these wishes by offering an acoustical valve and speaker as an option on new Victrola 8-30's in 1927, thereby allowing the Orthophonic horn to be used as an amplifier for an independent radio set.

Eight-Thirty-Five
1928-1929 $300.00-$335.00

Although the Orthophonic Victrola 8-30 (the Credenza) had been a very popular instrument, Victor decided that it was time to redesign its "acoustic flagship". The result of the redesign was the Victrola 8-35, which was introduced in May 1928. Similarities between the two instruments were the basic operating principles and the price. The horn in this machine, while a folded exponential in cross section like those used in the earlier Orthophonics, was smaller than the one used in the Credenza. The smaller size allowed Victor to make the instrument lower than the Credenza, which, along with the exposed record album storage beside the horn, made the machine look more like an electrical phonograph, and less like an acoustical one (particularly so when ordered with the optional electric motor at $35). By the time this machine was put on the market, though, the price for an all-electric phonograph had fallen considerably, and it would soon be possible to buy a good Electrola for the same amount of money. The public had always preferred the electrical instruments and, when given the choice of acoustical or electrical amplification at the same price, usually selected electrical. The consequence of this was that sales of the 8-35 never approached those of the 8-30 and so this machine became the last deluxe Orthophonic in the Victor catalog. The 38.5 inch by 40 inch by 20.25 inch walnut veneered cabinet contained two small drawers above the record album shelves; the one on the right holding the needle cups and clips for the Tungstone needle tins.

Eight-Sixty
1926-1927 $650.00

This bizarre instrument was identical to the Orthophonic Victrola 8-30 (the Credenza) with one important addition: it contained a pick-up and amplifier for electrical reproduction of records. Using a single tone arm with two sound boxes, the 8-60 offered its indecisive owner the option of hearing records reproduced in the traditional acoustical manner, or in conjunction with the newest electronic technology. This state-of-the-art performance did not come cheaply, however; the addition of the amplifier, pick-up and speaker to the 8-30 doubled the price. The speaker used was the same as supplied with any of the Victrola-Radiola combinations of the period and used the Orthophonic horn for amplification. The inductive disc electric motor was standard, since the amplifier required AC power. A separate radio could be plugged into a jack at the rear of the instrument and share use of the amplifier and speaker, if desired. Included in the list price were eight record albums and gold plating on all exposed controls.

Cabinet dimensions were 46 inches high, by 31.25 inches wide and 22 inches deep.

FLORENZA (Nine-One)
1926 $475.00-$605.00

Initially priced at $550, this instrument was one of Victor's first phonograph-radio combinations. Employing the Radiola 25 chassis supplied by RCA (but built by General Electric and Westinghouse), the radio used five UX-199 tubes and one UX-120. Radio power was provided by three 45 volt, one 22.5 volt, one 4.5 volt and six 1.5 volt dry cells. Radio amplification was through the Orthophonic horn, a valve being provided to switch from radio to record reproduction. A loop antenna was concealed within the door and could be positioned for best reception. The radio was located under the left lid, while the Victrola was under the right spring-supported lid. A four-spring motor powered the gold-plated 12-inch turntable. Induction disc or universal motors were available for $35 and $55 extra, respectively. An output jack was provided for the attachment of an external speaker. A very similar two-tone walnut Italian style cabinet was used the following year on the model 9-15 Victrola-Radiola.

Dimensions of the instrument were 45 inches high, by 39.75 inches wide and 23.75 inches deep.

BORGIA II (Nine-Two)
1925-1926 $1000.00

This was Victor's most expensive Orthophonic Victrola since it also offered all-electric reproduction of records or radio. Built into the left side of the cabinet was a Radiola 28 AC chassis (RCA's finest). The AC power supply and the amplifier eliminated the need for batteries, although shelves were provided in the rear for batteries, just in case AC power was not available. Radio reproduction was through the Orthophonic horn, however a jack was provided for a separate speaker, if desired. The radio and amplifier used seven UX-199, one UX-120, one UV-876 and two UX-216-B tubes. Record reproduction could be had through the standard Orthophonic tone arm and sound box (acoustical) or through an electrical pick-up (supplied by RCA) grafted to the same tone arm. When the electrical pick-up was used, the reproduction was through the radio's amplifier and speaker, and volume could be controlled by a knob near the turntable. The left lid concealed the radio controls, including a wheel for positioning the built-in loop antenna. The right lid concealed the Victrola, and both lids were supported by air dashpots for automatic closing.

The instrument was equipped with an induction (AC only) electric motor for the 12-inch turntable. The left door concealed eight record albums, providing storage for eighty records, while the right door concealed the Orthophonic horn. A pilot lamp on the front indicated when power was on. The model designation was changed to 9-40 in 1927 when a hum control was incorporated into the amplifier, and the cabinet was modified to use four front doors instead of two. The cabinet was in the Italian Renaissance style with a blended finish on walnut veneer.

Dimensions of the instrument were 45.5 inches high, by 44 inches wide and 22.25 inches deep.

BORGIA I (Nine-Three)
1925-1926 $675.00

Just as the Alhambra II promised superior radio performance over the Alhambra I, the Borgia I was a step above the Florenza. Introduced concurrently with the other initial models of the Orthophonic Victrola, the Borgia I incorporated RCA's very best battery-powered receiver, the Radiola 28. This instrument also used the largest size of Orthophonic horn available, with the consequence that this machine presented the finest radio performance available in 1926. The Superhetrodyne circuit gave the radio a sensitivity superior to other circuits, while the large Orthophonic horn guaranteed a broader frequency response (100 to 5000 Hz) than was obtainable through any other means. The Borgia I was similar to the more expensive Borgia II, with the main difference being that the latter offered electrical amplification in addition to the standard acoustical amplification. Both instruments used a similar cabinet which was plainer in appearance than one might normally expect from the price. The simple lines of the cabinet in no way detracted from the quality construction, however. All of the customary features were present: built-in loop antenna, concealed battery compartment, four-spring motor, gold-plated controls on both the radio and the Victrola and a subtle two-tone effect given to the walnut cabinet. The cabinet measured 45.5 inches high by 44 inches wide by 22.25 inches deep.

Nine-Fifteen
1926-1928 $600.00-$655.00

The Victrola-Radiola 9-15, introduced late in 1926, replaced the Borgia I and became Victor's most expensive instrument not requiring AC power. In its standard configuration, the four-spring motor and battery-operated Radiola 28 made the unit ideal for high class installations where the supply of AC power was a problem. Naturally, Victor offered electric motor options (induction at $35 and universal at $55) and other companies (primarily Philco, which made a special unit for Victrola-Radiolas) offered AC-powered battery eliminators for those whose homes were or became electrified. The Radiola 28 tubes (seven UX-199s and one UX-120) and controls were housed under the left half of the split lid, while the Victrola hardware was under the right half. Beneath the Victrola turntable was the Orthophonic horn, so naturally the right door remained open while the instrument was playing. Behind the left door were four record albums and the control for the built-in loop antenna. Access to the six filament voltage batteries (1.5 volts each) was through the left front door as well (they were under the record albums), but replacement of the three 45 volt, and one 22.5/4.5 volt batteries required removing the back of the set. Spring-assisted lid supports and gold-plated controls were also featured on this instrument. The cabinet was finished in two-tone walnut, which was further blended by a darker stain near the corners.

Nine-Sixteen
1928 $750.00

The Electrola-Radiola 9-16 used RCA's Radiola 18 Special chassis (the "Special" indicates that this set used the AP-736-B Power Amplifier Unit in place of the Socket Power Unit SPU-30 used in the 7-11 and 7-26). The use of the Power Amplifier Unit permitted accommodation of the electrical phonograph pickup and electro-dynamic speaker at the expense of requiring a greater number of tubes. The consequence of this difference was improved performance, most noticeably increased volume, when compared to the 7-11 or 7-26. Normally supplied for use with 105-125 volts at 50 to 60 Hz, available special equipment allowed the set to be used in areas which had 105-125 volts at 25-40 Hz.

The Early English cabinet used for this instrument was the same as the one used for the 9-18. It was constructed of walnut solids with quartersawed oak veneer panels, and measured 55 inches high, 30.75 inches wide, and 17.25 inches deep. The hardware had what Victor termed a Light Flemish brass finish.

Nine-Eighteen
1928-1929 $925.00

RCA's Radiola 64 Superhetrodyne chassis formed the basis of this expensive radio-phonograph combination. Included in the purchase price were one UX-250, two UX-281s and eight UY-227 tubes. The Spanish-style cabinet had carved doors covering the speaker at the bottom and the record albums above. In spite of the high price, this was Victor's lowest priced combination instrument using the famed Radiola 64, one of the first radios to incorporate a tuning meter in the front panel.

The Early English cabinet used for this instrument was the same as the one used for the 9-16. It was constructed of walnut solids with quartersawed oak veneer panels, and measured 55 inches high, 30.75 inches wide, and 17.25 inches deep. The hardware had what Victor termed a Light Flemish brass finish.

Nine-Twenty-Five
1927-1928 $1150.00

The Electrola-Radiola 9-25 represented all that Victor knew about the electrical reproduction of music in 1927. As the price indicates, this was one of Victor's finest for that year -second only to the 9-55 which contained the same electronics plus the new Victor automatic record changer. The famous RCA Radiola 28 AC with the Radiola 104 loudspeaker was the heart of this unit. An electric pick-up converted the recorded vibrations to electrical impulses in this forerunner of the modern radio-phonograph, while a knob allowed control of the sound from "a whisper to full orchestra volume". The two small upper doors concealed the opening for the six-inch speaker, while storage for the record albums was provided behind the two lower doors. Like all Radiola 28 models, a built in-loop antenna eliminated the necessity of stringing a 100-foot length of wire between the roof and a sturdy tree, as was the practice with lesser radios of the day. The two-piece lid was spring-supported, and the electric induction motor was standard equipment. The universal motor and a different tube line-up was available for locations with direct current, but on special order only. The cabinet was Italian Renaissance in design, with a blended antique finish over the walnut veneer. Cabinet dimensions were 47 inches high, by 40.75 inches wide and 18.5 inches deep.

Nine-Forty
1927-1928 $1000.00

PHANTOM VIEW

This was Victor's updated version of their most expensive Orthophonic Victrola and offered the owner the choice of all-electric reproduction of records or radio in addition to the traditional acoustical reproduction of records. Nearly identical in appearance to the earlier Borgia II Victrola-Radiola, it incorporated a minor change to the amplifier (a hum-control adjustment was added) and substituted four smaller front doors for the clumsy double door arrangement of its predecessor.

Built into the left side of the cabinet was a Radiola 28 AC chassis (RCA's finest). The AC power supply eliminated the need for batteries. Radio reproduction was through the Orthophonic horn, however a jack was provided for a separate loud speaker, if desired. The radio and amplifier used seven UX-199, one UX-120, one UV-876 and two UX-216-B tubes. Record reproduction could be had through the standard Orthophonic tone arm and sound box (acoustical) or through an electrical pick-up (supplied by RCA) grafted to the same tone arm. When the electrical pick-up was used, the reproduction was through the radio's amplifier and speaker, and volume could be controlled by a knob near the turntable. The left lid covered the radio controls, including a wheel for positioning the built-in loop antenna. The right lid covered the Victrola, and both lids were supported by air dashpots for automatic closing.

The instrument was equipped with an induction (AC only) electric motor for the 12-inch turntable. The left door concealed eight record albums, providing storage for eighty records, while the right door concealed the Orthophonic horn. A pilot lamp on the front indicated when power was on. The cabinet was in the Italian Renaissance style with a blended finish on walnut veneer.

Dimensions of the instrument were 47 inches high, by 45 inches wide and 22.25 inches deep.

Nine-Fifty-Four
1928-1929 $1350.00

This handsome instrument utilized the new RCA Radiola 64 chassis and second generation Victor record changer to replace, in late 1928, the now obsolete (after only one year) 9-55. Until the introduction of the 9-56 a few months later, this was their very best (or at least most expensive). The massive carved walnut cabinet was styled in the Spanish influence which was so popular in 1928. Because the new Victor record changer required less room to operate than the old one (due to the more compact rejected-record compartment) the changer was positioned above the radio rather than next to it as in the 9-55. The result of this change was increased convenience, since the operator could stand more or less upright while loading or unloading records.

The changer and cabinet hardware were finished to look like wrought iron. The eight-inch speaker was located behind the lower right-hand door (the left door was a dummy). Six leather record albums (three of each size) were included. The Radiola featured single-knob tuning aided by a meter plus a built-in antenna plate.

The cabinet measured 60 inches high, 39.5 inched wide and 22.75 inches deep.

Nine-Fifty-Five
1927-1928 $1550.00

"It Has Everything!" sang the ads when the model 9-55 was introduced in November of 1927. And indeed it was Victor's first instrument to combine the three requisite features of the deluxe radio-phonograph of the future: radio, electric phonograph, and automatic record changer. This instrument was Victor's pride and joy in 1927 and is unquestionably the most impressive instrument they ever built. The 9-55 used the same automatic record changer introduced on the acoustical 10-50 a few months earlier, but was fitted with an electric pick-up in place of the Orthophonic sound box. The record changer and seven record storage albums were concealed behind the large single door on the left half of the instrument, while the radio controls and speaker were revealed by opening the double doors on the right. Since the top was fixed in place, Victor placed the entire radio chassis in a swinging enclosure which could be pivoted for convenient operation while sitting or standing. A control for the built-in loop antenna was located to the right of the speaker while the volume control was to its left. Records could be rejected by a button on the changer, or by one near the speaker. An ingenious power switch was provided which turned the instrument off if the double doors over the speaker were closed. The massive cabinet was carved in walnut and had an open-grained, shaded finish. Cabinet dimensions were 49.5 inches high, by 51.5 inches wide, and 27 inches deep.

Nine-Fifty-Six
1929 $1750.00

The elaborate Chinese Chippendale cabinet is all that differentiates this instrument from its less expensive catalog-mate, the Automatic Electrola Radiola 9-54. The hand-painted decorations did manage to account for a $400 difference in price, with the consequence that this has the distinction of being the most expensive standard instrument ever listed by the Victor Talking Machine Company. Hindsight has shown that 1929 was not the best choice of times to introduce an expensive toy, and it is unlikely that very many of these beauties were made. Like the 9-54, this impressive instrument utilized the new RCA Radiola 64 chassis and second generation Victor record changer instead of the original changer and Radiola 28 of the 9-55. As was also the case in the Automatic Electrola-Radiola 9-54, the new Victor record changer in the 9-56 was positioned above the radio rather than next to it as it had been in the 9-55. The result of this change was increased convenience, since the operator could stand more or less upright while loading or unloading records. Radio controls were at the proper height for convenient operation while sitting or standing. The 64.75 inch high by 38.5 inch wide by 20.75 inch deep cabinet had a black lacquer base with walnut veneer chest, satin wood banded doors and light statuary bronze hardware.

Ten-Thirty-Five
1928 $365.00

The 1928 Automatic Orthophonic Victrola 10-35 used the second style of automatic changer designed by Victor, which was somewhat simpler and less expensive than the original changer introduced nearly two years earlier. The cabinet was also simpler in construction and smaller in size than that of the original Automatic Orthophonic, the 10-50, with the result that the price of this machine was nearly half that of the older model. This was the least expensive instrument with an automatic record changer ever made by the Victor Talking Machine Co. There were no options with this Victrola—you liked the walnut cabinet and electric motor (the universal motor was available on special order for $20 extra) or chose a different phonograph. Standard, too, were all the expected deluxe Victor Orthophonic features such as the non-set automatic brake, speed adjuster, 12-inch turntable with antique brass finish, and four special record albums (all were 12 inches high, but two were fitted with ten-inch sleeves). The cabinet was 40.5 inches high, 34.75 inches wide, and 20 inches deep.

Ten-Fifty
1927-1928 $600.00

The Automatic Orthophonic, when introduced in March 1927, had the distinction of being the first popular phonograph and record changer combination designed for home use. A program of twelve records could be played through in its entirety (one side only) with no attention from the operator after the machine was put in operation—it even turned itself off after the last record. Victor issued special albums of complete classical works for use on this (and later) instruments, and the American public was soon irreversibly spoiled by this new-found luxury. A large Orthophonic horn occupied the entire right half of the cabinet and gave the instrument an impressive sound. If a more convenient volume control was desired than just adjusting the doors, it could be obtained for an additional $450 in the model 10-51 which had an electric amplifier. The French Renaissance style cabinet was finished in a blended walnut veneer. The AC induction motor was standard; however, the AC-DC universal motor was available for an additional $20. The changer compartment was lighted automatically when the left door was open. Some late production examples were equipped with a small window inside the upper molding of the left door, so that the operation of the record changer could be observed. Dimensions of the instrument were 49.25 inches high, by 48 inches wide and 25.5 inches deep.

Ten-Fifty-One

1927-1928 $1050.00

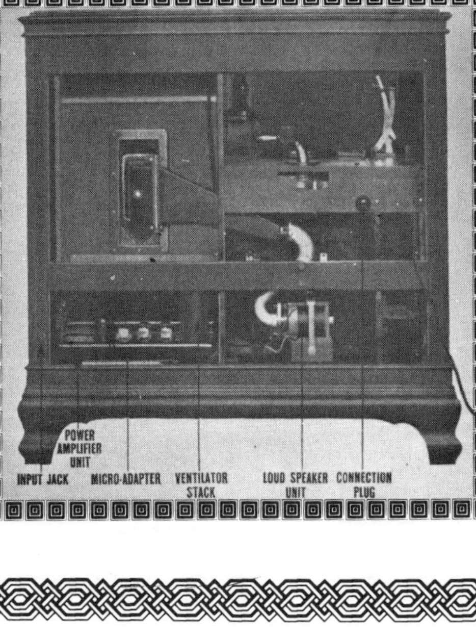

INPUT JACK   MICRO-ADAPTER   VENTILATOR STACK   POWER AMPLIFIER UNIT   LOUD SPEAKER UNIT   CONNECTION PLUG

The model 10-51 was created for people who wanted the convenience of automatic record changing combined with the novelty of electric amplification. Victor engineers made this instrument by taking an Automatic Orthophonic Victrola 10-50 and replacing the sound box with an electric pick-up. The signals from this pick-up were sent to an RCA amplifier located under the Orthophonic horn. An electrodynamic speaker unit (which Victor called the "Moving Coil Type"), was then used to reconvert the electrical signal to an audio one for further amplification by the Orthophonic horn. The advantage of this system over the standard purely-acoustical Victrola was that the volume could be continuously adjusted from soft to loud. In practice, this early electric system was capable of reproducing music only slightly louder than could an Orthophonic Victrola and had the disadvantage of adding noticable distortion and hum. The premium for these technical advances was $450 (when compared to the $600 10-50), but then America was at the dawn of the electronic age, and many Americans were rich, at least on paper. The early 10-51's contained the RCA AP-997 or AP-952 chassis which used one UV-876, one UX-210, one UX-199 and two UX-216-B tubes. Instruments above serial number 800 used the AP-736 (SPU-24) chassis which was standard in most of the Electrolas-sans-Radiolas of that period. Like the early amplifier, the SPU-24 used four tubes. These tubes (one UX-250, one UX-226, and two UX-281s) were of a more modern design than those used previously and allowed a significant increase in power. A jack was provided for attaching an independent radio set.

Dimensions of the instrument were the same as the 10-50, 49.25 inches high, by 48 inches wide and 25.5 inches deep.

Ten-Sixty-Nine
1928 $850.00

This Electrola used the second model Victor record changer and a later design of amplifier (RCA's SPU-24) to achieve improved performance at a lesser price, when compared to the model 10-70 which it replaced. The changer allowed some cost saving by virtue of its simpler design and more compact dimensions (which permitted a smaller cabinet). The amplifier, which was the same one used in the model 10-70 Electrolas above serial number 2600, was cheaper to produce than the earlier design because experience had allowed RCA to increase their productivity. The long, low cabinet designed to house this new mechanism was veneered in walnut and tastefully embellished with raised panels and carving.

Victor classified this cabinet style as "old English chest", and gave the oak veneer a "dusty antique" finish. The instrument came with six leather record albums (three ten-inch and three twelve-inch) and measured 38.5 inches high, 41.75 inches wide, and 21.75 inches deep.

Ten-Seventy
1927-1928 $1100.00

Introduced in October of 1927, the Electrola 10-70 combined the now famous Victor automatic record changer with RCA's amplifier chassis AZ 1073 to create Victor's first electric automatic phonograph with a cone speaker. The two front doors concealed the record changer, the six-inch speaker and eight record albums. The center pilaster contained the drawer into which the records were discarded after playing. A built in radio-record switch allowed easy selection between records and any radio receiver connected to the Electrola by means of the rear jack. The tubes used were one UV-876, one UX-210, and two UX-216-Bs. Instruments above serial number 2600 used a newer RCA amplifier, the AP-736 (SPU-24) which contained one UX-250, one UX-226 and two UX-281 tubes. The pilot light at the front of the instrument guarded against the possibility of inadvertently leaving the amplifier turned on after the last record had been played. The cabinet was walnut veneered with a blended antique finish.

Dimensions of the instrument were 51 inches high, by 40 inches wide and 24.25 inches deep.

Eleven-Twenty-Five
Eleven-Fifty
1928 $550.00-$950.00

The first Automatic Orthophonic Victrola (the 10-50) which Victor introduced in 1927 was a smashing success. It not only found immediate acceptance into the homes of America, but into her public establishments as well. Many restaurants used the 10-50 to entertain guests as they ate and were thus able to do without the services of a full-time orchestra. Other entrepreneurs found that this instrument was easily adapted to coin operation, and many 10-50's were converted (by just as many different people) for use in commercial establishments not wishing to give the music away. In 1928, Victor decided to pursue this market themselves with an instrument designed from the start to be coin-operated. They chose, naturally enough, the new Victor record changer for the heart of the machine. This record changer was theoretically an advancement over the one used in the 10-50 since it could play ten and twelve-inch records intermixed, although this was not a particular inducement for the commercial user. The commercial Victrola was offered in two configuations - one with the Orthophonic horn (the 11-25) and the other with electric amplification (the 11-50). The acoustical 11-25 was priced at the bargain figure of $550.00, actually $50 less than the 10-50 without a coin box! Even the coin-operated Electrola at $950.00 was lower than any similar instrument offered by the competition in 1928. For comparison, Gabel's cheapest acoustical jukebox was $700.00, while Seeburg's was $885.00. The electrically-amplified Capehart and Western Electric jukeboxes were each $1250.00. Victor believed that these two instruments put their dealers in a very strong position in the commercial marketplace. There were only two items that prevented the Victor coin-ops from dominating the business. The first was the rather inconvenient operation of the record changer, which required that the records be replaced manually into the hopper after they had played through (all the other jukeboxes recycled the records automatically), but the second reason was even more devastating. While the original Victor record changer worked slowly but faultlessly, the newer design contained a hidden mechanical imperfection of some sort which gave the device a very poor reputation in its own time.

CROMWELL (Twelve-One)
1926-1928 $450.00

This was one of Victor's earliest all-electric (non-acoustical) phonographs and initially was priced at $450. The amplifier, supplied by RCA, used one UX-199, one UX-210 and one UX-216-B tube. The speaker used RCA's ten-inch model 100 cone. An induction electric motor (AC only) drove the 12-inch turntable. Two front doors concealed the turntable, speaker and four record albums. A jack was provided to use this machine as an amplifier for an independent radio set. The Electrola could also supply 90 and 45 volts DC to the independent radio, if required. The Jacobean-style cabinet was finished in mahogany veneers with maple highlights, and the coloring was blended from light to dark, as were most of the Victor cabinets from this period. The hardware was gold-plated.

Dimensions of the instrument were 52 inches high, by 28 inches wide and 17.5 inches deep.

TUSCANY (Twelve-Two)
1926 $550.00

Like all of the early Electrolas, the Tuscany used components which RCA had developed for its AC-powered Radiola. The five-tube amplifier was very similar to the one used by RCA in their model 104 loud speaker, and well it should have been, as the cone speakers themselves were identical. The amplifier used one UX-199, one UX-210, one UV-876 and two UX-216 B tubes. An electric light near the turntable served both to illuminate the area for ease of operation in darkened rooms and to indicate when power was applied to the amplifier.

The electronics were contained in a mahogany-veneered wall type cabinet in Italian Renaissance style. Storage for 80 records was provided.

The cabinet was 52 inches high, 32.5 inches wide, and 18.25 inches deep.

Twelve-Fifteen
1928 $550.00

This early all-electric phonograph used RCA's AZ 744 amplifier chassis and six-inch cone speaker. The speaker was located behind the two front doors, while a spring-balanced lid covered the turntable and gold-plated controls. A vertical pocket on each side of the turntable held records either individually, or in albums (not included). A separate radio receiver could be connected to the Electrola, and a selector switch was provided for this purpose. The Georgian Style cabinet was walnut veneered with a blended antique finish. Tubes used on the earlier instruments were one UX-199, one UX-210, one UV-886 and two UX-281s. Electrola 12-15's above serial number 2600 used the newer RCA amplifier SPU-24, which contained one UX-250, one UX-226 and two UX-281 tubes.

Dimensions of the instrument were 45.25 inches high, by 27 inches wide and 19 inches deep.

Twelve-Twenty-Five
1927-1928 $625.00

The Italian styled Electrola 12-25 used a five tube RCA amplifier and a cone speaker. The outer two front doors concealed the eight record albums, while the center doors covered the speaker and turntable. A hinged panel enclosed the lighted turntable compartment, so that the record surface noise would be muffled during playing. A jack was provided for connecting an independent radio receiver. The cabinet was mahogany veneered with a blended finish, and measured 54 inches high, 34 inches wide and 19.5 inches deep.

HYPERION (Fifteen-One)
1926-1928 $900.00

This fancy instrument was one of Victor's first all-electric (non-acoustical) phonograph-radio combinations. The electronics were all supplied by RCA, with Victor building the cabinet and turntable. The radio was the famous RCA Radiola 28 AC and used seven UX-199, one UX-120, one UV-876 and two UX-216-B tubes. The electronics contained within this set were the same as those used in the Borgia II, with the exception of the speaker. A ten-inch cone speaker (RCA's model 100) was used here, making this one of the more advanced instruments of the period. A jack was provided for attaching a separate loud speaker, if desired. Victor's induction (AC only) motor drove the 12-inch turntable, while a rotatable loop antenna was concealed within the cabinet. Access to the sloping radio control panel was through the two drop doors at the top of the instrument. Two lower doors concealed the speaker and ten record storage albums. A pilot light indicated when the power was on. The hardware had the customary gold plating. Cabinet styling was Italian in nature, and the veneer was walnut with maple trim and light and dark shading. Dimensions of the instrument were 57.25 inches high, by 47 inches wide and 19.5 inches deep.

VICTOR LOUD SPEAKER
MODEL I
1925-1926 $35.00

The Victor Loud Speaker marked the company's first serious entry into the popular radio market. Victor had been licensed to apply the techology of corrugated paper cones developed by Louis Lumiere in France to its American products. As early as 1922, Victor had a test speaker operating under this principle in its research laboratory. Surviving lab notes indicated that Fenimore Johnson (Eldridge's son) evaluated the prototype speaker at his home in 1922 and found its performance to be very satisfactory. At that time, cone speakers were unusual, and it would have been a very unique product, had Victor been able then to place it on the market. When it did reach the market in September of 1925, as the first member of Victor's new line, it was still unusual, although the opportunity of introducing the first cone speaker had been lost.

The Victor-Lumiere speaker used two identical paper diaphrams, one rigidly connected to the moving element, and the other free to vibrate in sympathy with the first. This feature allowed the company to claim that the speaker radiated sound uniformly from the front and the rear. A control was provided on the top of the mahogany case to compensate for "atmospheric conditions."

R-Twenty
1926-1927 $135.00

Encouraged by the knowledge that the Orthophonic horn was the finest sound amplifier on the market in 1926, Victor decided to market their first-ever radio console. Coupled with a modern and efficient radio receiver, this new Victor instrument held the promise of providing the best performance of any of the radios available in 1926. Their new pact with RCA allowed them to select from among the best of the new radio chassis. RCA had only recently announced their new line of radios, and it included the set which Victor thought to be the ideal choice for their new console. The Radiola 20 was a low cost/high performance TRF circuit which would mate beautifully to the Orthophonic horn. Victor could have selected one of the more expensive Superhetrodyne chassis, but one of their design goals was to keep the combination relatively inexpensive. Those custumers who could afford to spend more would probably want a Victrola - Radiola combination, Victor reasoned.

It is probably not surprising that with the doors and lid closed, the R-20 looked just like a small Victrola, because, after all, that was what Victor knew best. Many customers were undoubtedly startled when, upon lifting the lid of what they presumed to be just another Victrola, they discovered the neat control panel of the Radiola - something quite foreign to a Victor showroom. The front doors revealed the Orthophonic horn when opened, just as in any of the new Victrolas, but nowhere on the instrument could be found a place to store record albums (not even a drawer for the radio log book?). The switch under the horn which is visible in the illustration controlled the power to an optional Philco socket power supply. This handy unit eliminated the need for certain batteries in radios such as the Radiola 20, and Victor recommended that their dealers carry it as a stock item, as it was a popular accessory.

Revere (Fourteen-One)
1926 $275

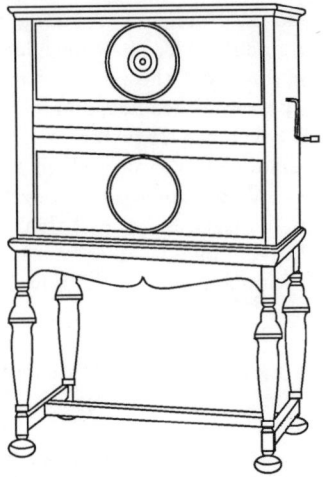

The Revere was one of the more unusual machines produced by Victor during the reign of the Orthophonic Victrola. What made this instrument so unique was the fact that the horn pointed towards the floor, instead of speaking to the front, as was the universal practice. Any student of acoustics will predict that this design will not favorably enhance the audibility of the higher frequencies. In spite of the fact that this rather expensive Victrola could not have produced the same audio experience as other instruments in the line (unless you were laying on the floor under the Revere), the company produced a modestly large number of these curiosities (3,035 to be exact).

The Revere was housed in a two-tone mahogany cabinet with shaded staining, as was popular on other Victrolas of the period. The only motor offered was the two spring motor, which had a capacity for playing ten minutes on one winding. The turntable was behind the upper door which was hinged at the bottom to open like a secretary. The lower panel was fixed, and covered the horn. Within the turntable compartment was storage storage for 50 records in albums.

The cabinet was 54 $3/4$ inches high, 35 $7/8$ inches wide, and 21 $3/4$ inches deep.

VICTOR ACCESSORIES

Like any well-run money making enterprise, Victor endeavored to guarantee that the purchase of a talking machine was only the beginning of a long and profitable relationship between them and their customers. They did this by offering a selection of accessories that, it was hoped, would be irresistible to the average talking machine owner.

Far and away the most important accessory, financially, was the record. Naturally, a phonograph was worthless without records to play upon it, but Victor's real genius lay in its early understanding of the importance of a large and varied record catalog. In order to elevate the "toy" image of the first disc Gramophones, Victor sought out the most respected performers of the day and attempted to sign exclusive recording contracts with them. Although the first celebrity recordings were imported from Europe, by 1904 Victor had established an American recording studio at Carnegie Hall for the exclusive use of its Grand Opera stars. Through its European allies, most notably the Gramophone Company Ltd. of London, Victor was able to secure the exclusive talents of the greatest opera stars of the day. Edison and Columbia also had a few renowned artists under exclusive contracts, but failed to pursue the project seriously as these celebrity records were not as profitable (in the short term) as were the popular tunes. Actually, Victor initially lost money on its Red Seal Recordings (as their celebrity series was called) when the advertising costs and high salaries were considered, but the publicity and prestige gained were almost priceless. By the end of the first decade of the new century, virtually every notable opera performer was recording discs exclusively for Victor in America. By the time Columbia realized the opportunity it had missed, most of the stars and prestige belonged to Victor. It stood to reason, in the customer's mind, that if all of the famous opera performers recorded only for Victor, then the Victrola must truly have been "The Supreme Musical Instrument", just as the ads stated. Caruso, Patti, and Melba must have sold a lot of Victrolas to people who had never seen an opera.

To understand the importance of opera at the turn of the century, one must look at the prevailing social temperment of the times. In those pre-income tax days, fortunes were being made right and left. The newly rich lived ostentatiously, flaunting their wealth for the envy of all. While few could afford all of the indulgences of the upper class, one of their favorite cultural pastimes, the opera, could be made available to all through the medium of records. As parents sought to give their children a vast cultural education, a knowledge and appreciation for classical music and the opera became one of its foremost symbols.

To emphasize Victor's commitment to fine opera, the company in 1912 published what was later to become one of the world's best known references on opera, the **Victor Book of the Opera**. The book described each major opera, giving a historical background and character analysis so that the listener would be in a better position to understand the work. As most operas were not usually sung in English, the book was of tremendous benefit when attempting to enjoy an operatic performance. Not coincidentally, the book also listed the Victor Red Seal records which contained selections from each of the operas described in the book. The book became so popular (it sold for $1.50 at Victor dealers) that it was updated frequently, and is in fact still available, although it is no longer published by Victor or RCA.

Although the **Victor Book of the Opera** was the company's best known venture into publishing, it certainly was not their only one. Other titles available at Victor dealers were **What We Hear in Music**, a general description of music and the musical instruments; **Educational Catalog and Graded List of Victor Records for the Home, School, and College; Music Appreciation with the Victrola for Children; The Victrola in Correlation with English and American Literature; The Victrola in Rural Schools, The Victrola in Music Memory Contests; The Instruments of the Orchestra by Sight, Sound, and Story**; and numerous others.

Additionally, Victor published monthly lists of new record releases to stimulate record sales. First issued around 1902, each of these lists was approximately four by six inches with a dozen or so pages, and illustrated artists performing, relaxing in their gardens, or listening to their latest release on a Victrola. Readers were encouraged to drop by their dealer's store to hear selections of the new records which they might be interested in buying. The technique was quite successful, and was soon common throughout the music industry, both for new record releases and for other allied products such as piano rolls. Since the monthly list contained only the most recent releases, Victor also published a large catalog listing every record available. These catalogs were updated yearly, and cheerfully given to anyone, for the asking, at each dealer.

Unlike Edison's cylinder, the Victor disc relied on the use of a soft needle which would wear rapidly to conform to the grooves of the record (in fact, the records were purposely made with an abrasive as part of their formula). The earliest Victor needles were made from steel, which proved to provide the proper combination of strength and softness. As might be expected, Victor designed and manufactured its own needles, and these soon became a very profitable product in themselves, as it was recommended that the needle be changed for each record played. The first needles came in cardboard or oak boxes which contained a separate compartment for used needles. Because of the chisel-like point which developed as a needle played, serious record damage could occur if a used needle were reinserted or turned in its holder. For this reason, it was (and still is) important that new and used needles not be mixed up. Victor provided a convenient covered receptacle in its Victrolas for used needles, and several independent companies offered similar clip-on cups (designed to fit outside horn Victors) for the same purpose.

A few years after the disc phonograph became popular, new types of needles appeared on the market which claimed to offer improvements in performance or convenience over the standard steel needle. One of the most successful of these was the fiber needle. First introduced by the B & H Fiber Needle Company, these triangular slivers of bamboo offered a much gentler treatment of the record than that provided by the steel needles. Because of the less rigid nature of the material, the fiber needle produced a softer rendition of the record, but many people found this desirable. The company even claimed that record quality improved with each playing, apparently because the needle tended to clean out the grooves (and remove the source of some of the unwanted noise). These needles became very good sellers within a few years, in spite of the fact that the needle holder in Victor sound boxes would accept only the smaller, round size of the standard steel needles. This was not an insurmountable problem, as one simply had to use an adapter to enjoy the benefits (real or imagined) of the fiber needle. Victor was obviously not unaware of the popularity of the fiber needles, and joined the market in 1909 with the simple expediency of buying the B & H Fiber Needle Company.

After their acquisition of the fiber needle facilities, Victor provided a triangular-shaped needle receptacle in all their sound boxes. Older sound boxes could be retrofitted with the new needle holder for $.50. Although the softness of the fiber (bamboo) used in the needles caused them to wear quickly, it also allowed them to be easily repointed with a simple accessory. Bamboo needle cutters were available in a variety of configurations from many different companies, as well as from Victor. The needle was sufficiently long to allow it to be trimmed as many as a dozen times, providing a significantly longer life than was available with a steel needle.

Natural thorns provided a good source for needles as well. Those not blessed with a supply of cactus or other thorny plants in their own yard, could purchase them prepacked. Some users preferred the soft thorns to the steel needle for the same reason that fiber needles were popular: reduced record wear. Again, as was the case with fiber needles, repointing tools were sold which allowed the owner to extend the life of needles when they became too blunt for good reproduction. While Victor never sold or recommended thorns for use as needles, they were widely used in Victor products as the standard round (and later triangular) needle holders accepted them easily.

Just before World War I, Victor introduced a new type of phonograph needle which they called the Tungstone. The name was derived from the fact that the needle was constructed by inserting a very thin constant-diameter tungsten rod in a brass shaft, and the new design helped to reduce Victor's requirement for war-critical steel once rationing began. Victor initially claimed that Tungstone needles were capable of playing as many as two or three hundred records before needing replacement, but later revised these figures downward towards a more realistic fifty plays. Even so, the Tungstone stylus with its added convenience was more cost effective than a single-play steel needle, so they consequently sold very well into the 1940's, when longer-lasting sapphire-tipped needles became popular. The Tungstone stylus had the interesting characteristic of not damaging the record if it were rotated in the sound box— in fact Victor, recommended it! This feature allowed the phonograph owner to interchange "soft tone", normal, or "loud tone" needles at will without fear of damaging the records or wasting part of the needle.

Shortly after the first disc-playing talking machines were introduced, it became apparent that some kind of disc storage container would be very desirable, as many users started to amass a collection of recordings. The first containers sold by Victor were cardboard or oak boxes with partitions to separate the records. These usually held 30 to 50 seven-inch diameter records in a vertical position, and sold for one or two dollars each. After the introduction of ten-inch (and later twelve-inch) records, storage boxes were made in these sizes as well. Within a couple of years, Victor changed the design of the storage containers to the more familiar album configuration which bound several (usually a dozen) individual record sized envelopes together. This arrangement provided both better protection for the recordings and improved portability. The user could buy as many albums as he needed, and store them conveniently on a shelf in his home.

TWO HERZOG CABINETS FOR THE VICTOR VI

For those people who required more deluxe accommodations for their recordings, Victor (and others) sold cabinets in which to place the albums. Since all the Victors at that time were tabletop machines, the cabinets were designed to accept placement of the Victor on top at a convenient operating height. Cabinets ranged in design from utilitarian to extremely fancy, depending on the machine they were designed to hold. Some companies catered to the very wealthy Victor clientele by offering Victor mechanisms built into custom cabinets. The Douglas Phonograph Company was particularly expert in this field and produced many outstanding cabinet-type Victors. With their introduction of the Victrola in 1906, Victor began the tradition of including record albums with the purchase of their better instruments.

CUSTOM CABINETS FOR VICTORS BY DOUGLAS

In addition to offering record storage cabinets, some companies concluded that if record collections were going to be portable (and require portable containers), then the phonograph itself was probably going to be carried about and could consequently benefit from some kind of protective container. With typical Yankee ingenuity, these companies produced a variety of suitcases designed to hold various models of Victors. Victor, too, offered cases for selected models, and took the idea one step further by introducing a talking machine built into its own carrying box in the early 1920's.

THE ADAPTOR ILLUSTRATOR

In addition to the more common accessories described above, some strange aftermarket items were also made by various companies to delight the audiophile of the day. One of the most curious, yet prophetic, of these was the slide-projecting attachment available for outside horn Victors (and later, for Victrolas as well). This product combined a standard magic lantern device with a horn elbow to allow the Victor owner to project images through the horn as if it were a lens! The exact advantage in combining these two devices in this manner has been lost to history, but it certainly looks logical.

TURNTABLE LIGHT FOR THE VICTROLA

As electricity became more common in the average home of the time, electrical accessories began to appear in dealer's windows across the country. One of the first to become popular was the turntable light. Changing records in a dimly lit room was a nuisance at best, and this invention provided a simple means of illuminating the interior of a Victrola. Available in a variety of styles, it usually consisted of a lamp holder at the end of a cord and clipped or screwed to some convenient location in the cabinet. Electric motor equipped Victrolas came with such a light as standard equipment and also inspired a second popular electrical accessory—the automatic spring winder. By removing the crank and attaching this handy gizmo in its place, the formerly tired but now happy owner never had to concern himself with winding his record player again. The built-in electric motor automatically kept the spring wound at a prescribed tension. Natually, electric motor replacements for the standard spring motor also became available, allowing the owner to update his instrument to a more convenient and modern style.

As radio became popular in the early 1920's, several new Victrola accessories appeared on the market. The combination of a radio and a phonograph appeared to be an obvious one, and years before such products were formally produced, several radio receivers designed to be incorporated into a phonograph cabinet were available to the do-it-yourselfer. RCA sold a chassis, the Radiola IX, specifically for this purpose. This ultra-thin chassis actually fit inside the concave lid of any Victrola. While its use was not restricted to lids, this installation was a natural. When the batteries were placed in the record storage compartment, this accessory permitted the owner to create a radio/phonograph which occupied no more space than the phonograph alone. A simple speaker, much like that found in the average headphone, was attached in place of the Victrola sound box and allowed the radio program to be amplified by the Victrola horn. Such speakers were also available separately to adapt any type of radio to the Victrola. Variations on this theme also appeared, such as radio speakers designed to replace the record on the turntable and vibrate the needle just as a record would (this must have represented the ultimate in convenience).

Turnabout is fair play, or so they say, so if devices designed to play the radio through your phonograph were feasible, why not build an attachment to play records through your radio? Apparently there was no reason not to, as electrical sound boxes became a popular, low-cost means of duplicating the performance and convenience of the electrically amplified phonographs of the late 1920's.

TURNTABLE MOTION-PICTURE ATTACHMENT

The list of available accessories offered to the Victor owner over the decades is nearly unlimited. The items cover the spectrum from simple to ridiculous, useless to invaluable, but all remain fascinating today, as examples of the best (or worst) that the inventive mind can concoct.

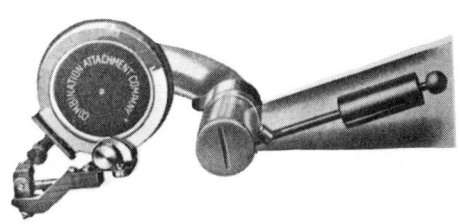

ATTACHMENT FOR PLAYING EDISON DISCS

VICTOR PATENTS

EXPERIMENTAL VICTROLAS

The files of the U.S. Patent Office reveal a fascinating look at the behind-the-scenes research being conducted in Camden during the first quarter of this century. While the conservative-looking machines manufactured by Victor gave the impression of an unimaginative and/or stagnant management, the patents assigned to Victor chart a path of continuous and ongoing research. Most of the research, if the patents granted are a good indication, was in the area of sound box improvements or methods of stuffing a larger horn into a Victrola cabinet. Strangely, improvements in these two areas were seldom considered in conjunction with each other so that they could be matched to each other's special characteristics. Ironically, the systems engineering technique, where all aspects of the design are optimized for each other, was first applied to a Victor talking machine not by Victor, but by a telephone company, the Western Electric division of Bell Telephone. The irony is further compounded when the relationship of Western Electric to the Columbia Phonograph Company is considered (Alexander Graham Bell played a major role in the development of both companies).

Several of the designs chosen for this chapter show unorthodox, sometimes even bizarre, horns, but even for all their experimentation, Victor failed to produce any real breakthroughs in horn design. All the pre-Orthophonic Victrolas were merely refinements of the original 1906 design.

PATENT # 834,511

Application filed November 12, 1904
Granted October 30, 1906

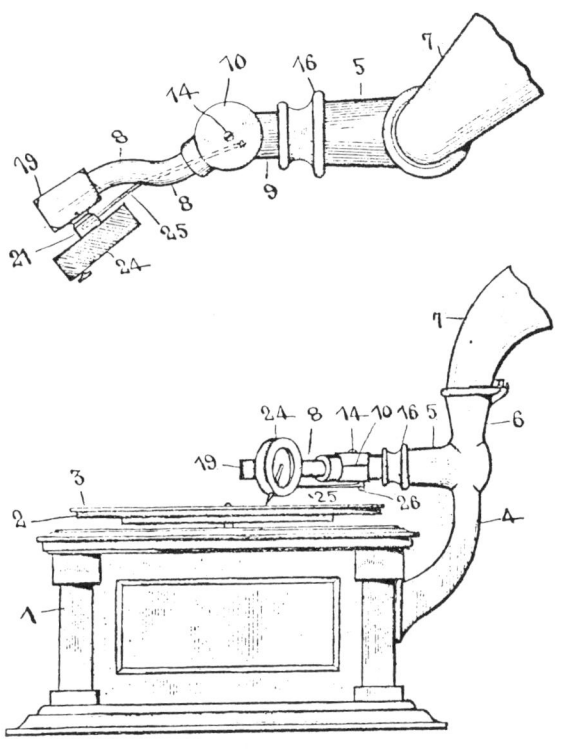

This invention by John English of the Victor staff, is an early acknowledgment of one of the chief deficiencies in the design of the tone arm as used on most record players. The typical tone arm which swings in an arc as it traverses the record's surface positions the needle tangent to the grooves only at one point on the record. The misalignment of the stylus relative to the grooves can cause distortion, reduce volume, and accelerate record wear. Mr. English's invention provides a mechanical link which rotates the sound box as the arm swings to maintain the desired stylus-groove relationship. While no Victors were sold incorporating this feature, it has appeared on several subsequent instruments. In the 1930's, this same arrangement was used on the famous Capehart turn-over record changer and it can still be found on some modern record changers.

PATENT # 951,158

Application filed March 29, 1905
Granted March 8, 1910

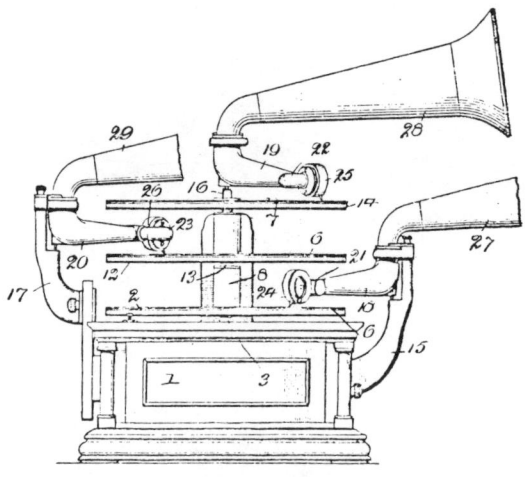

This invention, assigned to the Victor Talking Machine Company by Clarence Vogt—a U.S. citizen residing in Germany—proposed to provide improved volume and tone by incorporating a plurality of records, sound boxes and horns in a single instrument. Sychronization of recordings was provided by pins in each turntable which engaged alignment holes in each record, and by uniform starting grooves in each record. It was Mr. Vogt's intention that each record contain different information. As an example, three records (the description does not limit the patent to three however, but only to any number greater than one) might contain bass, middle and treble instruments, or perhaps accompaniment, theme and vocal. Also discussed in the patent was the possibility of changing the rendition by selecting from an assortment of compatible records. In this way a tune could be reproduced as an instrumental, a vocal with a choice of accompaniments, a duet, and so forth. The possibilities were quite intriguing.

It is clear that this invention was a forerunner of today's multichannel sound reproducers although the inventor did not specifically address the advantages of the spacial separation of channels of which the machine was obviously capable.

PATENT # 1,011,419

Application filed July, 7 1905
Granted December 12, 1911

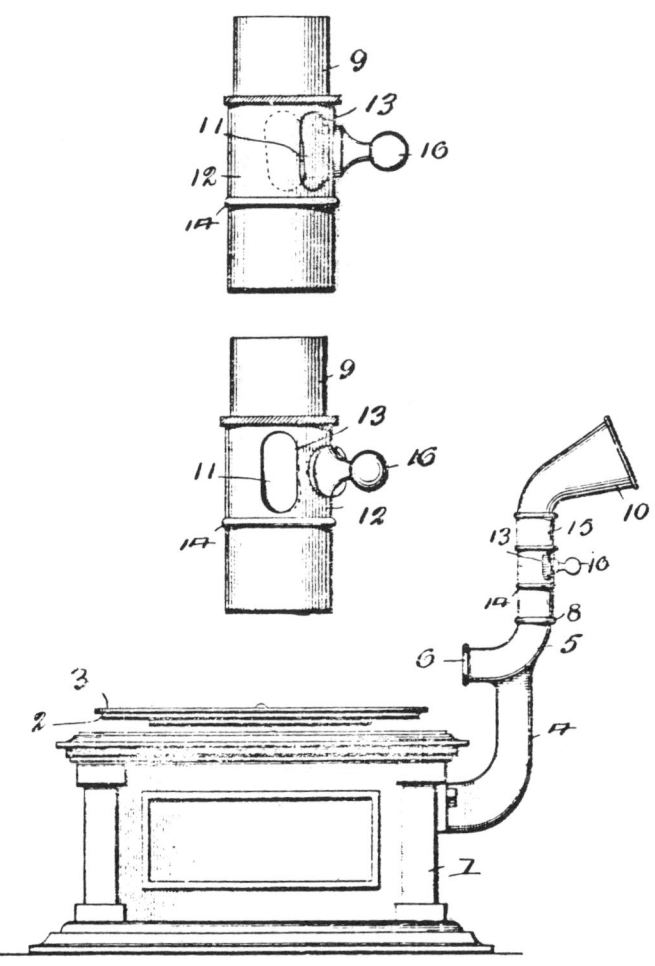

This patent for an early volume control for an outside horn Victor was filed by John English, one of the most proficient inventors on the Victor payroll. Quite simply, his invention provided an adjustable opening in the horn support to release a portion of the acoustical energy prior to amplification.

PATENT # 1,015,322

Application filed July 10, 1909
Granted January 23, 1912

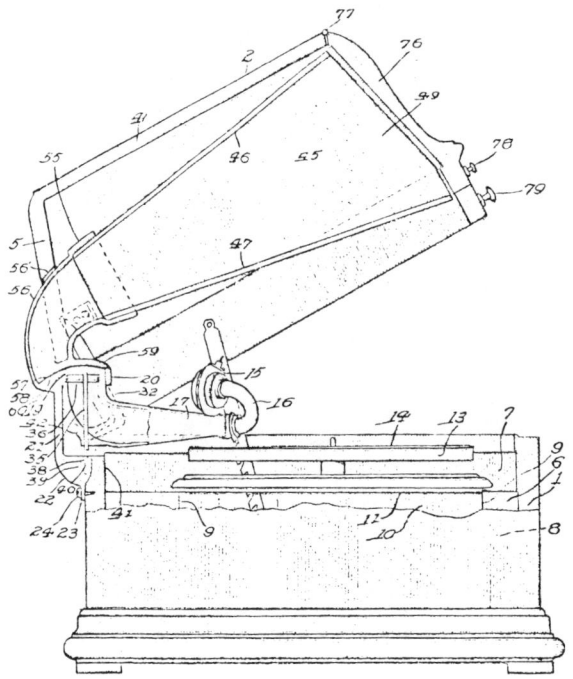

The design of this instrument deviates quite obviously from the norm in the treatment of the amplifying horn. It is difficult to decide whether to classify this instrument as a Victor with a cover, or as a Victrola with the horn on top. As illustrated here, the instrument had a horn positioned above the turntable and capable of pivoting about the point labeled 27. Spring and gear 68 and 65 could be utilized to hold the horn at any of several elevations. The cover also rotated about point 27, but was usually independent of the horn (the two could be secured together by means of a thumbscrew). The chief claimed advantage was that a variety of volume and tone qualities could be produced by varying the positions of the cover, horn and front door.

PATENT # 1,016,255

Application filed February 20, 1909
Granted February 6, 1912

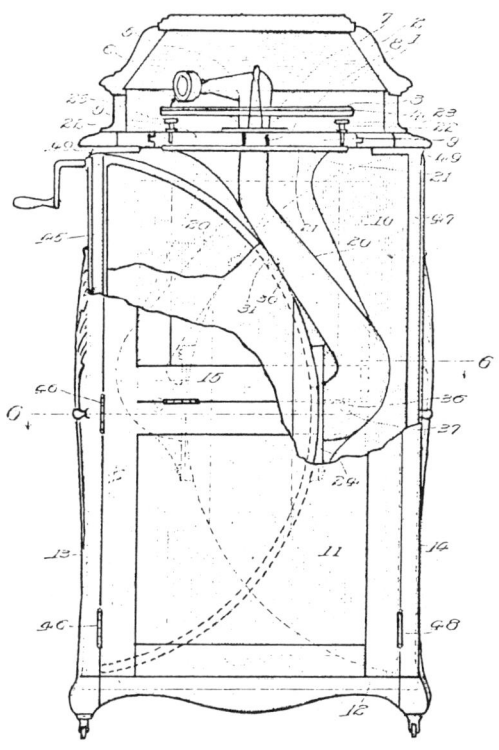

The most distinguishing feature of this design was the full length horn occupying the entire rear portion of the cabinet. Doors were provided at each side of the cabinet, and the horn could be mounted to speak through either one. Thumb screws attached the horn to the cabinet, and a door at the rear of the cabinet aided repositioning the horn. The instrument was intended to be positioned in a corner, so that the sound waves could be reflected off the wall into the room. The sides of the horn were tapered in thickness, as were the slats at the horn's mouth, to provide an effect similar to the sounding board in a piano. For this reason, the front of the horn was floating and mechanical support was provided only at the horn's rear. Since the sides of the horn vibrated like a sounding board to amplify the recording, the rear door could be opened to reflect the vibrations upward. The front of the cabinet was devoted entirely to record storage since the horn did not face forward. In other respects this instrument was similar to a standard Victrola of the period.

PATENT # 1,075,288

Application filed October 3, 1910
Granted October 7, 1913

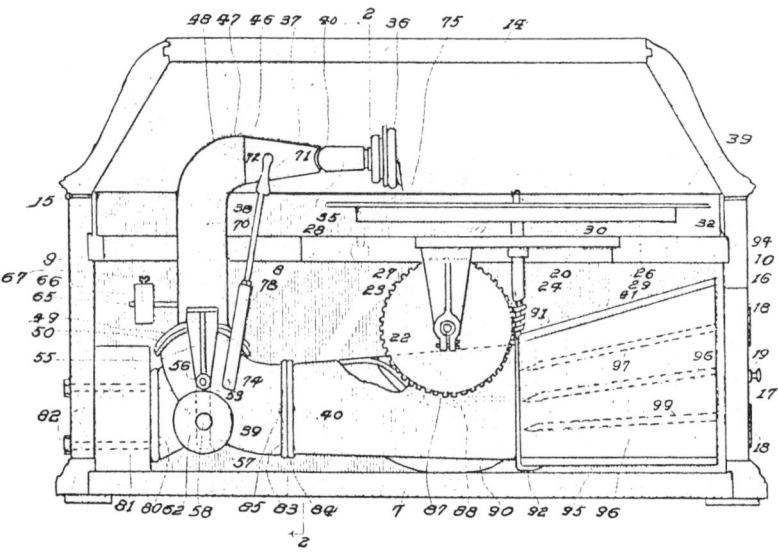

This invention filed by Eldridge Johnson and John English is an interesting variation on patent # 834,511. Instead of rotating the sound box as it swung in an arc across the record, the design allowed the tone arm to travel in a straight line from the edge to the center of the record (the exact same path followed by the record cutter when making the master). In this way, the needle again contacted the grooves at the proper angle everywhere on the record. The drawing filed with the patent shows how the tone arm was allowed to rotate about point 56 as the needle transversed the record. Strut 70 maintained the horizontal portion of the tone arm parallel to the record surface at all times while weights 62 and 66 counterbalanced the entire assembly to prevent unequal force on the inner walls of the record grooves. This design would have been expensive to manufacture and, consequently, it too never saw production under Victor, but the principle of a "staight line tracking" tone arm remained attractive. In the late 1960's, Marantz produced a turntable incorporating a remarkably similar tone arm, and other variations have appeared on subsequent record players.

PATENT # 1,187,892

Application filed August 14, 1909
Granted June 20, 1916

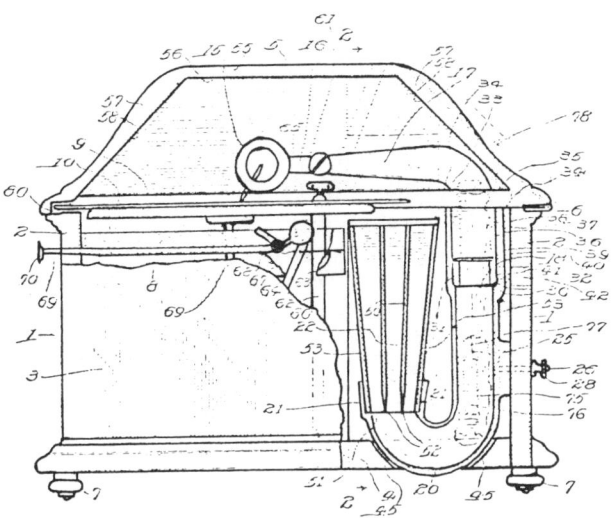

Perhaps the most striking feature of this tabletop Victrola, is the extreme volumetric efficiency of cabinetry allowed by the horn/lid design. The lid, when opened, was designed to form a part of the horn, and its position could be fixed at any point in its arc to direct the sound in a variety of directions. A friction cam was provided which would allow free movement of the lid when raising it, but prevent the lid from closing until the push button on the front was pressed. A dashpot was provided to prevent the lid from falling unrestrained—a feature that did not appear on production Victrolas until 1924. The cabinet was so compact that a recess was cut into the cover to accomodate 12-inch records. The Victrola No. 50, Victor's first true portable phonograph, utilized a horn design somewhat like the one shown in this patent.

PATENT # 1,217,869

Application filed April 23, 1915
Granted February 27, 1917

This invention, patented by Eldridge Johnson and John English, is one of the most interesting of those assigned to Victor since the design is unusually complete. A separate design patent (# 47,398) for the cabinet was filed on March 30, 1915, suggesting that this instrument was close to production just prior to our country's involvement in World War I. The instrument would seem to have been a replacement for the then-obsolete Auxetophone, as it would have been competitive in function and high cost. The patent application reinforces this speculation by stating that this instrument was "especially suitable, among other purposes, for reproducing sound in auditoriums, and similar rooms of large size, and yet capable of ready transportation from place to place as may be required." The machine's huge size is apparent in the drawings, and special provisions were made for disassembling it into two cabinets "for the purpose of permitting the machine to be readily passed through a door of ordinary width." Two large doors at the rear gave access to the wing-nuts which secured the two halves, and ten (!) casters combined to support the beast in either configuration. Record storage was enormous—about three times that of other Victrolas—and the weight of a full compartment of recordings fully justified all the wheels.

Technically, this instrument broke little new ground, it simply incorporated the largest horn on wheels ever seen in New Jersey. The vertical positioning of the horn did, however, allow the lid to provide considerable variation in volume and direction of the sound. An integral sounding board/deflector within the lid theoretically aided the already formidable amplification. Fully closed, the sound could be muffled for a small room—a feat not possible with the Auxetophone.

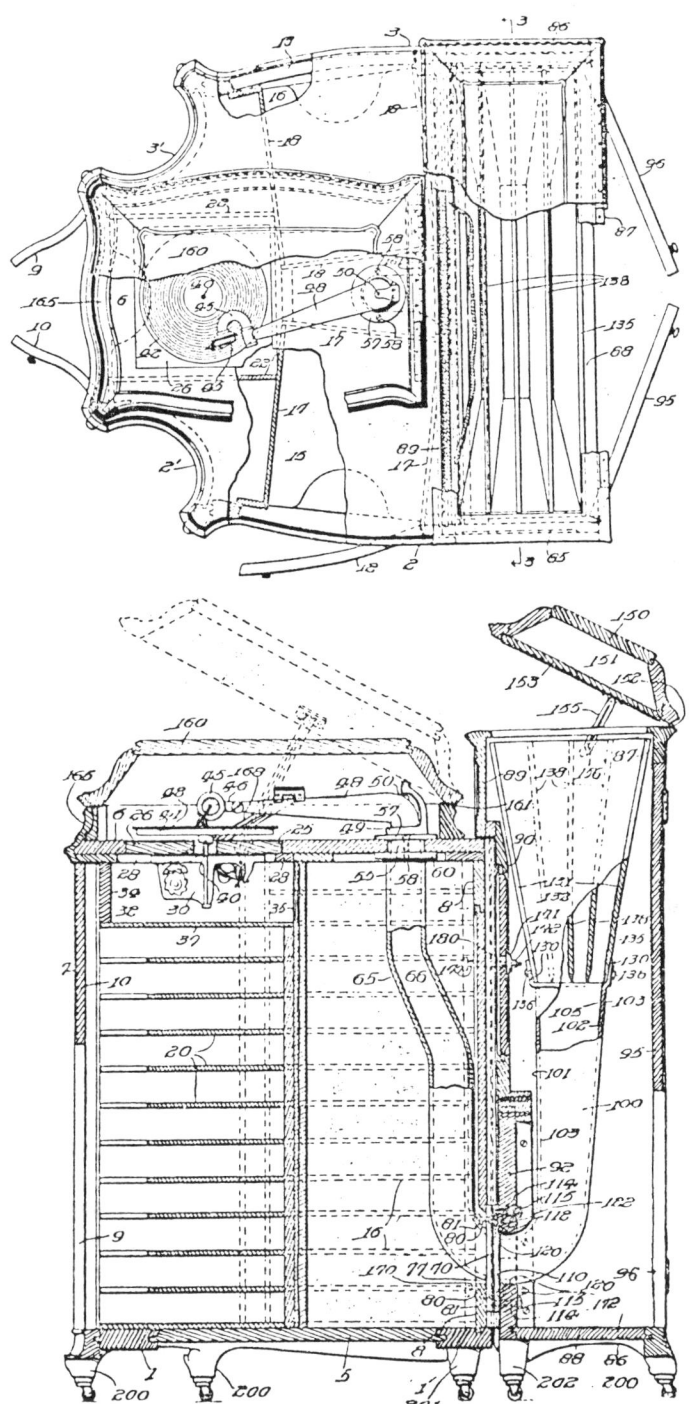

PATENT # 1,234,555

Application filed October 29, 1908
Granted July 24, 1917

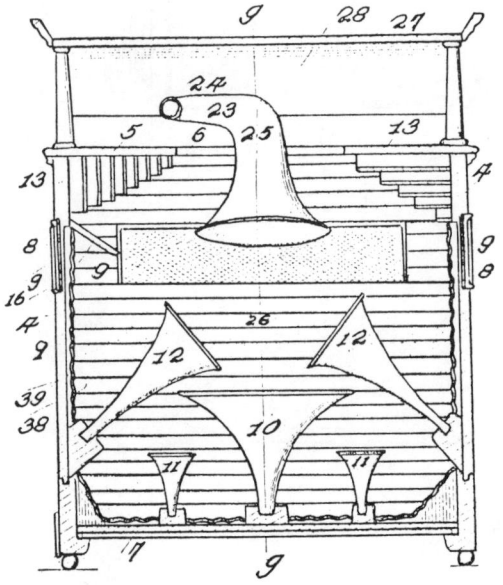

H. C. Miller's invention, assigned to Victor, consisted of a cabinet talking machine containing a variety of sympathetic resonators to amplify the recording. Recognizing that regular phonograph horns each have a specific resonant frequency at which they vibrate with greatest amplitude in concert with the recording, he proposed to add a series of horns, each with a different inherent resonant frequency, to augment the primary horn of the instrument. In this way, he reasoned, all tones and overtones would be amplified equally. To accomplish his stated goal, however, he would need substantially more horns than shown in the application since the typical resonant frequency band is rather narrow, but the idea is nonetheless interesting. A secondary advantage claimed for this design is the equal defusion of sound in all directions, rather than just towards the front of the machine, as was normal.

PATENT # 1,379,345

Application filed October 2, 1914
Granted May 24, 1921

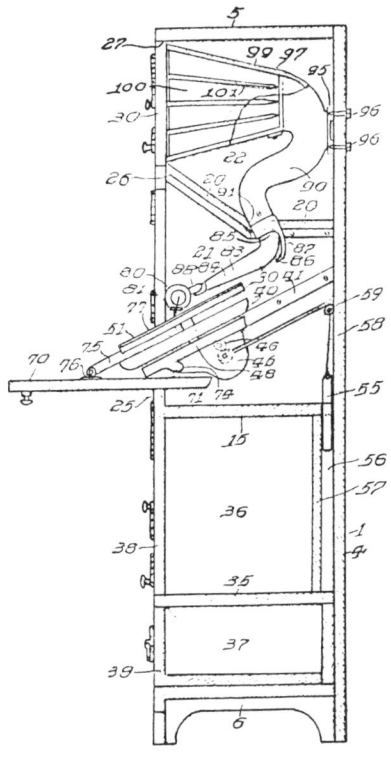

The unusual inclined mounting of the turntable in this instrument was claimed by the inventor (Eldridge Johnson) to improve accessibility and operating convenience. Since the mechanism (aided by a counterbalancing weight) withdrew into the cabinet when not in use, the overall cabinet depth was less than in an ordinary phonograph where the turntable was perfectly horizontal. The inclined motor board (40) and turntable compartment ceiling (20) were claimed to act as a secondary amplifier for "any sound wave which might be directed against (their surfaces) as a result of the external action of the sound box." It should be noted that these surfaces would also amplify the record surface noise and the noise made by the motor which was exposed when in playing position. When the instrument was equipped with a spring-powered motor, the crank was designed to slide forward in a slot in conjunction with the turntable. A door was provided in the cabinet for access to the crank which occupied an otherwise useless compartment.

PATENT # 1,652,257

Application filed August 20, 1925
Granted December 13, 1927

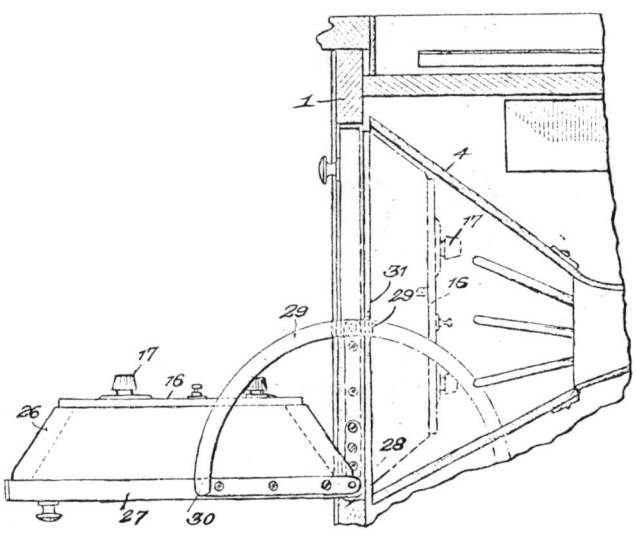

This invention proposed to combine a radio receiver and a Victrola door/horn muffler in a single unit. The primary advantage of this arrangement was that a radio chassis could be incorporated into a standard Victrola console for locations where space was at a premium. Interestingly, before this application was filed, RCA had marketed a chassis (the Radiola IX) so thin that it was actually designed to be mounted in the recess of the concave lid of a standard Victrola. The batteries for the Radiola IX however, remained quite bulky and had to be stored in a separate cabinet and connected to the chassis by a thick cable—a disadvantage also shared by this Victor design.

PATENT # 1,672,063

Application filed December 17, 1924
Granted June 5, 1928

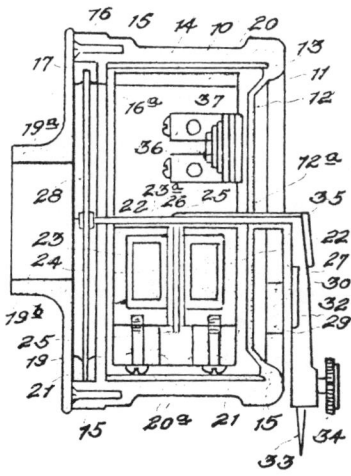

The application for this patent was filed just as Victor began to concede the inevitability of the success of radio receivers and electrically amplified phonographs. In this sound box, a single stylus bar was connected to both an acoustical diaphram and an electrical pick-up coil (the few Victrolas built in 1926 and 1927 which offered both acoustical and electrical amplification used two separate sound boxes on a common arm, a less elegant arrangement). This invention did more, however, than just replace two sound boxes. Since the stylus bar/diaphram/coil assembly vibrated as a unit when playing a record, why not reverse the standard procedure, feeding an electrical signal to the coil (from a radio receiver) and cause the diaphram to vibrate? Presto—a loud speaker! And if one were to yell into the phonograph horn, he would vibrate the diaphram and again produce a proportional electrical signal. In a single device, Victor had therefore incorporated an acoustical sound box, electrical pick-up, loud speaker, and microphone. About the only limitation of this device was that it could operate in one mode at a time, so that an electrical phonograph or public address system would have required a separate loud speaker.

BIBLIOGRAPHY

The primary source of dated references within this book are from Victor's own press releases as reported in the two major Victor trade journals of the day, **The Talking Machine World** and **The Voice of the Victor**. The issues of **The Talking Machine World** which were available for reference were January 1905 through December 1919 inclusive. A nearly complete set of Victor's publication to its dealers, **The Voice of the Victor**, covering the period from September 1912 through 1930, was also made available to the author, and supplied many of the facts and figures contained in this book. Additional sources of specifications, photographs and/or drawings of Victor products were found in original Victor sales brochures graciously made available by private collectors. The author would particularly like to acknowledge the assistance of Harold Crosby, Steve Oliphant, Bo Broock, Harvey Roehl, Mac Lackey Jr., and William Moran. All illustrations of Victors in this book are original factory-authorized pictures, and show the Victors as they appeared when new.

For readers who desire to learn more regarding the software for Victor Talking Machines, the author would like to recommend the monumental work by Ted Fagan and William R. Moran:

The Encyclopedia of Victor Recordings

This work covers all recordings, whether issued as records or not, made by the Consolidated Talking Machine Company, Eldridge R. Johnson, The Victor Talking Machine Company, and its successors. Volume 1 covers recordings made between January 12, 1900, and April 23, 1903, and contains as an appendix a reprinting of the fascinating history of the Victor Talking Machine Company detailed by B. L. Aldridge. Volume 1 will be published in the Summer of 1982 by Greenwood Press, 88 Post Road West, Westport, Conn. 06881.

Further references are:

The Victor Talking Machine Company, B. L. Aldridge, 1964

From Tin Foil To Stereo, Oliver Read and Walter L. Welch, Howard Sams and Co., Inc. 1976

His Master's Voice Was Eldridge R. Johnson, E. R. Fenimore Johnson, 1974

Journal of the Audio Engineering Society, Phonograph Centennial Edition, October - November 1977

A Wonderful Invention, James R. Smart and Jon W. Newson, Library of Congress, 1977

Electrical Phonograph Recording, J. P. Maxfield, Science Monthly, January 1926

What Is The Best Loud Speaker, and Why?, H. Winfield Secur, Radio News, March, 1927

A Portfolio of Early Phonographs, L. A. Schlick, 1966

Talking Machine World Trade Directory, Talking Machine World, Edward Lyman Bill, Inc., 1922

Collecting Phonographs and Gramophones, Christopher Proudfoot, 1980

The New Wave-Transmission Phonograph, Henry C. Harrison, Popular Radio, January 1926

The Other Side of the Record, Charles O'Connell, 1947

A Pictorial History of Radio, Irving Settle, 1960

Music and Romance for Youth, Hazel Gertrude Kinscella, 1930

Educational Catalog and Graded List of Victor Records, Victor Talking Machine Company, 1918

Music Appreciation for Children, Victor Talking Machine Company, 1923

RCA Victor Service Notes for 1923 - 1928, RCA Victor Company, Published approximately 1932

RCA Victor Service Data, Volume I, Radio Corporation of America, 1944

Victor Service Bulletins Numbers 1 through 5, Victor Talking Machine Company, 1926 - 1928

Automatic Record Changers and Recorders, John F. Rider, 1941

David Sarnoff, Eugene Lyons, 1966

VICTOR SERVICE

SERVICE

The remaining pages in this book are included to help the owner derive the maximum pleasure from his Victor Talking Machine; for while an attractive cabinet may delight the eye, no Victor can deliver its full potential of satisfaction until it is performing as well as it did the day it left the factory. Whether the problem is a sluggish motor, rattling sound box, or air leaks in the acoustical amplifier, any malady will detract from the instrument's value. The later Orthophonic Victrolas and Electrolas, some in conjunction with a Radiola and/or a record changer, are susceptible to an even greater variety of problems than the earlier acoustical models, and receive a correspondingly larger share of attention in this section.

As has been true in the previous portion of this book, all the data presented in this section are from original Victor sources. For the most part, the information on the following pages has been reprinted verbatim from original Victor Service Bulletins in the author's collection. While this might make some of the information somewhat "dated" (as in the case where it refers to a special tool) it does not diminish the usefulness of the text; techniques which worked well in 1920, will nearly always work well today. The service notes for the first electrical pick-ups or speakers are particularly interesting, and offer some insight into the plight of the technician who had, perhaps for decades, been concerned with nothing more taxing than cleaning the grease from his coveralls after a long day of repairing Victrolas. Compare the instructions for adjusting one of the record changers with any of the operations required on an earlier Victrola, and you can perhaps sympathize with the repairman who is now charged with the maintenance of an instrument an order of magnitude more complex than any he had previously worked on. Imagine, if you can, earning your living in a profession which becomes suddenly obsolete, then endeavoring to grasp a new technology as foreign as an unknown language. That story is reprinted here as well, only it is written between the lines.

INDEX OF SERVICE NOTES

Catagory   Page

MOTORS

    Spring Motor (circa 1920) 261

    Universâl and Induction-Disc
    Electric Motors 271

SOUND BOXES

    Exhibition 274

    Orthophonic 277

    Electric Pick-up 279

SPEAKERS

    Orthophonic Horn 281

    Orthophonic Loudspeaker 284

    Moving-coil Type Orthophonic
    Loudspeaker 286

    Ten-inch Cone Type Loudspeaker 288

RECORD CHANGERS

    First Type 290

    Second Type 302

CABINETS

    Retouching Victrola Cabinets 320

Instructions for the Care of
Victor Spring Motors

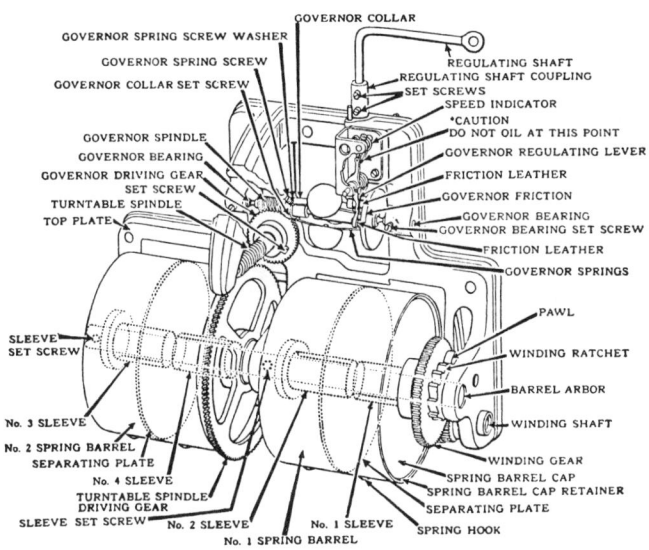

POSSIBLE CAUSE OF TROUBLE

Irregular running, noise or sluggishness can always be traced to one of three causes, *which are lack of lubrication, incorrect adjustment, or injured or broken parts.* When the motors leave the factory they have all been thoroughly lubricated, adjusted, inspected and tested in every way so that they run smoothly and quietly and will regulate properly. But occasionally they are handled very roughly in transportation and the parts are injured or knocked out of adjustment. Often, too, the motor may be exposed to dust or dirt so that its lubrication becomes dirty which does not allow it to work freely. Therefore, it is necessary, after each machine is unpacked and set up, to operate it and observe whether it is quiet and will regulate properly. If it will not, then it should be carefully gone over and the following points taken care of:

I. LUBRICATION

To lubricate the motor, raise the motor board so that the motor may be reached. To do this, remove the winding key and the turntable, take out the two screws in the front corners of the motor board and turn the automatic brake yoke to the left far enough to clear the edge of the board. Take hold of the knob in the left hand front corner of the board and raise the board to an upright position. If the lubrication is dirty, the motor should be taken entirely apart and thoroughly cleaned with gasoline. How to do this will be explained under the heading "To Take Down Motor". If it is not dirty, a thorough lubrication of the accessible parts may correct the noise or failure to regulate. This should be done as follows using Victor Spring Motor Oil and Victor Motor Grease.

First - Lubricate the governor friction leather, the governor spindle at each end of the friction sleeve and at each end of the spindle where it enters the governor bearings with oil and fill all the threads of the governor spindle, and all of the teeth of the governor driving gear with grease.

Second - Oil the turntable spindle in its bearings at each end and fill all its threads and all the teeth on the turntable spindle driving gear with grease.

Third - Oil the barrel arbor at its bearings in the top plate, the barrel sleeves at the bushings in the spring barrels and the bearings of the winding shaft; and fill all the teeth in the winding ratchet and the teeth of the winding gears with grease.

Fourth - Oil the speed indicator bearings and friction leather. *Be careful, however, not to put any oil in the slot in the indicator lever at the point designated by the "*" on the diagram.* Now lower the motor board into place, turn the brake yoke back into position, replace the turntable and be very careful to see that the brake is off so the friction leather will clear the turntable. Also replace the winding key. Then run the motor, observing whether it is quiet and regulates correctly. If not, its adjustments should be carefully gone over as follows:

II. ADJUSTMENT

First - the brake leather may have been pulled out of the brake lever a little in putting the turntable onto the spindle so that it is rubbing the turntable when the brake is off. If so, take off the turntable and cut a little off the leather so it will clear the turntable when the brake is off.

Second - The speed of the motor may be wrong or the speed indicator may be out of adjustment. See that its parts are all working freely and that its spring has tension enough to make the friction leather follow the action of the governor friction disc. The speed indicator, as its name implies, is a speed *indicator* and not a speed *regulator*. Its purpose is to show at what speed the motor is running, which should be 78 revolutions per minute. To prove this proceed as follows:

Put a small piece of paper under the edge of the record, count the number of revolutions of the turntable while playing the record, and, if necessary, adjust the speed of the motor by turning the speed regulating screw to the right to increase the speed, or to the left to decrease the speed, as shown on the speed indicator plate, until the turntable is running at 78 revolutions per minute. Now observe the position of the speed indicator pointer, and if pointing at 78 on the dial the speed indicator is properly adjusted. If not pointing at 78 slide the dust cap around, insert screw driver in shaft slot, hold the shaft from turning and gently move the pointer to 78 while the motor is running at 78 revolutions per minute. As long as the pointer is not disturbed, its position on the dial will be an accurate indication of the speed of the motor.

Should it become necessary to remove the motor from the motor board, be sure to first remove the speed indicator pointer. To do this remove the indicator plate from the motor board, take lock nut and spring washer off the shaft, then lift the pointer off, being careful not to bend either the shaft or the pointer.

Third - Raise the motor board in the same manner as for lubrication and examine the governor driving gear to see if the set screw is in the spot in the turntable spindle and properly tightened. This will bring the gear central with the threads on the goveror spindle, when the hub should clear the under face of the top plate about 1/64 inch or more. *Let the motor run down before making this adjustment.*

Fourth - See that the governor is free but not too loose endwise in its bearings. It should have from *three* to *five thousandths* of an inch end play, just so it can be barely felt. To make this adjustment see that the set screw in the governor bearing next to the turntable spindle is tight in groove in governor bearing, then release set screw in governor bearing nearest governor friction disc, and move bearing until end play is correct, then tighten set screw firmly. See that all screws in the governor springs are tight. See that set screw in governor collar is screwed tight into spot in governor spindle. If governor springs are damaged, replace with new ones.

Fifth - The governor springs may have been forced out of position on their seats, causing the governor sleeve to bind on the governor spindle. If the motor does not regulate properly, this may be the cause. To remedy this, loosen all the six screws holding the springs on the collar and friction disc sleeve so that they are free and can assume their normal position. Then adjust the screws until not quite tight, then go over them and tighten them firmly.

Sixth - It may be found that the speed regulating screw cannot be turned far enough to the right without striking the escutcheon plate to bring the speed up to 78, or far enough to the left without coming out of the escutcheon to bring the speed down to 78. This can only be caused by the set screw in the regulating shaft coupling not being in the countersunk spots on the regulating lever and regulating shaft. To correct this trouble, loosen the set screws and adjust the coupling until the screws enter the spots, then tighten the screws firmly. Lower motor board into place, start the motor, turn the speed regulating screw right or left until the turntable runs at 78 by test and see that the indicator pointer is at 78 on the dial. Now try the motor again for quietness and regulation. If it is not running correctly it should be taken entirely apart, thoroughly cleaned with gasoline and every part carefully examined for injuries of any kind.

III. TO TAKE DOWN MOTOR

It is recommended that, before taking down the motor or any other of the assembled parts, it is first carefully looked over so as to get a good idea as to where the different parts belong.

First let the motor run down completely, take off the turntable and remove the winding key, then remove the indicator plate and pointer, raise the motor board, detach support from stud, lift the board off its bearings and place it upside down on blocks to prevent injury to the brake. Take the two screws out of indicator frame and remove the speed indicator. Release the governor bearing set screws, take out both governor bearings and remove the governor. Release governor collar set screw and slide the governor off the spindle. Release the set screw in the governor driving gear, and pull turntable spindle out of top plate. Take the two set screws out of the barrel sleeves. (In the double spring motor take the set screw out of the barrel arbor bearing), then pull barrel arbor out of the bearings and the spring barrels, take out the spring barrels, pull sleeves out and remove the barrel caps. To do this, first remove the barrel cap retainer, take a screw driver, hold barrel firmly in the hand and pry one end of retainer from the barrel, turn the barrel over and remove the cap by striking the edge of the barrel on a piece of wood, being careful not to damage the barrel in so doing. Remove the outer spring by uncoiling, being careful to keep firm hold of spring while uncoiling, lift out separating plate using the hook and remove the inner spring in the same manner. Wash parts with gasoline being careful to take the turntable spindle thrust ball and governor spindle thrust balls out of their bearings.

(If it should be decided that the main springs are not damaged, they can be washed thoroughly and cleaned in gasoline and lubricated merely by removing the sleeves, leaving the springs, caps and retaining rings in place.)

IV. EXAMINATION OF PARTS

Examine the turntable spindle and barrel arbor bearing in top plate. If they are cut or badly worn, use a new top plate. Unless it is necessary to replace the top plate, do not remove it from the motor board, as to do so will disturb the alignment of the winding shaft with the winding key escutcheon. If the bearings are in good order, put a few drops of oil in each. Examine the thrust balls; if smooth and bright, put them into their bearings with a drop or two of oil. If rough, replace with new ones. Be sure that the barrel arbor, turntable spindle and governor spindle are straight and smooth, examining the theads of the spindles particularly. If any of these parts are bent or rough from wear, or damaged, replace them with new parts.

See that the barrel cap bushings and the barrel caps are in good condition. Note the condition of the teeth on the turntable spindle driving gear, governor driving gear and winding gears, and if any are bent or injured at all, replace with new gear. In the case of the turntable spindle driving gear and winding gear, use a new sleeve and gear group when these gears need replacing, as the gear teeth are located centrally with the hole in the sleeve, which can only be properly done at the Factory, which is equipped with the necessary tools for doing the work. Examine the spring hooks in the barrels; if any require replacing, be careful not to injure the barrels in doing so.

V. TO PUT BACK THE OLD MAIN SPRINGS IN 4 SPRING MOTORS

No. 1 or Right Hand spring barrel (having the winding gear). Hook the outer end of one spring into the inner hook in the spring barrel with the coils running from left to right, or clockwise, and, grasping the barrel and springs with both hands, wind the spring into the barrel, being careful to keep a firm hold on both, lubricate each spring with three teaspoonfuls of Victor Spring Lubricant, put in the separating plate and then the outer spring in the same manner as the first one, *except with the coils running in the opposite direction*, right to left or counter-clockwise.

No. 2 or Left Hand spring barrel (having the turntable spindle driving gear). Replace springs in barrel as directed above with the exception that the springs should be coiled in the opposite direction , the inner one counter-clockwise and the outer one clockwise.

IN 2 SPRING MOTORS

For two spring motors the inner spring is wound into the spring barrel clockwise and the outer spring counter-clockwise.

IN 1 SPRING MOTORS

For one spring motors the spring is wound into the spring barrel from right to left or counter-clockwise.

VI. TO PUT IN NEW MAIN SPRINGS

To put the inner spring into No. 1 spring barrel, take the spring in retainer and pull about 12 inches of the outer end out of the retainer, slide the retainer nearly off the spring and hook the outer end onto the hook in the spring barrel with the coil of the spring running from left to right, and press the spring with retainer down into the barrel. Put block with leather on faces on spring to protect the hand and with hook pull out retaining ring, letting the spring uncoil in the barrel. Lubricate the spring with three teaspoonfuls of Victor Spring Lubricant. Put the separating plate in place, then put in the outer spring pulling out about 6 inches in the same way as the first, only having the coils running in the opposite direction, or from right to left.

Rest the retaining ring on the edge of the spring barrel, and with a piece of leather to protect the hand, push the spring down into the spring barrel and out of the retaining ring. Put the springs into No. 2 spring barrel in the same manner as in No. 1 spring barrel, the inner spring having the coils running from right to left. Lubricate the spring with three teaspoonfuls of Victor Spring Lubricant. Put the separating plate in place, then put in the outer spring with the coils running from left to right and lubricate. (To replace the springs in the barrel of the double spring motor, proceed the same as directed for the No. 1 spring barrel. For the single spring motor, hook the spring onto the hook in the barrel, with the coils running from right to left.)

VII. RE-ASSEMBLING

Replace the barrel caps, forcing into place with the two thumbs, or tapping gently with a wooden block, and spring the cap retainers into position in the spring barrels. Put the sleeves in place so the milled slots will engage the formed ends of the springs, sleeve No. 1 having the winding gear on it going into the barrel cap end, and one plain sleeve going into the closed end of No. 1 spring barrel. The remaining plain sleeve going into the barrel end and sleeve No. 4, having the turntable spindle driving gear on it, going into the closed end of the No. 2 spring barrel. Put a few drops of oil in the barrel arbor bearing, rub a little grease on the arbor, place spring barrels into position with ratchet engaging the pawl on the top plate, and slide the barrel arbor through into the center bearing, the end having the drilled hole going in last. Tighten up the sleeve screws, being careful that the points of the screws enter the holes drilled for them in the arbor. See that the turntable spindle thrust ball is in place and put a drop of oil in each spindle bearing. Push the small end of the turntable spindle through its upper bearing in the top plate, slipping the governor driving gear with its set screw towards the lower spindle bearing on the spindle as it comes through. Push the spindle on down into the lower bearing, using a socket wrench and spanner wrench, if necessary, to bring the governor gear into place. With the turntable spindle in place on its thrust ball in the lower bearing, locate the governor driving gear so that the set screw enters the countersunk spot on the turntable spindle, and tighten its set screw.

Put a few drops of oil in the sleeve on the governor friction disc and slide it into the governor spindle until the set screw in the collar is over the countersunk spot in the spindle and tighten the screw firmly. See that the thrust balls are in both governor bearings, and put a couple drops of oil in each. Put the grooved governor bearing in place in the governor bearing hole nearest the turntable spindle, and tighten the set screw, being careful that the set screw enters the groove in bearing, and put the plain sleeve in the outer governor bearing hole. Put the governor in place with the friction disc between the friction leather and the outer bearing, and the threads in mesh with the governor driving gear, and slide the outer bearing onto the spindle. Adjust the outer bearing until the end play can just be felt, which will be when it is from three to five thousandths of an inch, then tighten the screw. Note whether the governor driving gear is in line with the center of the governor spindle. If not, release the set screw and adjust the gear until the point of the set screw is over the countersunk spot in the spindle, then tighten firmly. Replace the speed indicator, oil the friction leathers freely, and fill all the teeth on both gears and all the threads on both spindles with grease.

The motor is now ready for service unless it has been necessary to remove the top plate from the motor board. If this has been done, care must be taken to replace it correctly so that the winding key will align properly with the winding shaft. To do this, lay the motor on the bench with the top plate up and place the rubber washers, one over each top plate bolt hole. Place the motor board on the top plate, being careful not to move the washers or bend the indicator shaft. Put in the bolts and screw the nuts up tight on the under side. Put the motor board in place in the cabinet. In doing this, first see that the automatic brake yoke is turned far enough to the left to clear the edge of the board, and that the taper tube is turned as far to the right as possible. Then place the board in position so that the pivot bearings on the board slide over the pivots in the cabinet, and attach the motor board support to stud on cabinet. Let the motor board down into place and put the indicator pointer on its shaft *so that it points to the line on the dial nearest the word SLOW.* Replace the spring washer and lock nut, then tighten lock nut until pointer can be moved easily while holding shaft with screw driver. Insert the winding key, noting whether it screws into the winding shaft easily. If not, it is because the top plate has not been put back on the motor board in the correct position for the winding shaft to line up with the winding key escutcheon. To correct this, loosen all the top plate bolts just enough to allow the top plate to move and screw the winding key tightly into the winding shaft. Then tighten all the nuts again, replace the speed indicator plate, and put on the turntable, being careful not to strike the brake leather. Wind the motor and adjust for speed by counting until it is running at 78 revolutions per minute, and adjust the indicator pointer until it points at 78 on the dial when the machine is running.

As stated, the motors are adjusted so that they will run properly when they leave the factory, and if the foregoing instructions are followed, there will be no difficulty in restoring them to good running condition.

When not actually in service, the motor should be allowed to run down, as the pressure due to the tension of the main springs acting continuously in one direction for a long time may prove detrimental to the parts.

Motors should be run occasionally in order to keep the parts free in their bearings, as all lubricants will thicken more or less when exposed to the air. If possible, the motors should be wound up and run down again at least once a day whether in service or not, as this will keep all parts free and in good running condition. It is impossible to expect a motor, any more than any other machine, to run smoothly and freely if it has been standing still for any length of time. Under no circumstances should a machine be delivered to a customer without carefully testing and lubricating it.

ACTION WHICH TAKES PLACE IN SPRINGS, ETC., IN WINDING AND UNWINDING

The winding key turns to the right when the motor is in place in the cabinet, and being geared to sleeve No. 1 turns that sleeve in the opposite direction, or to the left, winding up the outer spring which is hooked to it, left-handed. From the sleeve, the outer end of this spring is connected be means of a hook to the inside of No. 1 spring barrel. The inner spring is connected at the left hand side of this No. 1 spring barrel and is wound up from the spring barrel down to sleeve No. 2. This No. 2 sleeve being connected to the shaft by means of a set screw, the winding is then carried from this to the No. 3 sleeve which is at the extreme left end of the No. 2 spring barrel. This No. 3 sleeve is connected to the shaft by means of a set screw and winds the outer spring up from the No. 3 sleeve.

This outer spring is connected at the outer end to a hook on the inside of the No. 2 barrel and the inner spring is connected to the right hand side of the No. 2 barrel to a hook, and is wound up from the outside into the sleeve. This is connected to the No. 4 sleeve to which the turntable spindle driving gear is attached.

When the brake is thrown off, the motor starts running and the springs unwind in the opposite manner from the way in which they were wound up. In other words, spring No. 4 beginning to unwind first following right through to spring No. 1.

Instructions for the servicing of

Victor Electric Motors

Universal Electric Motor

The Victor Universal Electric Motor is designed for universal operation at 32 Volts AC or DC. This operating voltage is obtained from a power line of 100 to 230 volts by connecting the proper resistance in series with the motor. In no case should the voltage across the motor terminals be allowed to exceed 36 volts, or go below 30 volts (as measured with a DC voltmeter). High voltage at the motor terminals will cause excessive wear and overloading of the brushes, dirty commutator, and noise in the motor.

The Victor Universal Electric Motor will not require any great amount of servicing with the exception of occasional lubrication and renewal of the brushes.

Induction Disc Electric Motor

The Victor Induction Disc Electric Motor is designed for use on Victor electric instruments operating on 105 to 120 volts, 25 to 60 cycles, alternating current, and consumes approximately 50 watts of power. One of three different motor coil types is used depending on service frequency and whether or not the motor is to be installed in an automatic instrument.

In the majority of cases, the only servicing which the induction disc motor will require is proper lubrication.

Servicing (Either Type)

1. LUBRICATION - It is important that the motor be lubricated at least once every six months and with the proper lubricants. A motor lubricating diagram is shown in all instruction books. Victor Motor Grease should be used on the teeth of the governor drive, governor spiral, and (on the universal motor) grease cups. Lubricate the governor bearings, governor friction sleeve, and turntable spindle bearings with Victor Motor Oil. If this oil is not available, a similar high grade oil of equal body may be used. Do not use an oil of a thinner body as this may prove injurious to the motor. Neat's Foot oil is recommended for lubricating the governor friction leather. If the leather has become hardened and glazed, it should be roughened with the sharp point of a knife so as to permit absorption of oil.

2. FAILURE TO MAINTAIN A CONSTANT SPEED - If the motor fails to maintain a constant speed, the following points should be checked.

    a. Hardened or Gummed Lubrication - If necessary, remove and wash gummed parts in kerosene. Replace and lubricate as described in subject 1.

    b. Shifting of Motor on Motor Board - Loosen the three motor board screws and re-tighten, alternately, while the motor is running until the binding has been eliminated and the motor runs steadily.

    c. Weak Coils (Induction Disc Motor Only) - If the lubrication and mounting of the motor have been examined as described in sections (a) and (b) above, and the condition still exists, replace one or both of the motor coils.

    d. Broken Armature Wires and Burned Commutator (Universal Motor Only) - Armature wires may sometimes become broken, causing intermittent contact. The commutator may become badly burned after a motor has been in hard service for a period. In such cases the motor should be returned to your distributor for repairs.

3. REDUCING HUM (Induction Disc Motor Only) - There are a number of causes for hum in the induction disc motor, but in most cases any existing hum can be eliminated by proper adjustment.

    a. Loose Coil Winding on Iron Core - This condition can be corrected by forcing a small wooden wedge between the outside of the coil and the core.

    b. Coil Loose on Top Plate - Tighten screws holding coil to top plate.

    c. Loose Laminations of Iron Core - Securely tighten the bolts clamping the laminations together. In some cases, however, it may be found that the hum can be minimized by adjusting the tension of these bolts.

    d. Motor Not Fastened Securely to Motor Board - Examine felt washers between the motor and the motor board and tighten nuts securely.

    e. Motor Board Not Properly Secured to Cabinet - Place a piece of felt between motor board and motor board rail, and tighten the four corner screws holding motor board to the cabinet.

4. REDUCING MECHANICAL NOISE - There are several features which may cause motor noise other than a hum.

a. Governor Springs - Loosen the screws on the disc end of the governor springs and allow the motor to run for a minute or so to allow the springs to assume their correct position. Stop the motor and re-tighten the screws. Replace any broken or out-of-balance springs.

b. Governor Thrust Bearing (Induction Disc Motor) - Hold one finger over the end of the bearing, and loosen the set screw which holds the bearing in position. Adjust bearing for most quiet running position, and re-tighten the set screw.

c. Governor Spindle - A bent governor spindle will cause binding in the gears as well as noise and should be replaced.

d. Governor Driving Gear - Remove the turntable spindle and examine the governor driving gear for wear. If the wear on the gear is greater on one side than on the other, the turntable spindle is bent. Replace both the spindle and gear.

e. Worn Commutator (Universal Motor Only) - A badly worn commutator or worn brushes will cause noise. This can be eliminated by the adjustments described in subject 5.

5. SPARKING (Universal Motor Only) - Excessive sparking is usually caused by badly worn brushes or brushes which do not fit properly. Examine the brushes, and if necessary refit them by placing a narrow strip of No. 7-0 or No. 8-0 sandpaper around the commutator with the sand side out, rotating the commutator with the sandpaper, at the same time placing pressure with the fingers on the tops of the brush holder spring latches. Do not use emery paper or cloth.

It is well when adjusting or renewing brushes to clean the commutator, while the motor is running, using a cloth dampened with kerosene.

6. SPEED REGULATION - The governor will maintain a constant speed of the motor within a range of sudden voltage changes of 8 volts (universal motor) or 15 volts (induction disc motor), providing all parts are correctly adjusted. All the topics under the heading of Servicing will have a certain effect upon the regulation of speed and should be taken into account even though there is no actual mechanical noise present.

Instructions for the Repairing of the
Victor Exhibition Sound Box

Causes for Poor Results

1. Rubber insulators buckled.

2. Diaphragm not centered, causing it to touch the sound-box cap.

3. Fulcrum bearings of needle arm not set on fulcrums of sound-box cap.

4. Needle-arm foot pressing on the diaphragm.

5. Needle-arm foot pulling on the diaphragm.

6. Needle-arm foot not securely fastened to the diaphragm.

7. Adjusting or lock nuts loose.

1. Place a new rubber insulator in the cap or top of the sound box, with the two ends of the insulator directly in the center of the sound-box cap fulcrum plate.

2. With a small camel's hair brush place a little orange shellac around the top of the rubber insulator to hold the diaphragm in position.

3. Place the diaphragm on the rubber insulator, making sure that the diaphragm is centered, i.e., clears the cap on all sides. This is important. Let the shellac dry - requires about one minute.

4. Place the second rubber insulator in position on top of the diaphragm with the ends of the insulator exactly opposite the ends of the insulator under the diaphragm.

5. Place the sound box back in position, tightening the three small screws securely in position.

6. Then place the sound box thus assembled in the left hand, with the thumb and first finger encircling the cap and place the needle arm in position, being careful to see that the arm is properly set or adjusted on the fulcrums of the sound-box cap.

7. With the sound-box arm in position, tighten both sound-box arm screws sufficiently to bring the needle-arm foot flat on the diaphragm. Careful attention should be given to this operation to see that the needle arm does not press tightly on the diaphragm or that it does not stand away from the diaphragm. For proper results the arm should barely touch the diaphragm. This may be accomplished by tightening the lower screw to raise the arm on the diaphragm or tightening the upper screw to lower the arm on the diaphragm.

8. When screws are properly adjusted, tighten the lock-nuts to prevent the adjusting screws from changing their positions.

9. With the sound box inverted, resting on a table or bench and held firmly in the hand, pierce the diaphragm at the point where the piercer will also run through the needle-arm foot.

10. With the sound box in the same position run a tap, using No. 00-112 standard size, through the diaphragm and needle-arm foot, taping the diaphragm for the insertion of the diaphragm screw.

11. Place the small paper washer on the diaphragm connection screw, and with the sound box in the same position insert the diaphragm connecting screw and tighten securely.

12. Heat an awl over an ordinary gas jet for about one minute, dip into a box of suitable wax. Place the awl over the sound-box needle-arm foot, and permit the wax to run off on top of the foot. Then turn the sound box over and repeat the operation by placing a drop of wax over the connection screw head.

13. If taper arm sound box, place the rubber back into position.

14. Place the needle-arm thumb screw into arm.

15. Test carefully for proper adjustment by playing over a record with which you are familiar. If the tone of the sound box is heavy, relieve the pressure on the diaphragm by slightly releasing the upper screw. It requires but half a turn sometimes to accomplish the desired results. If the sound box rattles, try tightening the upper screw slightly.

Instructions for the Servicing of the
Orthophonic Sound Box

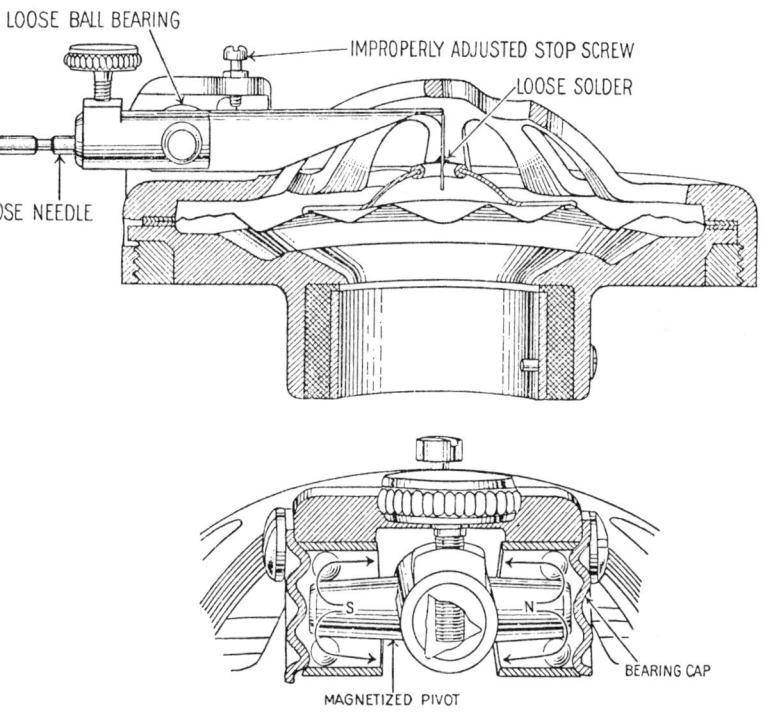

Care in Handling - The diaphragm is exceedingly thin metal -seventeen ten thousandths of an inch thick. Do not touch it in any manner, with your finger or any implement. Always lower the needle gently onto the record when starting to play.

If the reproduction is considered faulty, the following should be noted:

First - Loose needle or defective needle - Change needles and be sure needle screw is tight. Are you using a perfect Improved Victor record?

Second - Improperly Adjusted Stop Screw - If a new needle does not quiet box, remove stop screw completely. Play and note whether noise has ceased. If so, replace screw, thread in until noise starts on playing. Then back off screw two or three turns. Set lock nut.

Third - If the noise still persists, loosen the screws and swing the bearing caps to one side. You will note that the pivot is carried on ball bearings. The balls should be in a ring around the pivot, and if not, should be lightly pressed back into place.

This ball bearing is self aligning and self adjusting. The pivot is hard steel, magnetized and tapered, the magnetism drawing the balls up to a seat on the taper. Any slight difference in ball diameter is compensated by the taper, and the entrance of the balls into the housing. The balls must not necessarily all go in the same distance but they should be side by side. This assures a constantly tight bearing. The only requirement is that none of the balls has been displaced, and if so, may be replaced by pressing back into position. Do not attempt to take the bearing apart, as it can only be assembled with special tools. The bearing cap is not a part of the pivot bearing - it is simply a dust cap, and does not necessarily touch the pivot ends or the balls.

Fourth - Attachment of Stylus Arm to Diaphragm Spider - The stylus arm is at present soldered to the spider center. Through injury, this joint may be broken. Press lightly against the soldered members with a tooth pick, and determine whether the joint is tight. If not, the box should be returned to the factory for repair.

Fifth - The Sound Box should be air tight - This may be tested by blowing *lightly* on the opening for attaching to the tone arm. If not air tight the box should be returned for repair.

Sixth - Injured Diapragm - Return box for repair.

Instructions for the Servicing of the
Electric Pick-up

The electric pick-up is the introduction of an electrical method of sound reproduction.

The pick-up is mainly composed of three major parts:

First - The permanent magnet.

Second - A small generating coil.

Third - The vibrating armature on the end of which is the needle holder.

The generating coil, both ends of which run to the volume control, is placed in the center of the permanent magnet which causes a constant flow of magnetic lines of force through the coil. In order to generate current in the coil it is necessary to vary the magnetic field, so, in order to accomplish this, the vibrating armature is placed in the center of the coil with a needle inserted in the needle holder. As the needle vibrates back and forth along the grooves in the record the density of the magnetic field is changed correspondingly generating pulsating electric current which corresponds to sound waves of music. The advantage of this method of reproduction is that these electrical pulsations can be amplified many times by means of radio amplifying tubes.

When these pulsations have passed through the amplifying tubes they are then carried to the speaker unit where they set in motion its diaphragm thus generating sound waves in the air.

These sound waves may be generated in large volume by use of a large diaphragm such as the cone or, if a small diaphragm is used, may be ampified by use of a horn.

Another advantage of this method of reproduction is the ease with which volume of sound may be varied by the volume control which varies the amount of amplification of the electrical pulsations before delivery to the amplifying tubes.

The following data covers the servicing of the pick-up unit:

First - Place the pick-up on the tone arm of the machine, turn on the tubes and have the machine in readiness to play a record.

Second - Tap the needle lightly with your finger, first on one side and then on the other. Each time you touch the needle ther should be a loud click through the speaker.

(A) If the click is louder when stiking the needle on one side than it is on the other, the electric pick-up is out of adjustment. To determine this, remove the metal case from the pick-up and note whether the vibrating armature which is operated by the needle is directly in the center between the two pole pieces of the magnet. If the vibrating armature is off center remove the holding clamp from the magnet allowing further acessibilty to the working parts. You will then see two knurled nuts locked in place by two ordinary nuts. By loosening the lock nuts you can adjust the knurled nuts until the vibrating armature is again in the center of the pole pieces.

(B) If there is no click at all in the loud speaker, put a record on the turntable, start the motor, put the electric pick-up in place and let the record play.

(a) Take a pair of ear phones, place the tips across the two connections of the volume control to which the leads run from the pick-up. You should hear the record playing with very low volume.

(b) If there isn't sound at this point, remove the pick-up wires from the volume control and check for open circuit from this point through the pick-up. (Note:-Occasionally the contacts in the tone arm are not springing into position properly.)

(c) If it develops that the pick-up is open or impossible of adjustment it should be returned for replacement.

INSTRUCTIONS FOR THE SERVICING OF THE
ORTHOPHONIC VICTROLA
TONE CHAMBER

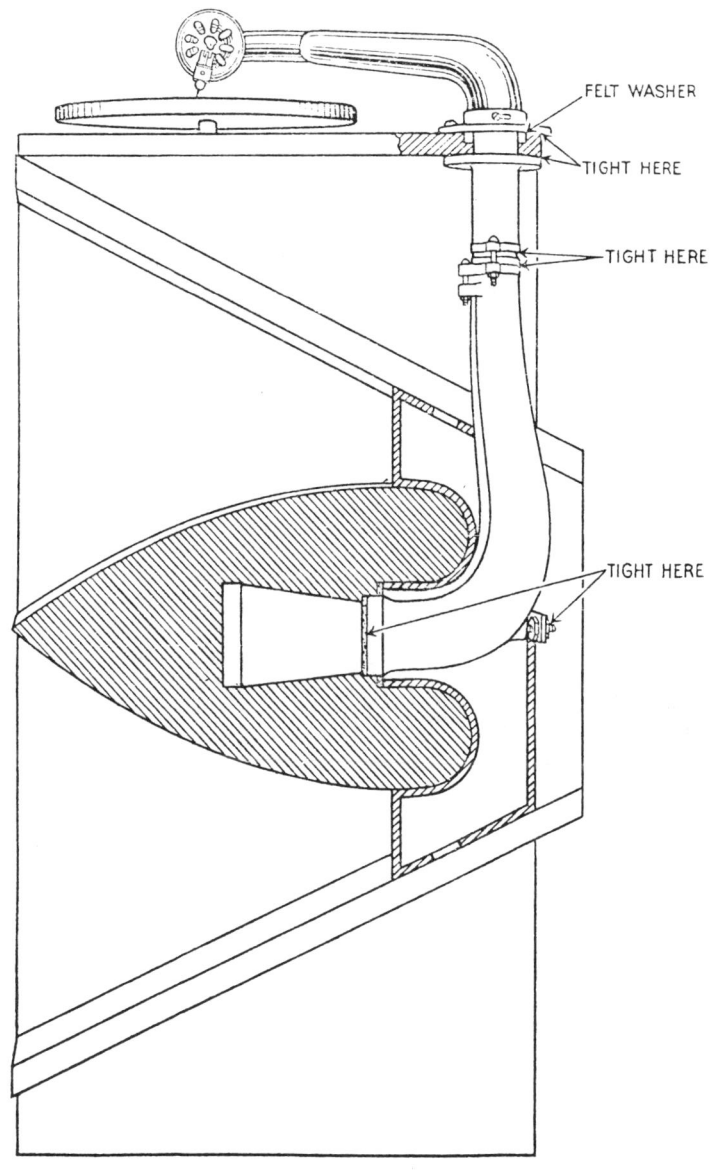

SOUND BOX CROOK AND TONE ARM

First - The sound box crook should be free, but without being loose. If loose, it may introduce a rattle, and should be adjusted. To do this, loosen the rest clip, and turn the crook cap until the crook is free, without shake. Replace rest clip. There must be no binding in the crook, as the sound box *must* be free to rise and fall with the record.

Second - Taper Tube Support Bearing - This likewise should be free, but not loose. Adjustment can be made by loosening three screws in the cap, and swinging the screws to the required position. There should be no "hard" or "bumpy" spots when swinging the tone arm through its arc of movement. The adjustment should be made to the side of looseness, rather than tightness, as the needle *must* pass freely over the record.

REPRODUCTION

If the reproduction of the instrument is not up to standard, with any of the boxes you know to be in good condition, with full tone Victor needles and Improved Victor records, the following points should be noted:

A loss of bass indicates an air leak in the tone chamber.

First - Remove the tone arm from the elbow rail. Make sure that the elbow flange is drawn tightly up to the bottom of the rail by the two screws. Next work a little heavy grease around the joint. Then pack the support bearing and felt washer in grease and replace the whole on the rail; drawing all four taper tube support screws down evenly and tightly.

Second - If the trouble persists, remove the back panel of the instrument and examine the joints in the cast iron elbow, and at the junction of the elbow and the wooden heart. All joints should be tight.

Third - Wooden Tone Chamber - Examine all wooden parts for injury and open joints. Remove the screen at the mouth, and inspect against a bright light. Place a light at the back, and look into the mouth. Then place a light in the mouth and look into the back. No light should be seen. Close any small leaks with wax. Major repairs should be done at the factory.

Due to the large volume of sound, and its vibratory effect on the cabinet, loose parts must be avoided. These will cause rattles. If an elusive rattle is present, try to locate any loose member that may be the cause.

The Orthophonic Victrola should always be played with the lid closed. As the sound box generates more volume and delivers it to the tone chamber, it also delivers more sound energy from the back of the diaphragm. The diaphragm sound is high pitched and piercing, and unpleasant on certain notes unless the lid be closed, cutting it off.

Instructions for the Servicing of the
Orthophonic Loudspeaker Unit

This unit is similar in construction and operation to that used in the ten inch cone type speaker. The armature, however, instead of being attached to a cone, is attached by means of an aluminum spider to an Orthophonic diaphragm.

Sound reproduction is attained by the vibration of the diaphragm against the air in the horn. The operating principles of the unit itself are the same as those of the ten inch cone speaker.

Before attempting to adjust the speaker unit, check the instrument with another unit to make certain that the Electrola or radio set is delivering the proper tone quality and volume.

It is possible, especially on the radio side, that the tubes are being overloaded by a strong signal, which will cause rattling of the speaker and distortion. The unit can only reproduce that which is delivered to it. If the delivery to the speaker is of poor quality, the reproduced sound will also be of poor quality.

If it has been established that the speaker is not reproducing properly, the following adjustment can be made:

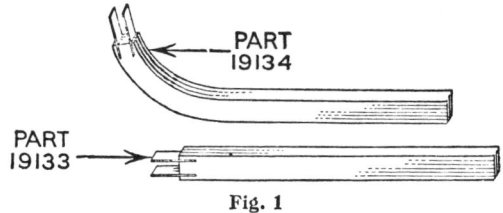

Fig. 1

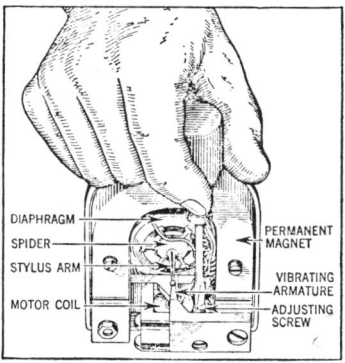

Fig. 2

First - Using a phosphor bronze gauge .125 inches wide and .010 of an inch thick, as shown in Fig. 1, check the vibrating armature to see that it is properly centered. The gap on each side of the armature should be .010 of an inch.

If the armature is off center, loosen the screw on each side of the motor coil as shown in Fig. 2, place the gauge on both ends of the vibrating armature, and retighten the screws.

Second - While checking the spacing of the armature, make certain that there is no foreign material, such as filings, interfering with the free movement in either direction. By using a thin piece of cardboard, most of the foreign matter can be removed.

Third - The stylus arm should be perfectly straight in all directions.

If, after making the above adjustments the speaker is still unsatisfactory, it should be returned to the distributor for replacement.

Instructions for the Servicing of the
Moving Coil Type Orthophonic Loudspeaker

The moving coil type Orthophonic loudspeaker unit operates on the same driving principle as the six-inch cone speaker. A voice coil mounted in the center of a 3.5-inch diameter Orthophonic diaphragm vibrates within the field of a powerful electromagnet. The coil is so attached to the diaphragm and the latter is so constructed that its movement is a combination of plunger and vibratory motion.

The voice coil is connected to the "Output" terminal of a power-amplifier unit containing a 25 to 1 output transformer. The field leads of the loudspeaker are connected to the "Field" terminals of the power-amplifier unit.

The moving coil Orthophonic loudspeaker unit when used in conjunction with the large Orthophonic horn affords a greater electrical and mechanical efficiency than any other Victor loudspeaker.

The only ordinary servicing necessary on this unit is the adjustment of the voice coil to eliminate diaphragm rattle. This adjustment must be made with *extreme* care. Unless a competent service man is available to do the work, the unit should be returned to the distributor. If it is felt that the work can be carried out satisfactorily, the diaphragm seal on the unit should be broken, and the following adjustment made:

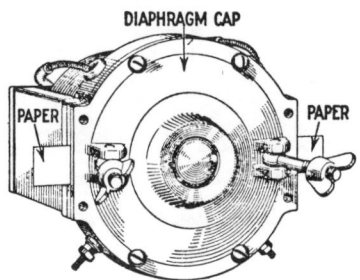

Fig. 1

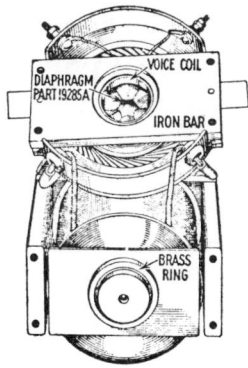

Fig. 2

First - Remove the four corner screws in the diaphragm cap on the front of the unit.

Second - Loosen, but do not remove, the other four screws on the circumference of the cap, as shown in Fig. 1.

Third - Insert two thin pieces of paper as shown in Fig. 1.

Fourth - Lift the diaphragm assembly from the field coil as shown in Fig. 2.

Fifth - *Carefully* center the voice coil within the hole in the iron bar as shown in Fig. 2.

Sixth - Remove the two pieces of paper, making sure that the position of the voice coil is not changed.

Seventh - Re-tighten, alternately, the four screws in the diaphragm cap, thus clamping the diaphragm tightly.

Eighth - Place the brass ring (see Fig. 2) in the iron bar so that it surrounds the voice coil.

Ninth - Carefully replace the diaphragm assembly on the field, fasten securely with the four corner screws.

If the above adjustment does not stop the rattle, or if the field or voice coil leads are broken, the loudspeaker unit should be returned to the distributor for repair.

Instructions for the Servicing of the
Ten Inch Cone Type Speaker

This speaker unit is of the free floating cone type. It is supported at the outer edge and held in central position by soft leather. This leather is supported in such a manner, that it does not interfere with the free movement of the cone. It is not susceptible to atmospheric changes, and is exceedingly pliable.

The loud speaker comprises the following main units:

First - The cone.

Second - The vibrating armature.

Third - The motor coil.

Fourth - The permanent magnet.

The motor coil with the vibrating armature centered therein is placed between the poles of the permanent magnet. The arm is soldered to one end of the armature and made secure to the center of the cone by means of small lock nuts. The function of this arm is to transmit the sound vibration from the armature to the cone itself.

When the motor coil is mounted, it is adjusted so that the armature is exactly in the center of the pole pieces. It is thus placed in the center of the magnetic field set up by the permanent magnet. In order to vibrate the cone for the production of sound, it is necessary to vary the magnetic field, so that the armature will be carried from side to side. The magnetic field variations necessary are produced through the electrical pulsations which are delivered to the motor coil of the speaker from the power amplifier unit. Through the vibration of the cone in this manner the electrical pulsations are again transformed into sound.

Before going into speaker adjustment check the unit in the machine with an external speaker to insure that the Electrola or radio set is delivering the proper tone quality and volume.

It is possible, especially on the radio side, that the tubes are being overloaded by a strong signal, which will cause rattling of the speaker and distortion. The speaker can only reproduce that which is delivered to it from the power amplifier unit. If the delivery to the speaker is of poor quality, the reproduced sound will also be of poor quality.

If it has been established that the speaker is not reproducing properly, the following adjustment can be made:

First - Use a gauge .125 inches wide and .010 of an inch thick of phosphor bronze and check the vibrating armature to see that it is properly centered. The gap on each side of the armature should be .010 of an inch.

If the armature is off center, loosen the screw on each side of the motor coil, place the gauge on both ends of the vibrating armature and retighten the screws.

Second - While checking the spacing of the armarture make sure that there is no foreign material, such as filings, interfering with the free movement in either direction. By using a thin piece of cardboard most of the foreign matter can be removed.

Third - The stylus arm and the connecting arm should be perfectly straight in all directions.

Fourth - The speaker being of the free floating type, there should be no tension on the cone. A slight tension can often be relieved by loosening the screw, located on the front of the magnet, holding the connecting arm in place and reightening after the cone has shifted.

Fifth - The locking nut in the center of the front section of the cone may have become loosened a fraction of a turn due to vibration. This nut should be retightened but great care should be exercised in checking this as the thread can be very easily stripped, or the arm entirely broken off.

If, after making the above adjustments the speaker is still unsatisfactory, it should be returned to the distributor for replacement.

Instructions for the Servicing of the
Automatic Record Changer
Used with Automatic Victrolas and Electrolas
10-50, 10-51, 10-70 and 9-55

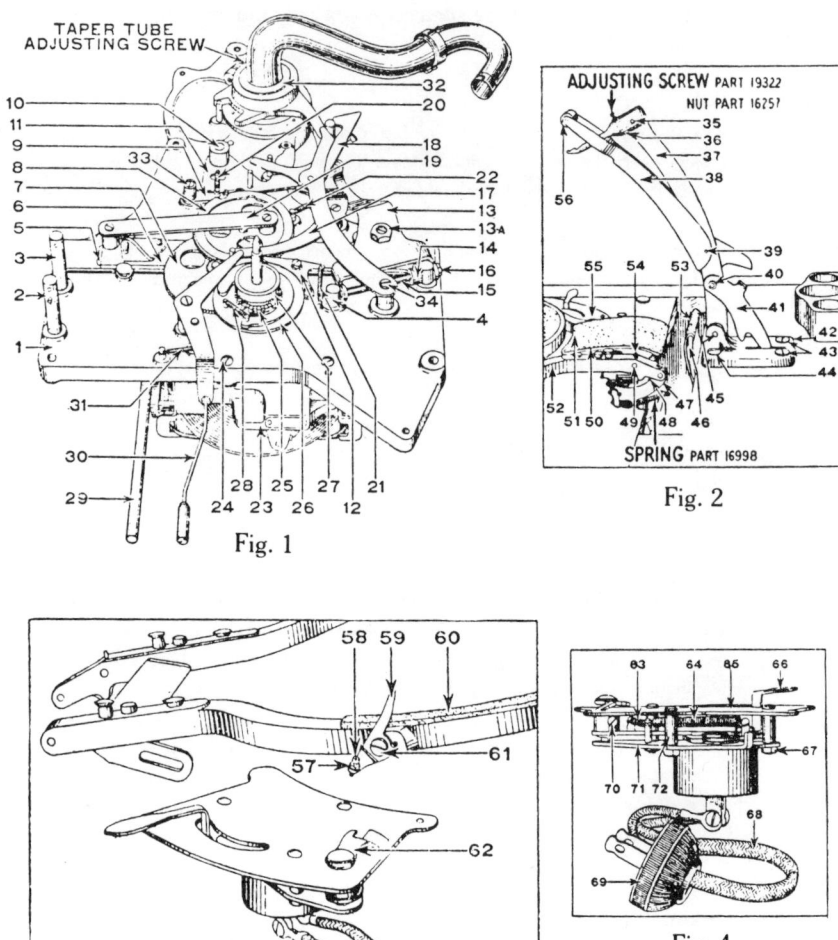

Fig. 1

Fig. 2

Fig. 3

Fig. 4

NOTE: - The operating unit of the Automatic Electrolas differs from that of the Automatic Victrolas in the taper tube return lever No. 18 Fig 1. All 10-50 units above serial number 8950, all 10-51 units above serial number 800, and all 10-70 and 9-55 have a motor plate with provision for mounting the electric pick-up shunt switch and the remote reject control.

NAME OF PART

1. Motor Plate
2. Lifter Ring Post Front
3. Lifter Ring Post Rear
4. Sound Box Lift Lever Stud
5. Side Spring (not shown)
6. Main Slide
7. Intermediate Gear
8. Cam Gear
9. Index Lever
10. Index Shaft
11. Sound Box Control Lever
12. Clutch Release Lever
13. Sound Box Lifting Lever
13a. Nut, Screw
14. Collar
15. Shaft
16. Nut
17. Trip Lever
18. Taper Tube Return Lever
19. Connecting Link
20. Spring
21. Spring
22. Spring
23. Motor - 60 Cycle
   - 25-30 Cycle
   - Universal
24. Screw
25. Thrust Washer
26. Pawl Carrier
27. Clutch Wheel
28. Spring
29. Index Control
30. Reject Lever
31. Spring
32. Taper Tube Assembly
33. Screw
34. Screw
35. Screw, Nut
36. Magazine Spindle
37. Magazine Stand

38. Tilting Lever
39. Screw, Nut
40. Nut
41. Latch
42. Base
43. Screw
44. Screw
45. Screw, Nut
46. Record Guide
47. Latch
48. Link
49. Shaft
50. Record Lift Pad
51. Felt
52. Record Lift Ring
53. Felt
54. Screw
55. Switch
56. Roller
57. Nut
58. Screw
59. Trip Lever
60. Felt
61. Screw
62. Latch Trip
63. Spring
64. Spring
65. Top Plate
66. Switch Lever
67. Nut
68. Cord
69. Plug
70. Screw
71. Bottom Plate and Switch Assembly
    10-50 Below Serial No. 8951
    10-51 Below Serial No. 801
    All Other Automatics Bottom Plate Only
72. Spacer
73. Switch

SERVICING

1. Should the sound box (or pick-up) fail to swing into the record groove after the tone arm has descended to the playing position:

Check to see that the machine is level. If the right side (facing the front of the machine) is lower than the left, the sound box will not swing over into the record groove. If the left side is lower, the sound box will skip the first few grooves of the record.

This is because the tone arm is mounted at a slight angle to the horizontal, allowing the arm to swing into the playing groove by force of gravity after lowering upon the smooth portion of the record.

2. If the record lift ring (No. 52, Fig. 2) fails to pick up record:

a. The magazine spindle is bent either towards the front or back of the instrument.

b. The magazine spindle (No. 36, Fig. 2) should either lowered or raised slightly as the case may warrant, by adjusting screw.

c. The record is warped.

d. Lift ring shaft is bent.

e. Operating unit and magazine stand are located either too far away or too close together, and will not permit the records to mount the buttons properly. Remove magazine stand and file bolt holes in board, if necessary, so that the stand may be placed in the correct position with reference to the operating unit.

3. If the record drops into the drawer after being lifted from the magazine spindle or fails to line up with the turntable spindle:

a. The magazine spindle is bent either towards the front or back of the instrument.

b. A warped record has been used.

c. Warped or bent lift ring.

d. Lifter ring posts (2 and 3, Fig. 1) out of line.

4. Should binding of the record lift pad (No. 50, Fig. 2) occur:

a. Remove the shaft (No. 49, Fig. 2.) If bent, it should be replaced with a new shaft.

b. Note if sides of record lift pad are binding against nut of latch and link of record lift ring. If necessary, file the sides so as to clear the ring. A bent shaft causes failure of the pad and lift ring to rise simultaneously. The record consequently is not raised from the turntable equally and is thus forced by the revolving turntable to strike the side of the record chute. This condition may cause breakage of records.

5. If the lift ring fails to discharge a record into the drawer after it has been played:

The small spring shown (Part No. 16998) in Fig. 2 may be broken or disconnected.

6. If the brake does not shut off at the end of the program:

a. The small screw (No. 58, Fig. 3) on the automatic stop is not properly adjusted.

b. Set screw (No. 70, Fig. 4) located under brass plate on switch trip may be loose.

c. One of the springs (No. 63 or No. 64, Fig. 4) on the brake may not be properly adjusted, or has become loosened.

d. The electric switch contacts are sticking.

On 10-50 below serial No. 8951 and 10-51 below serial No. 801 proceed as follows:

Remove the bakelite cap of switch and spread contact points to permit easier operation. WHEN TAKING SWITCH APART BE CAREFUL TO OBSERVE THE POSITION OF THE INSULATING WASHERS SO THAT THEY CAN BE PLACED IN PROPER POSITION WHEN REASSEMBLING.

On all other automatic instruments the following procedure should be used:

Remove bakelite top, loosen screws holding contact mechanism and with switch in closed position, move switch towards the shoulder of the latch, leaving enough clearance so that there is no pressure on movable contact arm. This will allow the contacts to open to their maximum point and prevent arcing and sticking. File and clean contacts.

e. Warped lift ring.

7. Failure to reject a record when the reject button is pushed may be caused by:

a. Reject button having been forcibly pushed in, bending connecting link to reject mechanism. This can be remedied by removing the front panel on which the index lever is mounted and bending the reject mechanism back to its original position.

b. Defective reject magnet circuit (models 10-70 and 9-55).

1. Bad switch - dirty contacts.

2. Burnt out coil.

3. Broken wiring.

8. Continued rejection when the button is not being pushed may be caused by:

   a. The button being stuck, having been forcibly pushed in by the operator.

   b. Heavy grease or foreign matter in the cam notches of gear (No. 8, Fig. 1).

   c. Excessive pull in spring (No. 28, Fig. 1) or worn teeth on pawl.

   d. Worn trip lever.

   e. Mechanism improperly timed.

   CAUTION: - Use nothing but specified springs throughout.

9. If the point of the needle rides over several grooves in coming to rest on the record, or does not rise high enough to clear the record on its return, proceed as follows:

   a. Place index lever in "Victrola" or "Electrola" position and permit mechanism to operate until tone arm is in playing position and free.

   b. Note the distance of point of needle below top of turntable. This should be between 1/12 and 1/16 of an inch.

   c. If the distance is not approximately the same as given in (b.), make the following adjustment: Loosen screws holding crook stop to tone arm and alter the position of the crook stop until the correct distance of the point of the needle below the turntable is obtained.

   d. Tighten screws.

   NOTE: - Carelessness in mounting the sound box or the pick-up on the tone arm, and failure to fit screw on pick-up in hole provided for this purpose, will often result in condition noted in the beginning of this section.

10. Should the mechanism trip when the index lever is in the "Victrola" or "Electrola" position, and it has been definitely found that the cause does not lie in any of the points mentioned in subject 8:

a. Remove back panel of the instrument and loosen taper tube adjusting screw (Fig. 1) one quarter turn.

b. Force the taper tube arm (the casting containing the adjusting screw) UP until the trip lever clears the ratchet by approximately 1/16 of an inch, and re-tighten adjusting screw.

NOTE: - The normal position of the collar should now be approximately 1/64 of an inch below the base of the taper tube, PROVIDING ADJACENT PARTS HAVE NOT BEEN BENT OR TAMPERED WITH.

11. If the sound box or pick-up does not lower at the proper position onto a ten- or twelve-inch record: falls into the record groove without first striking smooth outside margin: or does not reach the outside diameter of the record before lowering:

a. Place twelve-inch record on turntable with index lever in 12-inch position, start the motor and note the distance at which the needle strikes to the right or left of correct adjustment. (Needle should strike record at approximately middle of outside margin.)

b. Turn the index lever to "Victrola" or "Electrola", allowing mechanism to complete cycle so that tone arm is free and in playing position.

c. Stop motor.

d. Move the tone arm towards the center of the record, past the eccentric groove until it strikes the stop.

e. Slightly etch the record label at this point with the needle.

f. Remove the back panel of the instrument, allowing access to "taper tube adjusting screw" as shown in Fig. 1.

g. Loosen the screw one quarter turn so that the tone arm can be moved the proper distance in the casting either to the right or left of the etched mark on the record until the proper adjustment has been obtained. The adjusting screw should again be tightened, BEING VERY CAREFUL THAT THE TAPER TUBE ARM CASTING HAS NEITHER RAISED NOR LOWERED WITH RESPECT TO THE TONE ARM.

h. Remove twelve-inch record and replace with ten-inch one.

i. Start the automatic mechanism again and allow it to run until the taper tube return lever starts to draw the taper tube towards the record. Shut off power and revolve turntable by hand (if induction disc motor is used) noting the manner in which the needle comes to rest on the record. (If it is noted that the horizontal travel of the needle changes to a slope just before reaching the record and continues so, until the surface of the record is reached, it is evident that the mechanism is lowering the sound box or pick-up prior to the termination of the needle's horizontal travel towards the record.)

As a condition of this nature will sometimes cause the needle to drop outside of the record's edge and damage the adjacent mechanisms, or, due to the greater velocity obtained on the slope, brake down the walls of the first grooves, the following adjustments should be made:

j. Slightly loosen lock nut (No. 13a, Fig. 1) on cam button and with screw driver turn button about ten degrees in either a clockwise or counter-clockwise direction.

k. Tighten nut and start mechanism through its cycle, again noting the manner in which the needle strikes the record. Observations should show a needle path practically horizontal until the needle is almost directly over the margin of the record: then a gradual drop to the record's surface. In the event that this adjustment has not yet been reached, turn the cam button about ten degrees more in the same direction and repeat until the mechanism functions in the desired manner.

In order that this gradual adjustment is not carried too far and to prevent the cam button from resting too much on the slope of the main slide, a check may be made from the following requirements:

With the index lever in "Victrola" or "Electrola" position, and the needle resting on the margin of a ten-inch record, the clearance between the bottom of the fulcrum pin on the taper tube assembly and the fish tail of No. 13, Fig. 1, should be about 1/64 of an inch, providing that the fish tail has not been bent.

From the above description it should now be evident that the main function of the cam button is to determine the time or position relative to the horizontal travel of the sound box or pick-up, in which the needle is lowered onto the record, and its adjustment should not therefore be altered for other failures.

12. Should the pick-up shunt switch (shown dotted in Fig. 9) fail to close or should it momentarily open after the reject button has been operated, or fail to open when the first music grooves are reached:

> With roller "G" engaged in pawl carrier at point "H", Fig. 9, loosen screws holding pick-up shunt switch to the operating unit base, and adjust its position so that the contacts have a clearance of about 1/32 of an inch.
>
> If the condition cannot be corrected by the above adjustment, loosen the nut shown at 13a, Fig. 1, and turn the screw *slightly* as may be required.

13. Should the mechanism fail to trip in ten- or twelve-inch position:

> a. loosen set screw under crook joint collar of tone arm and tighten collar until all side play is removed, being careful, however, that the up and down movement of the crook is not impeded.
>
> b. Remove any possible bind from the trip pawl on fulcrum pin mentioned in (k), No. 11, above.

14. If the index lever does not point to the proper position on the indicator plate, adjustment can be made in the following manner:

a. Remove back of cabinet to give access to gears controlling index lever. The shaft and pinion are on a block which is attached to the top plate with two screws.

b. With a screw driver, loosen these screws until the gears are clear.

c. Set index lever until it points to the proper position on the indicator plate.

d. Re-tighten the screws and then replace the back of the cabinet.

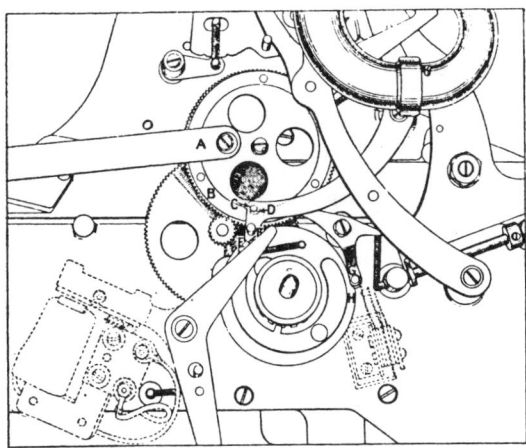

Fig. 9

Precautions necessary in reassembling:

a. Replace thrust washer (No. 25, Fig. 1).

b. Remount motor on bed plate.

c. Re-time mechanism in the following manner, referring to Fig. 9:

First - Hold cam pin against cam slide and revolve gear in clockwise direction until pin strikes side of rise of cam.

Second - Mark tooth of intermediate gear parallel with slide bar.

Third - Revolve cam gear in counter-clockwise direction until cam pin touches opposite side of cam.

Fourth - Mark tooth of intermediate gear parallel with slide bar.

These preliminary actions will allow the determination of the extremes of the cam and permit the distance to be referenced on the teeth of the intermediate gear.

Fifth - Divide the distance between the two marked teeth on the intermediate gear and set the gear in a position where the third mark will be parallel with the slide bar.

The trip lever pin will now be centralized with reference to the cam sides.

Upon replacing pawl carrier, "G" and "H" should be in position, as shown in Fig. 9.

The center line of the connecting rod "A" should be slightly beyond the center of gear "B" as shown. The face of the pawl "E" will then be against the trip lever "F".

d. Replace clutch wheel and tighten set screw in spotted point on turntable spindle.

e. Replace reject lever.

RE-ADJUSTING TONE ARM

After installing the sound box or electric pick-up, it may be necessary to re-adjust the overall horizontal position of the tone arm in order to permit the needle to lower onto the smooth outside rim of the record.

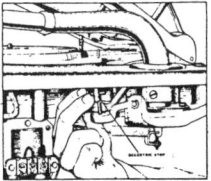

First - Loosen the 12" eccentric stop clamping screw in the taper tube arm casting.

Second - With a small rod or nail, turn the eccentric stop as shown in the illustration. In some cases it may be necessary to turn the stop to the right, and in other cases to the left.

Third - Check the setting after successive trials until the proper position is obtained, and then re-tighten the clamping screw.

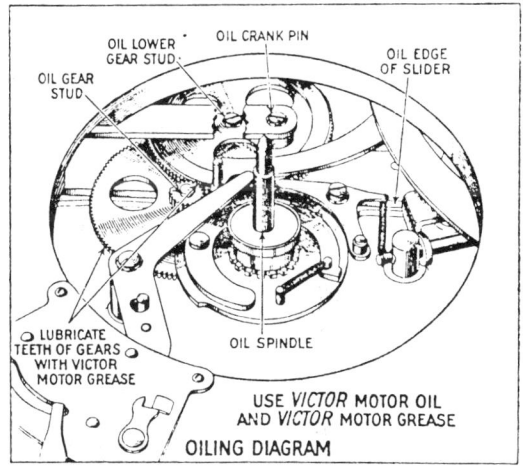

Fig. 7 - Oiling Diagram, Upper Mechanism

Instructions for the Servicing of the
Automatic Record Changer
Used with Automatic Victrolas and Electrolas

11-50
11-25
10-35 (above serial number 8126)
10-69 (above serial number 5001)
9-54 (above serial number 6401)
9-56 (above serial number 1701)

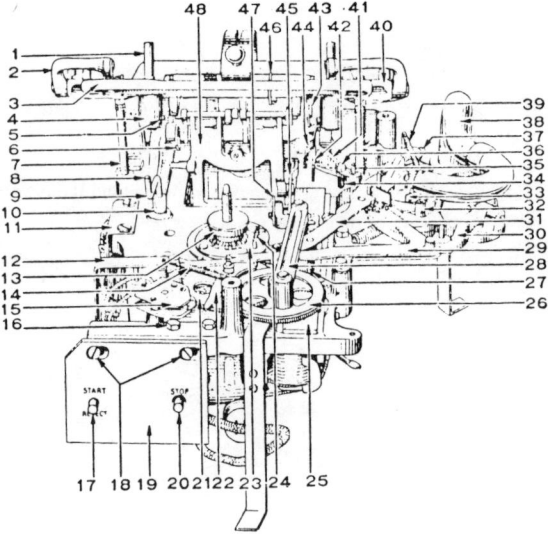

Fig. 1 - Automatic Mechanism with Motor Board Removed

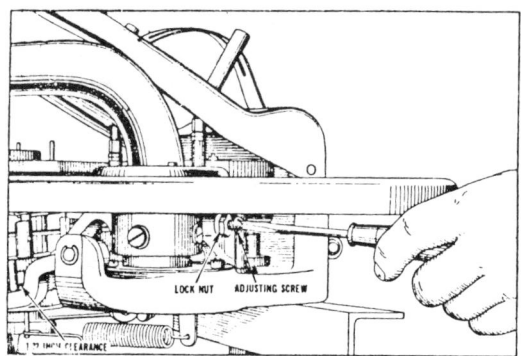

Fig. 2 - Adjusting Sound Box Lift Lever

1. FAILURE OF NEEDLE TO SWING INTO FIRST RECORD GROOVE - If the needle fails to swing into the first record groove after striking the smooth outside rim:

a. Determine if the instrument is level by placing a spirit level on the turntable.

b. If the right side of the cabinet is low, raise this side slightly be placing a thin wooden wedge or other available material under the feet of the lower end.

c. If the condition is not corrected by the above adjustment:

> Loosen the lock nut and adjust the sound box lift lever adjusting screw as shown in Fig. 2 until there is a clearance of approximately 1/32 of an inch between the underside of the taper tube arm casting and the top of the sound box lift lever as shown. This clearance can be checked by placing a thin piece of cardboard between the two points and observing whether or not there is a dragging on the cardboard when the tone arm is moved towards the center of the record. *This clearance is highly important and will affect other conditions of the mechanism if not properly adjusted.*

2. EXCESSIVE WEAR ON RECORDS - If excessive wear on the records is noted, the same adjustments as described in subject 1 above should be made. It may be possible that the needle will move into the record groove after striking the smooth outside rim, but will cause excessive wear of the record due to a slight contact between the two points shown in Fig. 2 where the 1/32 of an inch clearance should exist.

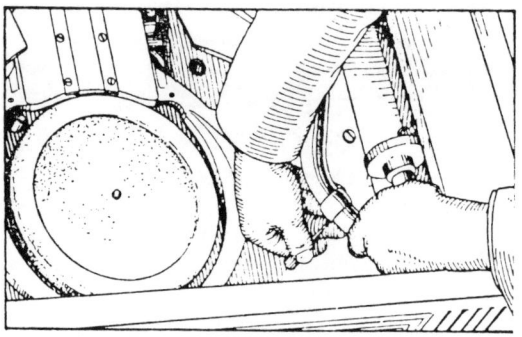

Fig. 3 - Adjusting Crook Stop

3. NEEDLE DOES NOT LOWER SUFFICIENTLY - When the 1/32 of an inch clearance described in c of subject 1 above is obtained, the clearance between the needle point and the record should be approximately 3/8 of an inch on the return of the tone arm. If this clearance does not exist:

> a. Examine the position of the tone arm cover plate. It should be so placed on the motor board that the tone arm does not touch the plate at any time. The screws in the plate can be loosened if necessary, care being taken not to turn these so far that the nuts on the bottom are dropped, and the plate then moved slightly to allow clearance of the tone arm. Re-tighten the screws securely when the proper clearance has been obtained.
>
> b. Examine the sound box or pick-up crook stop. Loosen the lock nuts and turn the stop screw, which is an eccentric, until the proper lowering has been obtained. Re-tighten the lock nut (see Fig. 3.)

4. NEEDLE DOES NOT CLEAR RECORD - If the tone arm does not rise sufficiently for the needle to clear the record on the return of the tone arm:

a. Examine the position of the tone arm cover plate and the crook stop making the same adjustments as described in subject 3 above except that the eccentric screw must be turned in the opposite direction.

b. If the condition is still not corrected, particularly if there seems to be a sluggish action of the return of the tone arm, remove the sound box lift lever spring as shown in Fig. 2, and increase its tension by shortening the straight section of the spring, bending it nearer the coiled section.

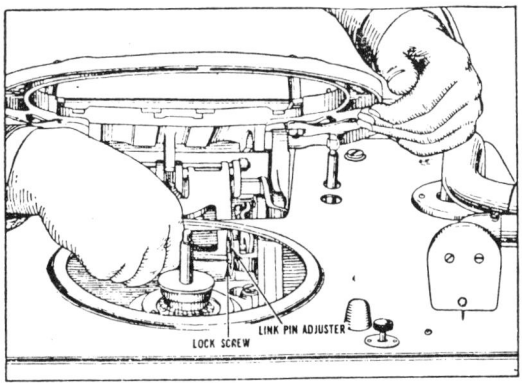

Fig. 4 - Adjusting Link Pin Adjuster

5. LIFT RING DROPS SLIGHTLY WHEN DESCENDING - If the lift ring suddenly drops about 1/4 of an inch when starting down, make the following adjustments:

a. Remove the turntable.

b. Loosen the lock screw in the link pin adjuster as shown in Fig. 4.

c. Turn the mechanism until the main slide is in its extreme forward position.

Turn the link pin adjuster until the rollers of the lift lever mechanism 48, Fig. 1, are in the slots pressing against the extreme end of their track (cam).

NOTE: - Do not advance the adjusters so far that the rollers are too tight against the end of the cam since there will be a strain and possible binding of the entire mechanism.

e. Re-tighten the lock screw.

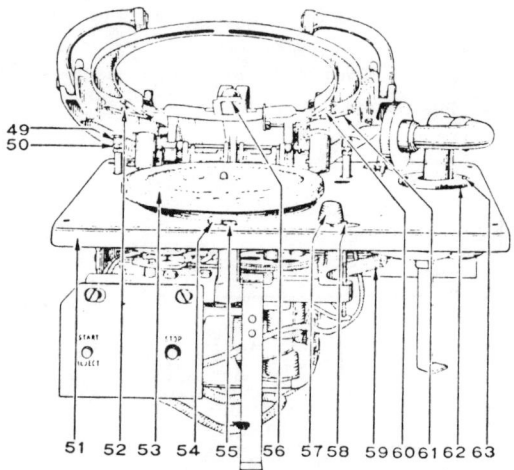

Fig. 5 - Automatic Unit Front View

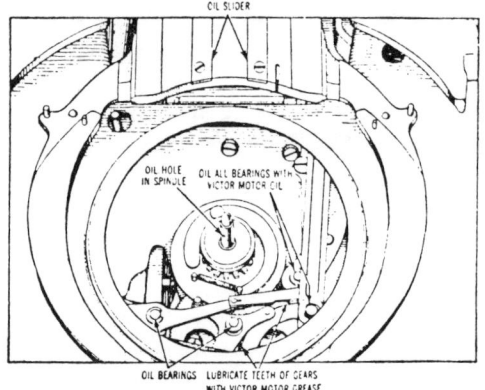

Fig. 7 - Oiling Diagram

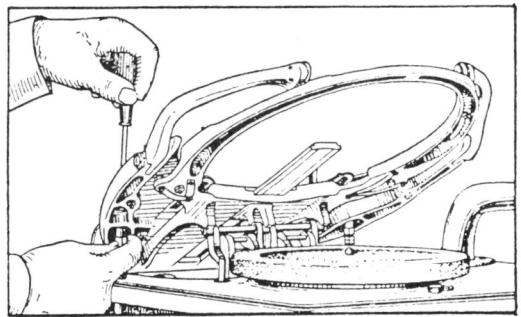

Fig. 6 - Adjusting Height of Hopper

6. LIFT RING FAILS TO REMOVE RECORD - If the lift ring fails to remove a record,

a. The record may be warped. Place the record on a flat solid surface in a warm room, and weight with books or other records.

b. The vertical height of the hopper (magazine) with respect to the lift ring is not properly adjusted.

First - Loosen the hopper support screws as shown in Fig. 6.

Second - With the lift ring in its highest position, turn the hopper adjusting nuts so that the top surface of the hopper is exactly flush with the top of the lift ring. A straight edge can be used as a gauge for this height.

This same method should then be used for gauging the height on the opposite side of the hopper. Turn the hopper support screws so that there can be an additional upward movement of the hopper of approximately 1/16 of an inch on each side with the hopper resting on each top adjusting nut. This amount of play will prevent any possible binding of the lift ring and hopper. Adjust the lift ring screws as shown in Fig. 8, until the ends touch the under side of the hopper when the ring is in its highest position.

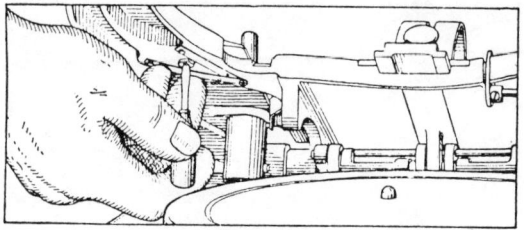

Fig. 8 - Adjusting Lift Ring Screws

Third - Note the action of the knives on the record support pins. Pushing the top of the record support pins down, insert a .065"-.070" gauge under each knife. This adjustment should be made when the lift ring is up and the knives turned inward. If the knife is too high or too low, it should be bent slightly by prying with a screw driver until the proper height is obtained.

With the lift ring down, insert a .120" gauge as shown in Fig. 9. There should be no play in the height of the knives and the sharp edge should be against the curved surface of the gauge. If this condition does not exist, loosen the set screws in the spiral cams as shown in Fig. 9. Using a socket wrench, make the necessary setting of the knives, pushing the spiral cams towards the back center of the mechanism, and then re-tighten the set screws.

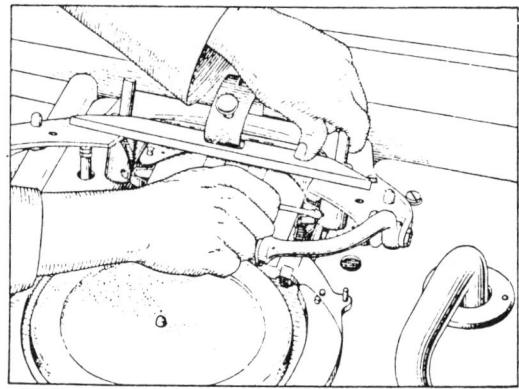

Fig. 9 - Gauging Record Support Pin Knives

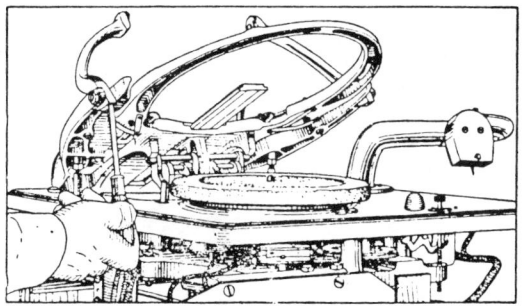

Fig. 10 - Adjusting Hopper Arm Screws

7. LIFT RING REMOVES TWO RECORDS - If two or more records are entirely removed from the hopper and deposited on the lift ring at the same time:

    a. Records are improperly loaded.

    b. Hopper improperly adjusted with respect to lift ring. See b of subject 6 above.

    c. Hopper arm improperly aligned, allowing the two bottom records to pass under the arms. Lower the hopper arms by turning the small adjusting screws as shown in Fig. 10, so that both hopper arm spacers touch the lift ring when the latter is in its raised position and there are no records in the hopper. Spacing for the gates on the hopper arms should be between .093" and .107".

8. RECORD CENTER FAILS TO ALIGN WITH TURNTABLE SPINDLE - The mechanism is designed to allow a 10" record to fall directly over the turntable spindle and a 12" record to fall 1/16 of an inch in back and then fall of its own weight forward over the spindle. If this condition does not exist:

    a. Records are not properly loaded in hopper.

    b. Record is warped.

c. Record guide pins 74 or 75, Fig. 11, not fitting properly in holes of lift ring. This fit should allow a free vertical motion of the pins, but a minimum side motion.

d. Hopper improperly adjusted with respect to lift ring. Make the same adjustment as described in b of subject 6 above.

e. Note the position of the record pusher pins on the back edge of the record. If both pins do not touch the back edge of the record as the latter is being moved into position, loosen the upper screw in the pusher plate, and adjust the plate until the proper contact is made, or, if one of the pins is below the record, bend the pusher spring slightly until proper contact is made.

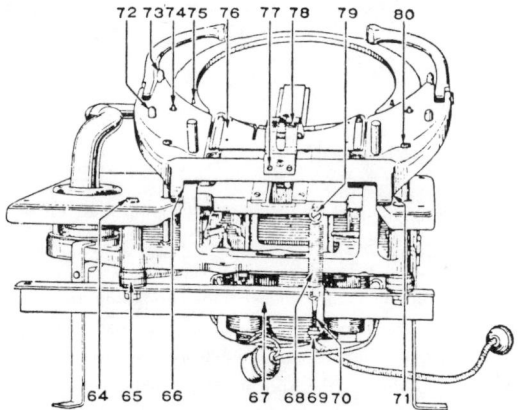

Fig. 11 - Automatic Mechanism Back View

9. LIFT RING RISES TOO SLOWLY - If the lift ring rises too slowly with a resulting strain on the mechanism, or if it descends too fast, increase the tension of spring 68, Fig. 11, in the back of the mechanism in the following manner:

a. Loosen the two lock nuts on the eye screw.

b. Increase the spring tension by turning first the top and then the bottom lock nut toward the eye in the screw.

c. Test the adjustment by trial until the proper rising of the lift ring has been obtained and the ring descends slowly without a record. The ring should slightly overbalance the spring when the former is in its lowered position.

10. LIFT RING RISES TOO FAST - If the lift ring rises too fast, if it descends too slowly, or if it touches the under side of the record on the turntable during playing, decrease the tension of the spring 68, Fig. 11, in the following manner:

a. loosen the two lock nuts on the eye screw.

b. Decrease the spring tension by turning first the bottom and then the top lock nut away from the eye in the screw.

c. Test the adjustment by trial until the proper rising of the lift ring has been obtained, and the ring descends slowly without a record.

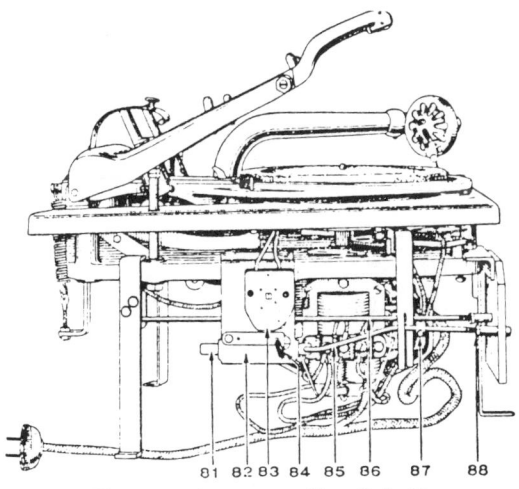

Fig. 12 - Automatic Unit Side View

11. LIFT RING VIBRATES IN DESCENDING - If the lift ring does not descend evenly:

a. Oil the bearings of the lift lever rollers.

b. Examine the pusher plate and the portion of the lift ring over which the plate moves, noting if there is any binding between the two when the pusher plate is advancing. Usually if there is contact between the two, a worn line will be noticeable on the lift ring, being produced by the contact of the bottom of the plate on the lift ring. This condition can be readily eliminated by bending up the plate slightly on the side which is touching the ring.

c. Examine the pusher slide, noting if it is properly lubricated, or if there is any grit or other foreign matter in the channel of the slide. *It is important that this channel be clean and well lubricated at all times.*

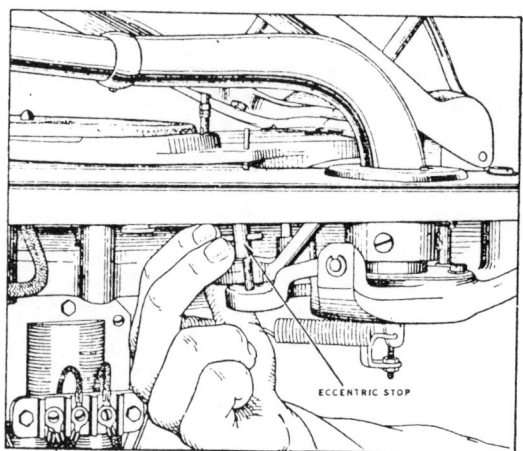

Fig. 13 - Adjusting 12" Eccentric Stop

12. NEEDLE LOWERS OUTSIDE 12" RECORD DIAMETER - Should the needle fail to lower on the smooth outside rim of a 12" record, but lowers outside the record:

a. Loosen the clamping screw for the eccentric screw, 32, Fig. 1, in the taper tube arm casting.

b. With a rod or nail, turn the eccentric adjustment as shown in Fig. 13.

c. Check the setting after successive trials until the proper position is obtained, and then re-tighten the clamping screw securely.

d. If the needle does not fall at the proper position on a 10" record after making the above adjustment, refer to Fig. 13.

First - Place a socket wrench over the lock nut on the under side of the 10" eccentric stop 35, Fig. 1, and a short screw driver down through the hole in the motor board and into the slot of the 10" eccentric stop.

Second - Loosen the lock nut and turn the eccentric in either direction as may be required.

Third - Make a test after each successive trial until the proper setting has been obtained.

13. NEEDLE LOWERS INSIDE 12" RECORD GROOVES - If the tone arm swings inwardly too far before the needle lowers on a 12" record, but not as far as the 10" position:

a. Make the same adjustments as described in subject 12 above, but turn the 12" eccentric in the opposite direction.

b. Check the 10'" position, making any necessary adjustments as described in d of subject 12 above.

14. NEEDLE LOWERS OUTSIDE 10" RECORD GROOVES - Should the needle lower outside the diameter of a 10" record, but lowers properly on a 12" record, make the same adjustments as described in d of subject 12 above.

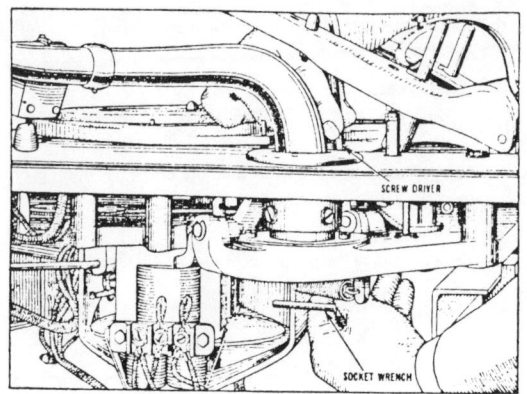

Fig. 14 - Adjusting 10" Eccentric Stop

15. **NEEDLE LOWERS INSIDE OF 10" RECORD GROOVES** - Should the needle lower inside the record grooves of a 10" record, but lowers satisfactorily on a 12''' record, make the same adjustments as described in d of subject 12 above.

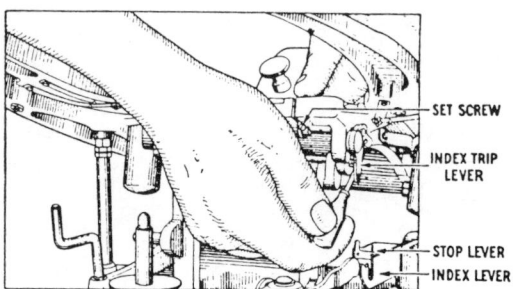

Fig. 15 - Adjusting Index Trip Lever

16. **FAILURE TO SELECT 10" AND 12" POSITION** - If the mechanism does not select the 10" and 12" position, that is, if the needle lowers to the 10" position on a 12" record, or on the rubber support block when a 10" record is on the turntable:

    a. Records are improperly loaded in hopper.

b. Tighten the set screw on the index lever trip cam, as shown in Fig. 15, so that it is against the flat of the index trip lever shaft. Loosen the lock nut in the index trip lever as shown in Fig. 15, and adjust the screw until the inside pin lowers on the stop lever and the outside pin lowers in the larger slot of the index lever when the lift ring comes down without a record.

c. If the mechanism still fails to select properly, adjust the lock nuts 36, Fig. 1, over the index lever so that the taper tube return lever strikes near the top of the 12″ stop face on the index lever casting 41, Fig.1, when set for a 12″ record and the approximate mid-point of the 10″ eccentric stop pin when set for a 10″ record.

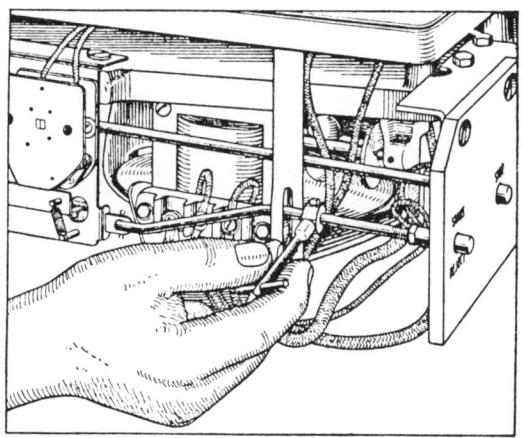

Fig. 16 - Adjusting Reject Collar

17. FAILURE TO REJECT RECORD - If the automatic mechanism does not trip when the "Reject" button is pressed, and the record is therefore not rejected:

a. Note that the condition is not caused by a wire between the reject rod collar 87, Fig. 12, and the fork portion of the trip lever.

b. If the condition is not yet corrected, loosen the set screws in the collar as shown in Fig. 16, and set the collar approximately 1/8 of an inch away from the trip lever. Re-tighten the set screws.

18. CONTINUED REJECTION - Continued rejection may be caused by any one of the following:

    a. Collar on reject rod set too near trip lever, preventing latter from disengaging from end of pawl.

    b. "Start" and "Reject" button stuck or binding.

    c. Pawl 23, Fig. 1, sticking between teeth of clutch wheel.

    d. Mechanism improperly timed. (See subject 26, below.)

19. FAILURE TO TRIP ON ECCENTRIC GROOVE - If the mechanism does not trip when the eccentric groove is reached:

    a. Observe the action of the sound box crook, noting if it is too loose on the tone arm. The crook should be so tightened that it is free to move up and down, and yet sufficiently tight to prevent any side motion.

    b. If the crook is found to be correct, remove the back of the cabinet, and with the aid of a flashlight, observe the action of the latch trip blade 33, Fig. 1, which is mounted on the 12" eccentric screw 32, Fig. 1. If the blade does not make contact with the latch plate, loosen the screws in the latch trip, and move the blade until proper contact is made with the plate.

20. FAILURE TO EJECT - If the eject lever 9, Fig. 1, fails to remove a record from the turntable, and the record lift ring raises the record, eliminate any binding in the eject lever cam 6, Fig. 1, near the end of the eject lever, by prying the cam away from the lever with a screw driver. The cam may be stuck slightly because of dirt or other foreign matter becoming lodged between it and the eject lever.

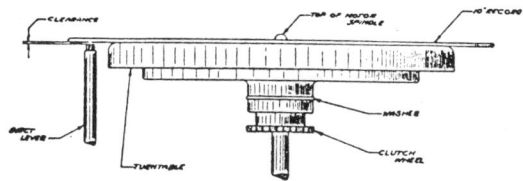

Fig. 17 - Correct Height of Record on Turntable Spindle

21. SLUGGISH ACTION OF EJECT MECHANISM OR RECORD EJECTS TOWARD FRONT OF CABINET - If the record is not entirely ejected from the turntable before the lift ring starts to rise, or if a record is ejected toward the front of the cabinet rather than in the discharge compartment:

a. Note the height of the record on the motor spindle, and compare this height with the correct height as shown in Fig. 17. If the record is considerably lower, raise the height by placing one or more cork or fiber washers under the turntable.

b. Examine the leather on the end of the eject lever. if this is worn smooth, roughen it by scraping with a sharp knife or file.

22. FAILURE TO START - If the mechanism fails to start, look for any of the following:

a. Open circuit in power supply. Check all plug connections both inside and outside the instrument.

b. Defective motor coil.

c. Open or shorted 3 Mfd. condenser.

d. Start switch position 83, Fig. 12, out of adjustment, preventing switch slide 81, Fig. 12, from tripping switch.

d. Defective start switch 83, Fig. 12.

23. FAILURE TO STOP WHEN STOP BUTTON IS PRESSED - The mechanism will not stop if the button is pressed during a cycle until the cycle has been completed. If the mechanism still fails to stop, look for any of the following:

    a. Defective start switch 83, Fig. 12.

    b. Defective cycle completing switch 15, Fig. 1.

    c. Improper adjustment of mechanical adjustment between stop lever 44, Fig. 1, and start switch. When facing the back of the mechanism, adjust the right hand collar on the stop shaft until the collar on the stop rod just touches the stop arm on the switch when the stop button is out.

24. FAILURE TO STOP AFTER LAST RECORD - If the mechanism fails to stop after the last record has been played, look for any of the following:

    a. Improper adjustment of index trip lever, Fig. 15. See b, subject 16, above for proper adjustment.

    b. Defective start switch 83, Fig. 12.

    c. Defective cycle completing switch 15, Fig. 1.

25. PICK-UP SHORTING SWITCH FAILURE - If the pick-up shorting switch fails to open before the needle reaches the first music grooves, or fails to close after the eccentric groove has been reached:

    a. Remove the turntable.

b. Loosen the screws in the switch with a small right angle screw driver, and adjust the position on the switch until the contacts are approximately 1/32 of an inch apart when the tone arm is in the playing position.

c. Examine the bakelite arm of the switch, noting if there is any binding. Such binding should be removed by prying the arm loose with a screw driver.

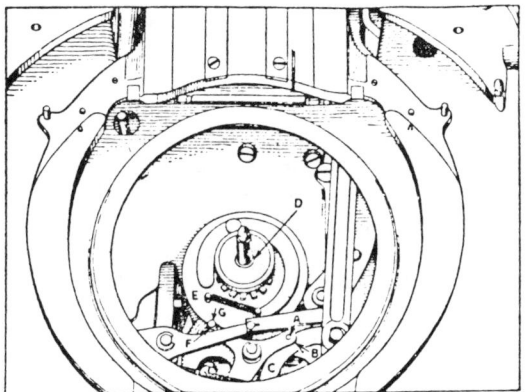

Fig. 18 - Method of Timing Gears

26. TIMING MECHANISM - When the motor or any of the gears has been removed, it will be necessary to re-time the mechanism in the following manner:

a. Remove the turntable.

b. Turn the mechanism by hand until the roller "A", Fig. 18, is engaged in the slot "B" of cam gear "C".

c. Loosen the set screw in the clutch wheel "D", lift the wheel, the pawl and the carrier "E", and turn the latter until the roller "F" is in line with slot "G".

d. Lower the pawl and pawl carrier and the clutch wheel, and then re-tighten the set screw, aligning the screw with the spot in the motor spindle.

Retouching Victrola Cabinets

Victor issued the following directions to its dealers to aid them in repairing Victrola cabinets which had suffered damage at the hands of clumsy movers or careless customers. While the instructions do not address the repair of varnished woods which have suffered the effects of old age, the tips are still useful. To refinish badly deteriorated varnish finishes, the reader is referred to the section of this book which describes a tour of the Victor factory in 1917, as this section details the original finishing process. The lacquered finishes of the Orthophonic Victrolas and Electrolas show the effects of age much less than do the older varnished Victrolas and many of these later lacquered instruments can be returned to showroom appearance rather easily by following the instructions given in the section for retouching post-1925 Victrolas.

Varnished Finishes (pre-1925)

CLEANING

By mixing three parts benzine to one part paraffin rubbing oil you will have the best possible cleaner and polish for a Victrola cabinet. Rub briskly, always lengthwise of the grain, cleaning off any surplus polish. Brush out all the corners with a brush, preferably a soft, round 000 bristle varnish brush.

RED MAHOGANY AND ENGLISH BROWN MAHOGANY

If paper has become stuck to the cabinet, it can easily be removed with a cloth and water. The cabinet should then be carefully dried and the surface rubbed with a 000 pumice stone, a soft felt and paraffin rubbing oil. Care should always be taken to rub lengthwise of the grain.

Never sponge a cabinet and then expose it to the sun in the show window. The glass intensifies the heat, which may blister the varnish, or fade the whole finish.

Bruises or scratches should be rubbed out with a piece of soft felt, a 000 pumice stone and paraffin rubbing oil. Go only so far as the body varnish will permit and rub only lengthwise.

If the bruise or scratch is too deep to rub out, it will have to be burned in with shellac cement, the spot leveled up with fine sandpaper and touched up to the required color. It will then be necessary to French polish it with a solution of shellac, alcohol and raw linseed oil, using a piece of cotton covered with a piece of fine linen cloth. This requires skill and experience, and should *never*, under any circumstances, be attempted on a large flat surface by a novice.

Rubbed spots and white corners on a red mahogany cabinet can be touched up with a spirit stain made from Bismark Brown dissolved in alcohol, to which a little shellac is added. For English Brown-finished cabinets add a little Nigrosine to the above-mentioned solution.

AMERICAN WALNUT - WAXED

Remove scratches with fine sandpaper and rewax. If too deep, the surface should be scraped by an experienced cabinet maker, and stained with Walnut Stain filled with Walnut Filler, shaded with Vandyke Brown to the required color, and given a thin coat of shellac. When dry, sandpaper and wax.

AMERICAN WALNUT - VARNISH FINISH

Follow the same procedure as mentioned in the foregoing in refinishing mahogany where the cabinet is scratched or paper has stuck to it. Edges and white spots may be touched up with a mixture of Dry Vandyke Brown and Nigrosine mixed in alcohol, and a little white shellac to the required shade; afterwards, French polishing to restore finish. Deep bruises, where the fibre of the wood is not broken, may be taken out by saturating a cloth with hot water and applying to bruises - holding over the same a hot iron and raising the bruised part level with the surface. Let dry thoroughly and sandpaper smooth, and French polish.

EARLY ENGLISH OAK - POLISHED

GOLDEN OAK - POLISHED

Scratches may be rubbed out with Rotten Stone and Paraffin Rubbing Oil; small surfaces, French-polished to required luster. If the entire cabinet needs polishing, take three parts turpentine, one part paraffin rubbing oil.

Dampen a piece of soft cheese cloth or canton flannel with the polish, and, if available, use a little of the powdered rotten stone, rub the varnished surface briskly until dry and the required luster is restored. Clean out all carvings, corners and moldings with a soft brush, and wipe dry with a soft clean cloth. Edges of Golden Oak may be touched up with Vandyke Brown and Shellac solution; Early English with Nigrosine solution.

GOLDEN OAK - WAXED

On waxed or flat finished cabinets, scratches may be sandpapered or scraped out. Bruises, if not too deep, may be raised with the hot iron, burned in with prepared cement, or pieces inserted by a skilled cabinet maker. If the finish is removed to the bare wood it must be restained with Golden Oak Stain, filled with Golden Filler, and given one coat of white shellac, sandpapered and waxed with a first-class prepared cabinet wax or floor wax, rubbing same until a proper surface is produced. Edges or white places to be touched up with Burnt Umber, Vandyke Brown and Yellow Ochre dissolved in alcohol, with a little shellac added to desired shade.

WEATHERED OAK - WAXED

Treat as all general finished waxed cabinets, using a stain for white places, edges, etc., of Vandyke Brown and Nigrosine in the alcohol solution, mixed to desired shade.

FUMED OAK - WAXED

This finish is the most difficult to repair of all the art finishes, as it is produced by chemical action. If scratched or bruised to the extent of white wood showing, and has to be refinished, the instrument had better be returned to the factory for repairs. Edges and small spots may be touched up with Vandyke Brown dissolved in alcohol and a little shellac.

If, after treating the cabinet in any or all of these ways, scratches and marks still show, it will be necessary to employ a skilled polisher to French polish the whole cabinet to the desired finish, which must then be dulled off with a soft brush dipped in 000 pumice stone and cleaned up as before.

Pyroxylin Lacquer Finishes (post 1925)

CLEANING

By mixing one part benzine to three parts paraffin rubbing oil you will have a satisfactory cleaner and polish for a lacquered Victrola cabinet. Rub lightly, always lengthwise with the grain, cleaning off any surplus polish. Brush out all the corners with a soft bristle brush.

ABRASIONS, BRUISES AND SCRATCHES

After carefully cleaning the cabinet a close scrutiny should be made for any defects deeper than the film of the lacquer. When this occurs "burning in" should be practiced. This process consists of holding a piece of wood cement of the proper color over the bruise and touching it with a pointed heated piece of metal, allowing the cement to drop into the defect and there harden, then leveling off with a piece of 000000 sandpaper dipped in paraffin rubbing oil and padded up with a mixture of intermediate lacquer reduced with ansol alcohol. Application of the material to the cabinet is made by dampening a small pad with this material and slowly applying it with a light rubbing motion of the hand parallel with the grain of the wood.

No attempt should be made to repair by this method any large defective surfaces. Should there be such, the cabinet should be turned over to an experienced finisher, as finishing is a trade, and requires considerable education to meet its particular conditions.

INDEX

Aeolean Company 45,53
Automatic Brake 52,77
Automatic Record Changer ....
.... 156,158,204,207,208,209,
...... 210,211,213,214,215,290,302
B & H Fiber Needle Co 229
Baumbach, Robert .... i,ii
Bell, Alexander ix,9,239
Bell Telephone Co ....
.... 116,149,239
Berliner, Emile.ix,9,10,20,21
Berliner Gramophone Co.... 10
Brunswick-Balke-Collender Co.
.... 61,155,179
Carnegie Hall 227
Capehart 241
Circassian Walnut 50,86,90
Columbia Phonograph Co ......
.... ix,12,47,53,70,150,227
Consolidated Talking Machine
.... Company 10
Cross Bands 61
Custom Victrolas ....
.... 48,53,55,86,89,148
Douglas Phonograph Co ... 232
Edison, Thomas ix,9
Electrola ....
.... 1,2,155,195,211,213
English, John.241,243,246,248
Franklin Institute 9
Front-Mount Tone Arm....14,24
Gabel, John 156
Gabelola 156
Gramophone ....
.................ix,9,10,21,29,227
Gramophone Company Ltd .....
.... 43,223 227
Graphophone 12
Johnson, Eldridge .... ix,
.... 8,9,10,12,20,21,25,45,55,
.............59,63,83,112,116,156,
.... 246,248,251
Jones, Joe 12
Lumiere 223
Marantz 246

Miller, H.C 250
National Gramophone Co ix
Orthophonic Victrola ....
.... 2,13,151,181
Panatrope 155
Parsons, Sir Charles 15,43
Period Victrolas 53,123
Philco 154,201
Phonograph (Edison's) ....
.... viii,11,53,227,229
Pianola 45
Pooley Furniture Co 45,83
Radio 55,105,
.... 106,117,118,119 153,181,183
Radio-Victor Corporation of
America 159
Radiola 2,154,179,181,
.... 182,184,185,186,196,197,
.... 199,200,201,202,203,204,
.... 206,207,209,213,219,222,234
Rear-Mount Tone Arm.....14,24
Red Seal Records 227,228
RCA ix,153,159,179,
.... 182,183,184,185,186,197,
.... 199,200,202,203,204,206,
.... 207,209,213,214,215,218,
.... 219,220,221,222,228,234,252
Rigid Tone Arm 12,35
Sarnoff, David 55,154,159
Scull,Andrew 59
Seligman, J & W 156
Speyer and Co 156
Standard Machine Shop 59
Tapering Tone Arm ....
.... 12,13,26,35,63
Universal Talking Machine Co.
.... 10,13
Vernis-Martin 62
Victor Talking Machines
-$3.00 19
-Type A 1,10,20,21
-Type B 10,21
-Type C 10,22
-Type D 14,23,38
-Type E (Monarch Jr.) 1,14,24

-Type M (Monarch) 1,14,24,25,26,27,36
-Type MD (Monarch Deluxe)26,27
-Type MS (Monarch Special) 1,26 37
-Type P 15,28
-Type R (Royal) 1,28,29
-Type Z 14,15,30,32
-Junior 15,31
-0 15,16,32
-I 14,15,30,33,35
-II 14,35,36
-III 14,36
-IV (Inside Horn) 49,70,71,94,163
-IV (Outside Horn) 26,37
-V 14,16,23,38
-VI (Inside Horn) 49,71,72
-VI (Outside Horn) 14,39,45,79,83,91
-VIII 49,72,77
-IX 49,73,77
-X 47,51,73,74,77,79,95
-XI 47,51,61,76,79,96
-XII 47,77,78
-XIV 47,50,51,62,80,100
-XVI 46,47, 48,51,79,81,85,89,90,91,102
-XVII 52,88,90,104
-XVIII 52,89,90
-XX 47,90,91
-XXV 16,40,54,191
-35 92,166
-50 93,94,247
-80 56,95,173
-90 96
-100 97
-105 98
-107 99
-110 100,101
-111 101,102
-120 101,102
-125 103,108
-130 103,104,108
-210 105
-215 106,107

-220 107
-230 108
-240 109
-260 110
-280 111
-300 54,112
-330 113
-350 114,116
-360 114,114,116
-370 114,116,119
-400 114,117
-405 114,118
-410 116,119
-1-1 163,164
-1-2 164
-1-5 165
-1-6 165,166
-1-70 167,168
-1-90 168
-2-30 169
-2-35 170
-2-55 171
-2-60 172
-4-3 173,176
-4-4 175
-4-7 176
-4-20 177
-4-40 178
-7-1 179
-7-2 180
-7-3 182,183,187
-7-10 183
-7-11 184,202
-7-25 185
-7-26 186,202
-7-30 182,187
-8-4 188
-8-7 189
-8-8 191,192
-8-9 191,192
-8-12 174,193
-8-30 194,195,196
-8-35 195
-8-60 196
-9-1 197
-9-2 198
-9-3 200

-9-15 197,201
-9-16 202,203
-9-18 202,203
-9-25 204
-9-40 205
-9-54 207,209,302
-9-55 157,207,208,209,290
-9-56 209,302
-10-35 159,210,302
-10-50 156,208,211,213,290
-10-51 157,212,290
-10-69 214,302
-10-70 157,214,215,290
-11-25 216
-11-50 216
-12-1 218
-12-2 219
-12-15 220
-12-25 221
-15-1 222
-R-20 224
-R-80 56
-Adam 144
-Alhambra I 179,181,182,200
-Alhambra II 180,200
-Auxetophone 15,16,39,42
-Borgia I 200
-Borgia II.155,198,200,206,222
-Chippendale 138
-Chinese Chippendale 140
-Colony 152,174,179
-Consolette............ 152,173,174
-Credenza ....
.... 151,155,175,193,194,195,196
-Cromwell 218
-Empire 130
-Florenza 197,200
-Granada 152,174,175
-Hepplewhite.................. 142
-Gothic 124
-Hyperion 222
-Jacobean..................... 132
-Loud Speaker I 223
-Louis XV..................... 126
-Louis XVI.................... 128
-Queen Anne 136
-Sheraton 146

-Tuscany 219
-Victor-Victrola 39,45,82
-William and Mary 134
Victrola 1,2,45
Vogt, Clarence 242
Wanamaker, John 49,86
Yielding Turntable Shaft 39
Zonophone 10,13